# DECEMBER

# 25th

A SOCIAL HISTORY

# DECEMBER

# 25th

## THE JOYS OF CHRISTMAS PAST

★ Phillip Snyder ★

DODD, MEAD & COMPANY ★ New York

To my v            ughter, Eve,
th                  cated.

Copyright © 1985 by Phillip V. Snyder

Published by Dodd, Mead & Company, Inc.
79 Madison Avenue, New York, N.Y. 10016
Distributed in Canada by
McClelland and Stewart Limited, Toronto
Manufactured in the United States of America

Designed by Phillip V. Snyder

First Edition

*Library of Congress Cataloging in Publication Data*

Snyder, Phillip V., 1936-
December 25th.

Bibliography: p.
Includes index.
1. Christmas—United States—History. I. Title.
II. Title: December twenty-fifth. III. Title:
December twenty-five.
GT4986.A1S68  1985    394.2′ 68282′ 0973    85-1583
ISBN 0-396-08588-1

# Contents

# CONTENTS

CHRISTMAS—the best day of the year.
                    —GEORGE TEMPLETON STRONG

Each December, millions
of Americans express a longing for
an old-fashioned Christmas.
Nearly everyone is convinced
that Christmas isn't what it
used to be. Yet except for vague
images of trees lighted with
candles, and Currier and Ives's
sleighing scenes, fewer
and fewer people have any idea
of what the sights and sounds and
aromas of old-time
Christmases were really like.

# Preface

Today, who knows about firecracker Christmases as noisy as an old Fourth of July, or gas-lit Christmas trees, or the Belsnickel, that devilish old counterpart to our jolly Santa Claus? And who can still remember armies of European immigrants going home for Christmas from points as distant as Oregon, or balance-of-payments problems created by holiday gifts of money sent to relatives in the Old World?

The idea for this book took form as I was reading nineteenth-century newspapers on microfilm while researching my book on antique Christmas ornaments. Although I read papers from many cities, it was particularly in the six principal New York City dailies that I discovered a gold mine of descriptive detail about old Christmases.

As successive waves of European immigrants poured into the port of New York, they placed their stamp upon the city's Christmases. Old World customs from many countries combined to yield hybrids. Many customs, including the Santa Claus we know today, were literally New York inventions that spread in a remarkably short time to all corners of the continent. Some have endured, such as the German immigrants' Christmas tree. Many have been forgotten.

Indeed, when it comes to the fascinating subject of old Christmases, myths and misinformation are legion. In this country, Christmas has been virtually overlooked by historians. The surprising and heartwarming story of the development of our American Christmas customs and traditions has remained largely untold.

# Preface

I have tried in these pages to make old-fashioned Christmases as real as they became to me during my research. I want to acknowledge my particular debt to the many anonymous nineteenth-century newspaper reporters who left detailed and endlessly surprising descriptions of what they saw and heard on Christmases past. A number of them, such as a picture of New York's markets and one of the shopping districts on Christmas Eve, are drawn from as many as one hundred or more of their eyewitness accounts. All the dialogue was recorded by a reporter present at the time. I have been privileged through thousands of hours of pleasurable reading to enjoy vicariously almost two hundred Christmases. For a decade, it has snowed eleven months of the year inside my head. I hope the book that has resulted will take you back to bygone pleasures and add to the joys of many Christmases to come.

PHILLIP SNYDER

## WHEN CHRISTMAS WAS CONTROVERSIAL

**B**efore the 1850s
Christmas had a tremendous
struggle trying to establish
a foothold in America.
Even in 1874 Henry Ward Beecher, the preeminent Protestant clergyman of his day, told a Pittsburgh congregation, "To me Christmas is a foreign day, and I shall die
so." Beecher was one of many who, having grown up
without Christmas, never adopted the custom.

The Christmas Americans celebrate today is largely a
late-nineteenth-century creation: a blend of Old World
history and traditions melded and altered by an emerg-
ing American culture. In addition to customs rooted in
the Nativity, the day incorporates folkways associated in
Europe with St. Nicholas Day (December 6) and festivities transferred to Christmas from New Year's Day—a
more important day for many Americans, only a century
ago, than Christmas.

still reported: "The greater part of the citizens of Pennsylvania pay no regard to such days as Christmas." However, even among the strongly anti-Christmas Quakers, there is some evidence that the old resistance was diminishing. The diary kept by Deborah Logan, a Philadelphia Quaker, records that she carried out a vigorous housecleaning before December 25 and baked mince pies and doughnuts and shopped for presents for her family. While the Pennsylvania German Mennonites, Brethren, and Amish shared the Quakers' general disdain for Christmas, celebrations were commonplace in the parts of Pennsylvania settled by Lutheran, Reformed, Moravian, Episcopal, and Catholic congregations.

Nonetheless, in 1867 the Reverend Henry Harbaugh, a Reformed Churchman who had spent eighteen years writing and preaching to promote Christmas among other Protestant faiths, found himself "exiled" in a Scotch-Irish community near Harrisburg. In frustration, he wrote: "Here where I am living—in the westerning Pennsylvania hills—they want to hear nothing of Christmas. They spend the day working as on any other day. Their children grow up knowing nothing of brightly lit Christmas trees, nor Christmas presents. God have mercy on these Presbyterians—these pagans."

In the first half of the nineteenth century, the holiday season fared best in New York, where it was a particularly joyful time among the Dutch, the first settlers there. However, Santa Claus visited Dutch children not on Christmas Eve, but on New Year's Eve—New Year's Day, with its open house and gifts for children and adults alike, being the principal holiday. Until after the Civil War, Santa Claus had to work two nights of the year in New York.

After the English won control of the city from the Dutch in 1664, the Dutch settlers were soon greatly outnumbered, and English customs—the two opposing English views of Christmas among them—became the norm. The city grew rapidly, and by 1800 it had gained first place in the United States and a cosmopolitan character it has never lost. When it came to the celebration of Christmas, the city's high society, prone to Anglican affiliation, showed the way. Harriet and Maria Trumbull, daughters of the governor of Connecticut, Jonathan Trumbull, spent the holiday in 1800 visiting in New York. "We went to church [Anglican] in the morning, it was all decorated with evergreen bushes," wrote Harriet on Christmas Day.

In the nineteenth century, New York was the principal port for European immigration. Cultural customs, including Christmas traditions, were as yet unblended into the proverbial American melting pot. Countless immigrants settled in the city temporarily while awaiting the opportunity to migrate to the hinterland. Here they learned how other nationalities celebrated Christmas, adopted the ways that pleased them, and then took with them all across the continent a Christmas that was, like the new country itself, a mixture of strands from many cultures.

Many of the immigrants' Christmas observances were purely secular: they stressed children, the spirit of hospitality, and seasonal good cheer, as well as military parades and special performances in theaters and music halls. These could be enjoyed without a thought for ancient religious quarrels. An 1831 publication, *Festivals, Games and Amusements,* printed this anonymous "stranger's account" of old New York on Christmas Eve:

> Whole rows of confectionary stores and toy shops, fancifully, and often splendidly, decorated with festoons of bright silk drapery, interspersed with flowers and evergreens, are brightly illuminated with gas-lights. . . . During the evening until midnight, these places are crowded with visitors of both sexes and all ages, some selecting toys and fruit for holiday presents; others merely lounging from shop to shop to enjoy the varied scene. But the most interesting and most delightful of all, is the happy and animated countenances of the children on this occasion. Their joy cannot be restrained.

By 1850 Christmas was well on its way to becoming New York's favorite day; places of business were generally closed on the holiday. And New York showed the way for the rest of the country: By the end of the century, Christmas had swept even reluctant New England into its camp. In 1887 a Christmas carnival, the first ever held in New England, took place in Bridgeport, Connecticut. The week-long festivities began on December 20 with a torchlight procession that resembled a New Orleans Mardi Gras. There were illuminated tableaux on wagons and all sorts of grotesque figures representing Kriss Kringle and the Belsnickel, Eskimos, clowns, imitation elephants, and a woman whacking a stuffed lion. All the streets were arched over at short intervals with gas piping wound with evergreens and festooned with hemlock boughs. The arches were decorated with colored glass lights, and over the sidewalks were strings of Chinese lanterns. Fireworks were shot off without stint, and on the roofs of all the highest buildings pots of red and green fire were burned.

Gradually the numerous elements of Christmas, religious and secular, fused into a truly national festival of extraordinary popularity. Within the formerly Puritanical Protestant sects, the day was losing its Roman Catholic associations and being recognized as part of the general inheritance of Christendom. There was a gradual lessening of hostility between militant Protestants and Roman Catholics. Participation in the secular aspects of the day did much to promote tolerance of denominational differences. By the last quarter of the nineteenth century, Christmas had become a dual holiday, embracing religious as well as folk celebration.

## Chapter 1

## CHRISTMAS EVE MARKETING IN OLD NEW YORK

**E**very year
on December 24, an army
of fatherly men and motherly
women invaded Fulton and
Washington markets in
New York City, eagerly seeking
a turkey and other raw materials for the Christmas feast.
On Christmas Eve—considered the best time to buy a turkey in the days before home refrigeration—the city's two great downtown entrepôts of the turkey trade were stuffed, like a turkey itself, with marketers. There was never a lack at either market of wherewithal to make a dinner table groan.

By the 1880s Washington Market and Fulton Market were household names throughout the United States. Food supplies to and from them were carried by rail and steamer as far as two thousand miles.

A market had occupied the site of Washington Market

since 1772. New buildings were erected in 1813 and again in the 1880s. Indeed, Washington Market continued to be part of many New Yorkers' Christmases until the late 1950s. It was to Washington Market that Clement C. Moore was bound by sleigh on the evening of December 23, 1822, when he conceived the idea for his famous poem, *A Visit from St. Nicholas.* Today the twin towers of the World Trade Center stand on the site.

The east end of Fulton Street near the East River had also developed early as a marketplace because of its accessibility to the fishing fleet and the ferry bringing food from the farms of Long Island. A vestige of the old Fulton Market building, which had opened in 1821, remained as a wholesale fish market until only a few years ago.

In 1875 the traditional Christmas dinner for a well-heeled New York family was described in *The New York Times* as invariably commencing with oyster soup and featuring roast turkey. According to the editor:

> If the lady of the household is ambitious, the bird is stuffed with oysters, and if she rules her husband, she orders him to purchase the oysters and turkey himself. Almost all the good old gentlemen consider it part of their religion to go down to Fulton Market, which is the aristocratic one.

Indeed, on the day before Christmas, gentlemen went down to Fulton Market in great numbers. After fortifying themselves for the task in one of the nearby oyster rooms, they made the rounds. Epicures first had a look around the stands where game was displayed, subjecting

# CHRISTMAS EVE MARKETING IN OLD NEW YORK

themselves to the blandishments of salesmen who tempted them with saddles of venison, with red-head and canvasback and mallard ducks, with hindquarters of bear meat, with woodcocks and snipes, with ruffed grouse and wild turkeys, with hares, rabbits, squirrels, even with raccoons, fattened on purpose for the great dinner of the Christian year.

Standing atop one butcher's stall was a huge, fat ram with a cross of evergreens on his breast and a crown of greens on his head, while on each shoulder were small epaulettes of blue and red ribbons. The ram had distinguished himself in life by getting fatter than his brethren, and he was being honored accordingly. The turkey-hunting gentlemen stopped to stare and admire his wondrous proportions. Ladies stood entranced before him, and small boys gazed from a distance in respectful wonder.

Nearby were stalls piled up with steaks and chops and joints. Other stalls were loaded with smelts and haddock, flounder and lobsters, pickerel, salmon, and seemingly every other fish that the oceans produce, glistening fishes of many a mark and spot, laid out in assorted rows—for this was the city's and the nation's premier fish market. Completion of the first transcontinental railroad in 1869 had multiplied the demand for Fulton Market oysters. By 1892 thousands of barrels of incomparable Long Island saddlerocks and bluepoints were shipped each Christmas to Denver and other Western cities. Every steamer that left New York after the first week of

# CHRISTMAS EVE MARKETING IN OLD NEW YORK

December carried large shipments of American oysters for holiday consumption abroad.

At one fish stand, the display was particularly artistic. Immense silvery salmon, with the tiniest of little fish grouped around them, contrasted their white sheen with the fiery red of the Southern red snapper. As a fringe around the whole were prawns, crayfish, and shrimp, some in their natural state with mailed bodies of blue and green, others boiled pink and scarlet. Crowning the display was a diminutive Christmas tree, its branches hung with small crayfish that were brilliantly pink or blue against the green. Small shells of mussels, clams, and scallops, some in their natural state, others bronzed, silvered, or gilt, made dainty ornaments.

At adjoining stalls were the objects of the gentlemen's quest. Mountains of turkeys, some so fat their skins appeared about to burst, as well as corpulent geese and chickens, reposing on beds of evergreen, were surrounded by eager crowds picking their favorites, bargaining and joking with the dealers, refusing what was offered, and insisting on selecting what had been selected and paid for by others, amid a hubbub of laughter and good-humored jostling.

The narrow passages between the market stalls were jammed with an assortment of humanity as diverse as the fish and game offered for sale. Standing next to a pale, pinch-faced young woman in a red shawl stood a lady clad in sealskin and silk, accompanied by a servant. She was considering a fat turkey with a red paper rose on its breast that a persuasive man with a black face and

# CHRISTMAS EVE MARKETING IN OLD NEW YORK

white apron was endeavoring to sell. Cozy old gentlemen and stout old ladies with fat purses elbowed their way through the crowds and held conferences, short, sharp, and decisive, with the marketmen. Now and again, undernourished young mothers looked longingly at the plump turkeys and geese and turned sadly away to fill their baskets with less expensive provender for consumption by the Tiny Tims at home.

Not every turkey that left the market was dead. On Christmas Eve in 1887, a man with a confident, self-satisfied air stood on the front deck of the Fulton Ferry bound for Brooklyn. Neatly tucked under his arm was a live turkey, with its head sticking out behind and an ample array of tail feathers in front. The ferry had scarcely started when the turkey began to gobble vigorously, to the dismay of its owner and the astonishment of the other passengers.

"Maybe you're carrying him wrong," suggested a kind-hearted passenger. "Why don't you keep his head up front?"

"Well, you see," said the owner, "this is a country bird. He's no city bird. I just bought him in the market and he seemed so lively and pert I was afraid he'd shy at the horsecars and elevated. I'll tell you how it is," he added, confidently tucking the turkey's head into his pocket to keep it quiet. "We got pretty badly left at my house at Thanksgiving time. The price of turkeys goes up so high around Thanksgiving that we bought our turkey the week before, and the weather being very warm, when the day came around, the bird was spoiled—and Thanksgiving without a turkey ain't worth foolin' with. I made up my mind I wouldn't run no risks at Christmas, and I wouldn't pay no fancy prices, so I've bought a bird on the hoof and now I don't care if it gets hot enough to melt butter."

He walked off the boat and started up Brooklyn's Fulton Street with his bird gobbling merrily every few yards.

By nightfall the Brooklyn men had purchased their turkeys on their way home, and the gentlemen from Fifth Avenue had returned uptown carrying flour bags from which a pair of yellow claws protruded—this being the New York method of bundling up a turkey. The business in Fulton Market was about over, but it was just beginning in and around Washington Market. For Washington Market, like a city, had its outlying suburbs. Each Christmas, the streets approaching the market, such as Vesey Street, lighted its entire length with flaming torches, were transformed into an outdoor bazaar, offering every commodity from game and fruit down to penny whistles. The section of Vesey Street that ran unevenly downhill to the Hudson River was the city's wholesale Christmas tree market. But the great attraction of the street stalls was poultry—unlimited, cheap poultry, neither as fresh nor as good nor as expensive as that sold inside the market. Outside, nobody thought about rice-fed Maryland turkeys with black legs. They were just turkeys. The tea and coffee stores, on other days the specialty of the street, could only be approached on Christmas Eve through a veritable maze of dangling ducks, geese, chickens, and turkeys.

By seven o'clock throngs of people had gathered. Here the shoppers were mostly women. Some were accompanied by little children who held tightly to their mothers' skirts with one hand and blew tin trumpets, purchased from a nearby stall, with the other. But most were alone and pushed along resolutely with their great baskets on their hips or in front of them, until they were wedged tightly into a mass before some poultry stall that had particularly low prices.

Inside Washington Market, butchers and tradesmen were particular about the starching of their white aprons or long blue gowns. But the tradesmen outside the market had lower standards of dress—and decorum. They would seize ladies by the arm, imploring them to look at chickens they were "sacrificing" at eight cents a pound. On a crowded street corner close to the market, an old woman with a weather-beaten face sat enthroned in a newly erected evergreen-trimmed booth. Her subjects were a hundred turkeys with the gobble gone out of them and a few geese. Her nationality was confirmed by the occasional *"Gott im Himmel!"* that crossed her lips when an adventurous customer had the audacity to offer her ten cents a pound for her turkeys.

A little farther down the street were piles of holly and mistletoe. A nineteenth-century Druid in a burlap apron stood by a barrel and sold his mystic berries quickly for ten cents a branch. The holly was made into wreaths and into stars, crosses, and anchors. A red-nosed, shaky-kneed man came wobbling along from the corner grog-shop. He eyed the red berries as he passed, stooped, and picked a tiny twig from the sidewalk; he stuck it in the lapel of his old coat and wobbled on with his head held high.

For squares about, the streets were blocked with grocers' carts and other vehicles. The cold night air was filled with the thousand and one cries of strong-lunged vendors, each offering prices they claimed would "defy competition." Among the milling crowd, silhouetted against the gaslights inside the market, was an old German woman dressed entirely in black, with the neck of a goose hanging limp over the side of her cloth-covered basket. Sailors from the steamships, whose black hulls loomed along the neighboring Hudson riverfront, or from the coasting vessels moored nearby, roamed in groups amid the bustling marketers.

Inside the market building, the air was heavy with the smell of cedar and fish, hams and cheese, fruits and vegetables. Forests of turkeys, groves of chickens, stacks of hams, barricades of butter and cheeses succeeded each other in bewildering variety. In the midst of the poultry was a brown-coated deer with gracefully branching antlers. At one stall were huge black bears, killed in the Adirondacks, and elk and deer from Minnesota, canvasback ducks from Maryland, English pheasants, and hares from Germany. A cluster of gray-haired opossums hung solemnly by their ratlike tails next to black and gray squirrels. Partridges, quail, squabs, and prairie hens dangled in long rows near quarters of antelope, great red sides of beef, and white legs of mutton, set off with ropes of laurel leaves, colored ribbons, and paper roses. Several hundred rabbits with soft brown fur, swinging against the outer wall, were regarded apprehensively by their live brethren, nervously nibbling cabbage leaves in cages.

Despite the rush for turkeys, the butchers, with paper bouquets on their broad, apron-covered chests, had no lack of customers. It was only on occasions like Christmas that they hung such large pieces of meat on the hooks, since the loss of weight from exposure to the air was from five to ten pounds in a single sheep. Ordinarily, butchers kept the carcasses in ice-houses, exposing only smaller parts for sale.

Interspersed among the meats and poultry were small mountains of vegetables: celery and parsley, lettuce and brussels sprouts, strings of red peppers and white onions. Bushel baskets and peck measures were heaped full and running over with cranberries. Mandarin oranges from Louisiana and lemons and oranges from Florida and the West Indies were piled in pyramids like cannon shot. Freshly opened boxes of fine pressed figs, Egyptian dates, apples, and grapes were displayed next to piles of brown-shelled walnuts, hickory nuts, and Italian chestnuts (preferred by educated cooks to French and American chestnuts for stuffing turkeys).

The main turkey market occupied a long gallery of approximately one hundred stalls at the northern end of the market. Most dealers displayed their poultry on long tiers of hooks that formed tall trellises of chickens and

triumphal arches of turkeys. The fowls, hung by their legs, were taken down and put up with a sort of boat hook, which was in constant use. Each dealer was busily taking down fowls here and hanging them up there, meanwhile reciting: "Shillin' a pound, shillin' a pound. Step right up, gents, step right up, ladies, and get yer Christmas turkeys. Finest corn-fed gobblers. Choicest thing in the market. Only twelve cents a pound. Here you are, finest Christmas turkeys, just waitin' to be ct."

All the while, the gaslight flickered and flared upon the long-necked cadavers, casting eerie shadows on the walls and ceiling.

Cruising around each poultry stand were all kinds of purchasers, from the inexperienced young housewife who took the marketman's word, to the wary old Hoboken landlady who took nobody's word and trusted only her eyes, nostrils, and fingers. There was no judging the age of a turkey by its tenderness any longer. Science had developed wonderful tricks since the days when honest farmers first raised turkeys and geese for the metropolitan market. Now, sharp old farmers poured spoonfuls of vinegar down their turkeys' throats to make them tender, and the owner of one poultry yard discovered that a turkey could be made plump if he skillfully inserted a quill into the areolar tissue and blew it up, and that this tempting plumpness could be preserved by tying a string around the bird's neck.

Throughout the evening there was no lull in the continuous flood of human beings. Many delicate creatures from the uptown districts were unaccustomed to such jostling and pushing as went on when, for instance, a burly two-hundred-pound Irishman sighted a fine fat goose, adorned with little American flags and evergreen wreaths, marked it for his own, and energetically elbowed his way to it.

"Send up a brace of your best ducks with that turkey," said a portly, comfortable-looking man, apparently a banker.

"Haven't you any chickens cheaper than these?" asked a woman with a thin, worn face, as she drew a tattered shawl more closely around her shivering form with a hand blue with cold, while the other rested on the shoulder of a little boy. Receiving a negative answer, she turned slowly away. "Never mind," she said. "We'll have a chicken New Year's."

Some of the "old country" buyers still held to their own ideas of the proper dish for Christmas, and the goose was still demanded in rich Irish brogue, while ribs of beef were ordered in the accents of London or Manchester.

In 1880 a *New York Daily Tribune* reporter described a Christmas Eve incident reminiscent of Charles Dickens:

> Occasionally an unusually large woman and basket filled the sidewalk and stopped all progress until a small boy, butting deftly with his head, suddenly propelled her forward. Everybody was hustled, crowded and trodden upon, but the good temper that prevailed was remarkable.
>
> A German Hausfrau, nearly six feet in height, plowed through the crowd carrying a brace of rabbits, still and

solid as bags of salt, in her left hand. Against her broad bosom, she hugged one great brown-paper parcel from which four yellow claws stuck out and another paper bundle with bananas and oranges. With her strong right hand, she smote a big turkey upon his wishbone so hard that she sent him swinging like a pendulum as she demanded the price. The marketman regarded her with awe and proceeded to haul down half his stock for her inspection. Others standing nearby wondered audibly how many she was planning to feed. She paid no heed to comments but bargained away with tremendous energy.

One didn't have to be descended from the Pilgrims to want turkey for Christmas. The air was filled with a babel of tongues. One butcher engaged a linguist to stand in front of his stall, who repeated over and over in French, "Here is where you get your mutton and turkey—*le bon mouton, le bon dindon.*"

Some of the German women were accompanied by their husbands, who did not deign to carry the baskets for their wives but did the purchasing in a grand and lofty manner. Their enjoyment over the stalls where different sausages were heaped was surpassed only by an exhibition of boars' heads decorated with colored sugars. Ham, tongue, and sausage stalls were busy as beehives on a July day. While stallkeepers sold bundle after bundle, the fingers of their wives and daughters, who had come down to help during the height of the rush, were swift at the cash drawers.

Mixed in the crowd were black men with a partiality for 'possums. Of all the gustatory delights known to them, the flesh of the opossum baked to the proper degree of brown, together with "sweet taters," was the dearest.

After ten o'clock the dealers became even more vociferous, keeping up their ceaseless announcements of "tender turkeys," "nice ducks," "elegant geese," and "fine jack rabbits." Sharp-eyed bargain hunters began to lay in their supplies, and among the crowd were many a shrewd, wizen-faced boardinghouse keeper and corpulent old gentleman puffing and blowing as they hurried along under the burden of huge turkeys scantily clad in red tissue paper, gigantic hams, and geese. A sturdy mechanic with a basket on each arm and pairs of fattened and featherless poultry slung over his shoulders collided with another mechanic with bundles of like appearance. Wishing each other a happy Christmas, they went off in opposite directions.

The market floor was slippery with ice and grease. Near the poultry stalls, a carpet of feathers was strewn; elsewhere the sawdust was churned up by passing feet. The rattle of stiff paper, the smack of the butcher's hand on smooth, hard beef, the jabber of a confusion of tongues—all melded together in a cheery hubbub. Outside, peddlers cried, doors swung and banged, wagons rattled, everybody talked at once, and another Christmas Eve passed swiftly for buyer and seller alike. The wind whistled and whipped through Vesey Street and about the gables of the old market, and the good-natured crowd stamped its feet and slapped its arms. Everywhere was a feast of bundles. Everybody had one, and almost everybody had two or three plus a basket filled to over-flowing, and often a holly wreath as well.

At midnight, although a large number of the stalls and stores still remained open and were well patronized, nearly all were depleted in stock, with a consequent plethora of cash on hand. In the cold night air, the glare of four great limelights illuminated Barclay and Washington streets with a strange green white hue and transformed the moving figures along the street into weird hobgobblin shapes. As late as twelve-thirty, the procession of large parcels with turkey legs protruding was still moving north, south, and east, as well as west over the river to the dark regions of New Jersey.

## Chapter 2

## THE FEAST OF CHRISTMAS

**B**y and large,
colonial America had
a prejudice against celebrating
Christmas. One of the chief
limitations of such
thinking was that it allowed
none of the joyful excesses of the Christmas table. But
Christmas celebrants had the last word, and in the early
years of the nineteenth century the tradition of Christmas Day dyspepsia spread rapidly. Signs that a woman's
concerns, even on the frontier, were little different from
those of more modern times exist in a diary account of a
Christmas on the banks of the Ohio River in 1819: "I
went one mile and a half, to borrow, from Mrs. Delight
Williams, six tumblers, for the use of our coming Christmas party."

The following Christmas, Richard Fowler, an Englishman, spent the holiday at Albion, Illinois. There, in the vast prairie wilderness, he and thirty-one other souls enjoyed a turkey as well as more conventional English dishes: mutton, roast beef, mince pie, and plum pudding.

The 1877 autobiography of Solomon Caswell, of Troy Township, Michigan, gives a good account of other frontier Christmas fare:

> In those early days [about 1835] the wild deer was plentiful in these parts. I have killed many on my own farm, which was a much quicker way of getting fresh meat than to go to Detroit for it.
>
> One Christmas some friends came to spend the day with us. My wife said she wished we had a good piece of venison to bake. I told her I would see if I could get a deer. I took my gun and went about 80 rods from the house and came to a track where five deer had just passed along. About six inches of snow had fallen that morning so I could easily track them. About 15 rods from me laid a large tree and I thought perhaps they might be behind that. I had my rifle ready. Pretty soon out stepped a deer. Crack went my rifle and the deer fell. The guests said to my wife, do you think he has killed one? To be sure he has, she replied. They helped bring it in. We soon dressed it and had baked venison for our Christmas dinner.

Even at the end of the nineteenth century, it wasn't always necessary to live on the frontier to shoot your own Christmas dinner. In 1899 a policeman named Lindemann bagged a wild goose from his front porch in New York City. On the Sunday night before Christmas, the sergeant had been enjoying a night off, a great event in

the days when New York policemen worked six and a
half days a week. After supper he went out onto his front
stoop to enjoy a smoke. His ear caught the honking of a
flock of geese, sounding at first like the distant barking of
a pack of dogs. He dashed into his house to get his Rem-
ington rifle. Right over his roof, he could plainly see by
the light of the moon a large flock of birds and could hear
the whistling of their wings. Taking aim at the middle of
them, he fired. In a few seconds, a fat goose plummeted
onto the sidewalk opposite his house and was brought to
him by his setter dog, an excited witness of the im-
promptu hunting scene.

Americans who clung to English tradition usually
gathered around a sirloin of beef or a goose for Christmas dinner, though at some New York tables, roistering
John Bulls carved saddles of genuine imported South-
down mutton flanked with succulent capons from Liverpool. But if there was some choice in the main course,
there were only two possible desserts at an English
Christmas dinner: the celebrated mince pie and the even
more revered cannonball-shaped plum pudding, the sort
Charles Dickens immortalized in *A Christmas Carol*. Superstition said that the pudding should be stirred by
everyone in the family when it was in preparation weeks
before Christmas. For the rest of their lives, many recalled the excitement when, as children, they had been
invited into the kitchen to stir on a Sunday afternoon in
early November. They stirred the ingredients in a clock-
wise manner—the direction the sun proceeds around the
earth, they were told—and each made a secret wish. To

stir in the opposite direction—"windershins," as one local dialect put it—was to ask for trouble. Every family had their own recipe for plum pudding, believed to be better than any other in the world. In New York in 1898, an old lady well versed in all matters connected with old-fashioned plum pudding gave as her recipe: "Put plenty of good things in, my dear, and plenty of good things will come out."

Regardless of the exact ingredients, the suet- and raisin-based once-a-year alcoholic delight was traditionally shaped into a ball, wrapped in a square yard of stout unbleached muslin, and hung up to ferment (to increase its proof) before it was taken down and steamed all Christmas morning. It was only at the turn of the century that the crockery bowl used today to shape and store the pudding came into use.

A charming bit of stage management commonly accompanied the arrival of the Christmas pudding at the table. Gaslights were turned low in anticipation of the moment the great pudding was triumphantly carried forth, flaming brandy forming a soft blue halo around the brown-speckled sphere, with a sprig of holly stuck into the top. The glory of just such a plum pudding was emotionally described in an *Illustrated London News* of 1848:

> Lo! the lid is raised, curiosity stands on tip-toe, eyes sparkle with anticipation, little hands are clapped in ecstasy almost too great to find expression in words. The hour arrives when the pudding, in all its glory and splendor, shines upon the table. How eager is the anticipation

of the near delight! How beautifully it steams! How delicious it smells! How round it is! A kiss is round, the horizon is round, the earth is round, the moon is round, the sun and stars, and all the host of heaven are round. So is plum pudding.

English aliens may have clung to tradition when it came to their Christmas dinner, but Germans, more than any other nationality, took many years to become even partially Americanized. Although American grocers in New York displayed many tempting articles at Christmas, for the Germans who wished their Christmas to be *gerade wie in Deutschland* ("the same as in Germany"), the German neighborhood delicatessen with its supply of the old familiar foods and aromas was far more attractive. Innumerable kinds of sausages, smoked beef, ham, hare, and wild boar were among the popular stock imported for Christmas. In 1900 boars were selling for a formidable fifteen to twenty dollars a head. That year, a reporter found a dealer in table luxuries in the German district of the city unpacking and arranging his holiday stock.

"These Karlstadter hams," said the grocer, ducking between hanging Holsteiner hares, "should be better than the ordinary article because of the treatment they receive. Instead of being cured in salt 'vater' they are prepared in salted milk. This gives the delicious flavor that cannot be achieved by other means. Another popular delicacy is the goosebreast, the greatest product of the German smokehouse, and no matter how well the goose may be fattened, nor how carefully it may be smoked in this country, it can never be made to resemble the taste of this real Pomeranian article."

Much sought after in his shop were such holiday comestibles as stollen, apple and pear butter, plum duff, and apricot jam, as well as astonishing quantities of honey, almond, and spice cakes fresh from the baker or imported in fancy boxes that teetered in great piles.

German bakeries were crowded from morning till night with basket-bearing Hausfraus all calling for *kuchen*. The *Lebkuchen*, or honeycakes, were probably the most common variety. Half a dozen of these large rectangular cookies, held together by pink paper labels or done up in bright green tissue paper, were sold for five cents. The *Lebkuchen*'s salient ingredient was honey, which gave it its characteristic flavor. In any well-run household or bakery, the dough was made from three to six months before the holidays. It was kneaded and put away in stone jars, where it underwent some mysterious change and became bakeable early in December. There was no yeast in the dough; the kneading and honey gave it such lightness as it possessed. In addition to *Lebkuchen* squares and oblongs, there were hearts and other fancy shapes, gaily iced with "For a good child" or some other appropriate motto. In Germany a handsomely frosted and decorated *Lebkuchen* with a holiday sentiment iced upon it was an acceptable gift between friends. In New York only an occasional latecomer still sent such a gift, but not a single German household in the city was without its plate of *Lebkuchen* left out like candy to be nibbled through the holidays.

# THE FEAST OF CHRISTMAS

Small round spice drops named *Pfeffennuch* were another popular cookie that sold in great quantities at that season of the year. Made of brown *Lebkuchen* dough, they were cut and rolled into round drops a little smaller than a golf ball, baked, and then dropped in sugar while still hot. When cool, they were roughly and deliciously coated with crystallized syrup.

Anise cakes, or *Springerle Kuchen,* also a staple article during the holidays, were little white squares and fancy shapes, not iced but stamped with quaint figures on top. Nothing was so sure to delight a German baby's heart as a gift of one of these cakes, for it served a double purpose: first as a plaything, and then as a meal.

The German bakeries were an inexhaustible source of wonder to the uninitiated American. In the pastry cook's window were elaborate gingerbread houses and castles with icing snow on the roofs and gingerbread generals in full uniform riding horses with trappings and manes of the whitest and shiniest icing. And there were gingerbread women with long skirts, their hair done up in nets made by threads of icing, their faces adorned with the roundest and pinkest cheeks.

Children and adults alike were attracted to the baker's counter by displays of little baskets overflowing with incredibly realistic peaches, pears, and apples, sausages, hams, little dolls, and animals, particularly the pig, a holiday good-luck symbol, all done in candy. Called "marzipan," they were made entirely from almond paste, sugar, and food coloring.

But the Germans were not alone in their *Weihnachts-*

*gebäck* ("Christmas baked goods") that filled the December air with scents of cinnamon and cloves, vanilla, and ginger. Every nationality had its own festive culinary traditions. Today one can put on ten pounds just thinking about all the food at an old-time Christmas dinner. Happily, in those days of more substantial viands, nobody counted calories. Our ancestors abandoned themselves with gusto to the pleasures of the table all year round. Then on Christmas they were ready for some really serious eating. From Maine to Pennsylvania in the 1890s, Yankee tables wouldn't have been considered ready for Christmas dinner without a huge chicken pie to supplement a turkey of extensive proportions. And in half those homes, it wouldn't have been Christmas without a generous dish of scalloped oysters as well.

In their book *Growing Up in the Horse and Buggy Days,* C. E. Ladd and E. R. Eastman recalled a typical Christmas dinner in western New York State. After second helpings from two turkeys on the table, scalloped oysters, baked squash, mashed turnips, and sliced cabbage, came apple or mince pie. Most of the men took both—and a piece of pound cake, fig layer cake, or marble cake that an aunt had brought along as well.

Many tables included both turkey and goose, and there would be several loaves of homemade bread and every form of preserve: grape, blackberry, raspberry, or strawberry; crabapple jelly; and sweet and sour pickles, not to mention a cut-glass dish of watermelon rind.

In those days, when the breakfast table alone was customarily laden with more food than is now consumed at all the meals of the day combined, someone with a Christmas appetite could wrap himself around astonishing quantities of food. One of the best accounts of "the groaning board," as the fully laden table was called, was recorded in Toronto in 1855. Believe it or not, this was Christmas Day fare for a typical middle-class family comprised of two grandparents, a bachelor son, two daughters, their husbands, and seven grandchildren:

BREAKFAST—lamb chops, toast, pork pies, deviled kidneys, porridge and coffee.

DINNER—four kinds of soup: oyster, chicken, gumbo, and mutton broth. The main course was comprised of eleven roasts: beef, pork, mutton, turkey, venison, three chickens, and three geese, as well as potatoes, carrots, turnips, parsley and onions.

DESSERT—trifles, suet puddings, a huge plum pudding, four kinds of fruit cake and three kinds of wine.

SWEETMEATS—for those who were still hungry—lozenges, fruit drops, sugared almonds, licorice sticks, and barley sugar rings.

SUPPER—ham, veal, pork, beef, chicken, tongue, turkey, brawn, headcheese, seven kinds of fruit jelly, and a dozen pies and cakes.

Apparently they joyously waded through it all.

On this side of the border, Americans were holding up their end of the table. The Christmas dinner menu of a Chicago hotel in 1855 gives some indication of the opportunities that lay before the Christmas gourmand. After bluepoints and soup came a choice of stuffed bass or boiled salmon. Then a choice of roasts—thirty-six to select from—among them turkey, broiled leg of mountain sheep, leg of moose, loin of elk, cinnamon bear, blacktail deer, loin of venison, saddle of antelope, opossum, black bear, and ducks innumerable. The chef offered canvasback duck, wood duck, butterball duck, brant, mallard, blue-winged teal, spoonbill, green-winged teal, and pintail duck, as well as sage hen, partridge, quail, plover, and fillet of pheasant. Among the ornamental dishes on the menu were a pyramid of wild turkey in aspic and an aspic of Lobster Queen Victoria.

In the North we believe that frost and snow sharpen Christmas appetites. To be objective, it must be said that Southerners did pretty well, as well. In 1907 a food editor for *The New York Tribune* interviewed a grand old Southern lady whose memories went back to Christmases in the 1850s.

> Christmas [she said] an old-fashioned Christmas! you folks know mighty little about it, because up to the war time Christmas lived down South. It was the day of days. We had the taste and smells of it. Never was, never will be such good eating again. And the things were nearly as good to look at as to eat—though we had never heard of orchids and never put a yard of ribbon on our tables. What we did put there was the best we had of everything—linen, china, silver, glass. And the dinner itself took up so much room there was none left for decorations, pure and simple.

# THE FEAST OF CHRISTMAS

But at dessert we came out strong—served our fruit, our oranges, apples and occasionally malaga grapes—we called them Sicily grapes—in tall openwork china bowls, white with gilt bands. Nuts came on the table in Wedgwood boats, our sweet homemade wine in gold stemmed glasses, our figs and raisins in the finest glass dishes we could muster.

But the Christmasiest thing of all was the egg nog. It was full man's size—but nobody slighted it. It began Christmas, in fact—about 4 o'clock in the morning.

We had turkey, of course, but no cranberries. Why should we bother with them when jellied apples were so much better and prettier?

We had cake pans in those days, to be sure, but never enough for the Christmas baking. It was a liberal education just to taste one of Mammy's oven pound cakes. They were baked between live coals, with only a greased paper between them and the iron, but they came out the richest brown, innocent of scores or streaks, even if they were six inches thick and sixteen across. Fine grained and light as a feather—and so good you felt like crying when you realized you couldn't eat any more.

Mammy made batter puddings—but on sufferance. What she reveled in was cheesecake—though she was fairly well affected toward sweet potato custard. She would have been perfectly happy in cooking if only she had been able somehow, someway, to grease butter and sweeten sugar. "I hates dese yere victuals whar yer hab ter wa'ar out yo' tongue tryin' to find de taste," she used to say.

Along with them went fried pies—made of sun-dried peaches, slowly stewed until very soft, mashed, sweetened liberally, then spread over rounds of crust and the unspread half turned over and pinched and the pie popped into boiling hot fat. In two minutes it was turned to brown the other side. A hundred was a good Christmas frying—and gone long before New Year. Our doctor boasted proudly that, "in good fettle, he could eat an acre of fried pies."

Speaking of pies, walking along a New York street just before Christmas in 1871, a reporter noted a pleasant aroma. It recalled memories of his mother's kitchen many years before. Like a bloodhound on the trail, he instinctively followed his nose. If it was not the smell of baked pies, what was it? From a large building came the din and clatter of chopping and pounding and a rattle of tin pans. Out in front stood many wagons and vans blocking the street, and boys and men with pies in baskets, boxes, and trays were rushing in and out, hurry scurry, as if life depended upon it.

"Why," he asked a driver, "do you have two horses to one pie-wagon?" He could understand two horses to a load of paving-stones, but not for a load of pies.

"Why, you see," said the driver, "a pie [he said poy] is a kind of delicate thing, and has got to be kept flaky. The heft of a pie is two and a half pounds, and as we carry 500 of them, and they is got to be carried along easy, a steady wagon with no shake is the thing. We loads up mostly with 500, but as we are driven nearly mad just now, we piles in all the pies the horses can pull."

# THE FEAST OF CHRISTMAS

"You don't mean to say that all those wagons are full of pies that are sold in a day, do you?" the reporter inquired.

"Five hundred—eight hundred—to a load, ain't nothing. I'll be back here today two or three times for more."

"What kind is most in demand?"

"They is running on minces just now, and is hot on cranberries. Jim, what's your load?" he inquired of another driver.

"Three hundred minces, one hundred apples, and the rest of the load is pumpkins and cranberries. Bless me, if there isn't one street I'm most afeered to go to, seeing I've had to disappoint 'em three days running on minces. It don't do to fool with women folks just now who has made up their minds to have mince pies for their Christmas dinners."

Without much trouble, the reporter entered the pie factory. Here whizzed a steam engine turning pie-making machinery, and there glowed a furnace throwing its ruddy glare on golden pies. Pies! He never saw so many pies in his life! Pies stacked up fifty deep, all around him higher than his head, coming and going, being baked. Men were slapping and banging about lumps of dough, rolling the pie crust into sheets, pricking them and marking them with an *H*, while scores of women were ladling out apples and other good things and cramming them into pies. Nearby stood hogsheads of sugar and a man distributing it around with a shovel in the most reckless way. Off to one side hissed and spluttered huge vats with cranberries cooking by steam.

"What is that awful-looking machine, grinding and rumbling away?"

"It is the mince-meat-maker," answered the proprietor.

"Are all those vats full of mince-meat?"

"Yes," replied the proprietor, "and we are dreadfully short, and can hardly keep up with the demand. That poor machine is worked beyond its capacity."

"How many pies do you turn out in a week?"

"At an average, 40,000 per week, but we are running much above that."

"How many mouths will that feed?"

"It's hard to say. Maybe it's according to whether they cuts them in four or across."

"How on earth did this colossal business begin?"

"In the simplest way. My wife commenced baking with a range, and when we had sold the first four we made four more. After a while—it was 1858—the range wouldn't stand the pressure—no, not a hundred ranges. The people was wild on our pies, and it's kept expanding in a kind of overwhelming way ever since. We make them honest. Try a piece of the mince."

A huge segment was offered to the reporter, who found it sincerity itself—in a pie sense. Thanking the worthy baker for his politeness, he left with his mouth full.

*Toothsome* was a word commonly used in the nineteenth century to describe the year's crowning gastronomical feast: Christmas dinner. Each Christmastide, "Toothsome!" was heard with remarkable frequency as Americans gathered about their dinner tables to enjoy a wealth of tasty game birds, of which the turkey, roasted golden brown and filled with savory stuffing was, of course, king.

The turkey, the bird Benjamin Franklin unsuccessfully proposed as our national symbol, had become instead our American Christmas dinner. No researcher can be quite certain about the origin of the bird's name, but a few facts are certain. The turkey is native to America. Spanish conquistadors discovered huge flocks of the Southwestern species (smaller than its Eastern cousin) in Mexico, and they introduced the strange bird to the Old World. The turkey is generally believed to have arrived in England in 1524. Three-quarters of a century later, when the first English colonists arrived in the New World, they greeted the wild turkey as an old friend and called it by the name we know today. Settlers wrote of great flocks that "sallied by our doors." In a seventeenth-century description of Maryland and Virginia, intended as a recruiting brochure for potential colonists, John Hammond exaggerated broadly in his description of their size, "so large that I have seen some weigh near three-score pounds." Be that as it may, the wild turkeys that inhabited the eastern half of the continent weighed from ten to thirty pounds and stood from two to three feet in height. Strikingly handsome, their plumage varied in color from greenish bronze to black and white. The wild turkey's keen sight made it legendary among woodsmen. Due to the placement of its eyes, the bird can detect the slightest movement within an arc of three hundred degrees.

Wild turkeys quickly became a staple of colonial diets. In those days, turkeys were skewered and hung over a fire. Basted frequently with salt and water, they were roasted until the breast emitted steam. Judging by the short roasting time recommended in early recipes, some pretty rare birds were consumed. According to one, a large turkey took "about an hour and 20 minutes."

From colonial times onward, the turkey was involved in a long rivalry with roast beef for its place on the Christmas dinner table of Americans of English ancestry. On Christmas Day in 1840, *The New York Herald* reported that New York's fire department had fought a fire at a lumberyard, then rushed to a chimney fire, and afterward "the firemen went to the enjoyment of their roast beef and plum pudding."

In New York in 1842, it was recorded that, for several days before Christmas, turkeys could be purchased on board sloops at the riverside at seven cents a pound. In other parts of the city they were available in butcher shops and from wagons driven through the streets, like oyster and potato carts, at prices ranging from eight to ten cents a pound. In 1845, on Broadway and other principal streets, one reporter said, "almost everyone seemed to be carrying either a turkey or a handful of evergreens. We saw many a poor fellow, tired, going along puffing under the weight of a huge turkey slung over his shoulder." On the day before Christmas in 1866, *The New*

*York Times* reported, "Everybody wanted to be on the front platform of the cars, for everybody had a turkey bundle which they did not wish to rub against their neighbor."

While extraordinary efforts had been made to develop oxen, sheep, and hogs to mammoth proportions, domesticated turkeys in the poultry yard were comparatively neglected until the middle of the nineteenth century. In 1860 a "monster turkey" weighing a fat and juicy thirty-four pounds was exhibited in New York City by a purveyor of provisions to several of the city's best hotels. The great excitement that the bird's rotund proportions evoked among the turkey trade suggested a wide field for experimentation in that direction. Within twenty years, forty-pound gobblers were recorded. On Christmas Day in 1893, the cafe at the Plaza Hotel served one that weighed sixty-one pounds.

In 1913 an eighty-pound turkey died a martyr to the cause as he tried to reach the ninety-pound mark. On December 19, "Buster," the champion heavyweight turkey of Crawford County, Ohio, suffered a heart attack at his farmyard at Bucyrus. His owner, Charles Aumiller, and Buster had taken prizes in many poultry shows in that section. After their last show, Aumiller began putting on the finishing touches so that Buster could be dished up for Christmas dinner. Buster cooperated and ate early and late. He had reached the dignified weight of eighty pounds when he dropped dead as he was being placed on the scales. According to *The New York Tribune*'s obituary, fatty degeneration of the heart had killed him.

Out on the frontier, in a lonely little fort miles from a railroad, any turkey, regardless of size, was as welcome as Christmas itself. In 1894 Elizabeth Bacon Custer, widow of General George Custer, recalled Christmases on the plains a quarter-century before for a reporter for *The Brooklyn Eagle.*

> To secure a Christmas dinner was even more important than to procure a Christmas tree. If we chanced to be near a little town, no one rode through the place without throwing a calculating glance into every yard or about the door yard of the less pretentious huts. A chicken, a duck, or a turkey was quickly noted and the owner was called out to find a booted and spurred cavalryman at the door, who accosted him with the usual frontier salutation: "I say, stranger, can I engage my Christmas dinner of you?"

In the same period, the middle of the nineteenth century, in St. Paul, Minnesota, only the rich could afford a turkey. The birds sold for the incredible price of $1.50 to $2.00 because they had to be transported from Iowa and Illinois by sleigh.

In large Eastern cities, no sooner had turkeys become established as the birds of Christmas than they became a fringe benefit given by benevolent employers to their workers. In 1882, for example, turkeys were given to the crews of the ferryboats that ran between New York and Hoboken. At nightfall on December 23, 350 ferry hands, ticket sellers, and men employed in the carpenter and machine shops gathered at the company's office between the slips in Hoboken. One by one, each man received his turkey from the hands of the company timekeeper. A drawing was held to determine who would take home the largest of the fowls. General good humor prevailed, and no dissatisfaction was expressed at the results, though the largest birds were twice the size of the smallest.

The following year Austin Corbin, a banker and the director of the Long Island Railroad, ran a special train loaded with plump Christmas turkeys from end to end of the island and presented a turkey to each of his employees. On Sunday, December 23, the thermometer registered zero at nine in the morning in the depot at Long Island City; outside, snow covered the ground. Engine number 31 stood chuffing great white clouds of steam. Coupled to it were a baggage car, a parlor car, and a dining car. Precisely at 9:15, the train thundered away on its mission, festooned with ropes of evergreen and decorated with holly. Running the length of each side of the baggage car was stretched the motto A MERRY CHRISTMAS. Inside, on a long table and in hampers, were twelve hundred frozen turkeys. Officers of the railroad and several representatives of the press were in the other two cars, heated as warm as ovens. Illness prevented Mr. Corbin from joining the fun himself. Nonetheless, his turkey express plowed swiftly across a white winter landscape, from mainline to spur and back again, delivering its special cargo. Each bird bore a tag with a name attached to its left drumstick and a letter expressing Mr. Corbin's compliments of the season. At Patchogue an extra engine was added, and between that point and Sag Harbor the train met frequent snowdrifts. At each station the assembled beneficiaries received the train with cheers—telegraph operators, station agents, porters, messengers, conductors, brakemen, and scrub women. When the train pulled out, little processions of employees wended their respective ways homeward, burdened with turkeys, faces wreathed in smiles, although it was so cold on the eastern end of the island that one old inhabitant alleged that the mercury in his thermometer was frozen solid.

In the afternoon, Mr. Corbin's guests tucked into a lavish dinner in the handsomely appointed restaurant car. The train whirled around the curves in such lively style that the diners had to keep their wineglasses drained or the champagne would splash out. If the guests were not full when they returned, it was not the fault of Daniel Webster, the rotund black purveyor of the road, who was as famous in gastronomy as his namesake was in oratory. After dinner, amidst aromatic clouds of Havana cigar smoke, the gentlemen amused themselves between stops with songs, stories, good-natured raillery, and, even though it was Sunday, a table or two of poker. The cars rattled and swayed and cinders streaked past the frosted windowpanes like black hail. After a run of 260 miles, the train arrived back in Long Island City with not a single turkey but with several score empty champagne bottles, several empty cigar boxes, and a crowd of passengers who didn't seem to have minded missing church that day.

# THE FEAST OF CHRISTMAS

By the last quarter of the nineteenth century, charity organizations increasingly saw to it that the poor enjoyed Christmas turkeys. In New York City, where the Department of Charities had begun to provide a special Christmas dinner for those under its charge, teams of horses labored through the streets dragging huge heavily loaded wagons. In 1884 one reporter said they carried enough chickens and turkeys "to populate a western prairie." That Christmas Day, at the county almshouse on Staten Island, five great cauldrons were filled to the brim with turkeys steaming vigorously. "We have to boil the turkeys," Keeper McCormick remarked, "because so many of the older inmates have no teeth, and by this method they get both the flavor and the full benefit of the fowl. The decrepit ones relish the soft method of cooking immensely."

Politicians in many cities were quick to recognize that votes could be bought for the price of a Christmas turkey. More than a few political machines, including Congressman "Big Tim" Sullivan's in New York, ran on turkey power. For more than a quarter-century, "Big Tim," followed by his son "Little Tim" as political boss of the Lower East Side, fed several thousand down-and-out voters from the Bowery a turkey dinner that was the best meal of the year for most of the profoundly grateful recipients.

In Chicago, on Christmas Day in 1898, Alderman John Powers of the nineteenth ward broke all records of previous years by giving away fifteen tons of poultry —28,000 pounds of turkeys and geese and 2,000 pounds

# THE FEAST OF CHRISTMAS

of chickens—to 3,000 families. In a store at 432 West Harrison Street, a huge pile of poultry reached almost to the ceiling. Doling out the fowl to a line that reached around the block took all day.

Theodore Roosevelt instituted the practice of giving Christmas turkeys to the White House staff. On December 23, 1907, under the President's instructions, Henry Pickney, White House steward, journeyed to Washington's Center Market with the black covered wagon belonging to the executive mansion. The next day found 125 fat turkeys heaped in a neat array on a long table, each with a numbered tag tied to a plump leg. On Christmas morning, every married employee of the White House received one of the birds. (It was presumed that the unmarried employees would be invited to have a little of "the light and dark" at the hospitable boards of those who had families.) The distribution included everyone connected with the White House, from the President's newest clerk to the policemen who guarded the grounds to the laundresses and the men of all work around the stable. All the turkeys were as nearly alike as possible, and the tickets were distributed by Pickney with absolute impartiality, so that the turkey drawn by William Loeb, the President's stenographer, was slightly smaller than that drawn by the man who dusted his desk.

The White House steward had long since ceased to give himself any concern about the huge turkey for the executive table. For thirty-eight years, a few days before each Thanksgiving and Christmas, a monstrously fat chestnut-fed live bird had arrived with the compliments

# THE FEAST OF CHRISTMAS

of a Rhode Island turkey farmer, Horace Vose. In 1904 *The Boston Herald* printed a story saying that the younger Roosevelt children, Archie and Kermit, had chased their great turkey all around the backyard of the White House, pulling out its feathers until the "poor old turk" fell exhausted. It was further stated that the President stood on the south portico and applauded the athletic efforts of his offspring. Roosevelt called the story false and angrily issued an executive order denying the *Herald*'s reporters access to executive and departmental news. James Wilson, the secretary of agriculture, construed the President's instructions so broadly that he directed the Weather Bureau office in Boston to withhold its daily weather predictions from the *Herald.*

Before mechanical refrigeration, most turkeys went to market live. Turkey drives used to be common in all parts of the country each fall. Once, a feathered jogger in a Vermont flock bound for Boston chose to roost for the night on the roof of a country schoolhouse. So many of his fellow travelers joined him that the roof collapsed, nearly killing the schoolmaster, who was working late. In 1863 a man drove a flock of five hundred turkeys the six hundred miles from Missouri to Denver. In good weather, prodded by two boy drovers, the birds made as much as twenty-five miles in a day. Mostly they lived off the land, feeding on hordes of grasshoppers. Where they couldn't forage, they ate shelled corn thrown from an accompanying wagon drawn by six horses and mules.

Once while the Comstock Lode was booming near Carson City, one Henry C. Hooker, accompanied by a couple of dogs and a helper, walked a flock of turkeys from Hangtown, California, across the High Sierras to the infant gold-rich capital of Nevada. He sold his birds for up to five dollars apiece and started a cattle ranch in Arizona with his profits.

To satisfy the demands of New York City, turkeys were walked and shipped from ever-greater distances. In 1856 a record supply was reported. The American Express company alone had brought in nineteen carloads of eight to ten tons each. By the end of the century, ten million pounds of turkeys were drawn from as far away as Canada, Iowa, and Tennessee.

In 1871 many of the choicest turkeys in the New York markets were supplied by E. M. Peck's poultry house outside Newtown, Connecticut. A report in *Harper's Weekly* gives an excellent idea of the modus operandi of his and similar operations. According to Mr. Peck, Connecticut was the largest turkey-raising state in the Union, followed by Rhode Island and New York. In Fairfield County, turkeys had not yet been raised in great numbers. Each fall, Mr. Peck scoured the country, buying only the choicest birds. The turkeys were carried to his farm in a wagon, fed for a few days on a light provender of corn meal to make them shapely for market, and then driven in a huge flock to the butcher's pen. Nearby was the picking-house, a veritable small factory. First, the feathers were picked from the legs, as the skin of the drumstick was too tender to be "scald picked." Next, the bird was immersed in steaming-hot water kept nearly at the boiling point, after which it was passed to a long table where, for a cent and a half a bird, women performed the tedious task of plucking the feathers. A skillful picker could dispose of seventy-five turkeys per day. The poultry was next placed on shelves to cool slowly, then packed in large boxes (with ice, if the weather was too warm) and shipped to New York. During a single week, Mr. Peck slaughtered 1,300 birds averaging fourteen pounds in weight, making nearly a ton of turkey meat.

By 1892 North Stonington was the banner town of Connecticut turkey country, and a farmer named L. Main of Swanton Hill was the crack raiser of the region. Somehow, the fame of Connecticut turkeys had penetrated into the royal kitchen of Queen Victoria, and word was sent to a large poultry house in New York to procure a forty-pounder for Her Imperial Majesty's Christmas dinner. Farmer Main got the order with all the speed that rural mail permitted, and in less than a week he had dispatched his best corn-fed, grasshopper-fattened, and dry-picked bird to New York. He received thirteen dollars for the fowl, and for years the region talked about the feast Queen Victoria must have had on their Jim Dandy turkey.

## Chapter 3

## A NOISY, OLD-FASHIONED CHRISTMAS

**W**hile it might seem hard to believe today, noise, ear-shattering noise, concussive, uproarious, tumultuous noise, used to be an integral part of old-fashioned Christmases. Guns, cannons, firecrackers, and tin horns were the principal noisemakers, but a good many others, both homemade and store-bought, contributed to the annual racket.

The firing of guns at both Christmas and New Year's predates the settling of this country. It has been suggested that the practice goes back to the idea that making loud noises would frighten evil spirits, which were believed by our ancestors to abound during the period of the winter solstice.

In Salem, Massachusetts, in his diary for 1705, a Puritan, Samuel Sewall, expressed the indignation that

# A Noisy, Old-Fashioned Christmas

Christmastime gunfire aroused. Christmas had been on Saturday, and the Anglican minority in Salem had celebrated noisily. Then, to make matters worse, on Sunday they went to the harbor "Rummaging and Chittering and Firing Guns and Setting Sail."

A fuller account of the custom was written in 1892 by John A. Chapman:

> Sixty years ago, the young men of Dutch Fork [South Carolina] retained many of the wild, frolicsome habits which their forefathers brought with them from the Fatherland. Perhaps the wildest of these customs was to ramble throughout the night on Christmas Eve, in companies of a dozen persons, from house to house, firing heavily charged guns. Having thus aroused the family, they would enter the domicile with stamping and scramble to the blazing fire, greedily eating the praetzilles and schneckilies, imbibe, with many a rugged joke and ringing peal of laughter, heavy draughts of a compound liquor made of rum and sugar, butter and alspice stewed together, and then with many a screetch and holler rush into the night to visit the next neighbor.

The earliest reference to firecrackers at Christmas appeared in *The Children's Friend,* a book published in 1821 in New York. In it Santa Claus says:

*To some I gave a pretty doll,*
*To some a peg top, or a ball;*
*No crackers, cannons, squibs or rockets,*
*To blow their eyes up or their pockets.*

# A Noisy, Old-Fashioned Christmas

When *The New York Times* reported that $1 million worth of fireworks were shipped south from New York manufacturers for the Christmas of 1902, it was reporting on a now-lost part of Christmas in the American South. Below the Mason-Dixon Line, Roman candles, rockets, pinwheels, crackers, torpedoes, and colored fire powder were set off during the last week of the dying year. From the 1840s to the 1930s, these and other noise-makers were an essential part of Southern Christmases. The din of exploding firecrackers on Christmas Eve, Christmas Day, and Christmas night equaled an old-fashioned Fourth of July in the North.

Those who couldn't get or afford real firecrackers often made their own. Years afterward, Thomas A. Hord recalled the cold, bleak Christmas Day of 1844 when he was six and his family was homesteading in Texas. Dallas was still mainly a collection of families living in tents on the prairie alongside the Trinity River. Despite the fact that neither he nor any of the other pioneer children received toys or playthings that morning, they were determined to have "Christmas fireworks." They drilled a deep hole in the ground, stole some gunpowder from their fathers' supplies, filled the cavity, and set it off. As the dust settled and their parents came running, some of the children were found to have been slightly burned, but worse injuries were inflicted on their backsides by their fathers.

In Vicksburg, Mississippi, in the 1850s, both boys and girls received small bunches of "popping crackers," Chinese style, which they fired off throughout the day, light-

# A Noisy, Old-Fashioned Christmas

ing them with hot coals brought from the house on a shovel.

An Englishman who spent the holidays of 1866 in Baltimore felt that he was almost in the midst of a war, for "every ten minutes or oftener a gun or squib was fired off." In 1871 the Washington correspondent for *The New York Times* reported on Christmas Day: "The distracting reports of fire-arms and fire-works, an absurd southern custom, has at times been hideous." Bad boys deliberately threw firecrackers near horses to see them rear up and slash the air with their iron shoes. One thoroughbred carriage horse was seen walking on his hind legs all the way down Capitol Hill.

Before the Civil War, the Christmas season was always celebrated by the blacks on the plantations with great glee. It was their season of high carnival and absolute freedom from the labors of the field. White Southerners who had just a little more to spend said, "Colored folks would spend their last cent for firecrackers and rockets." Poor black children who didn't have a last cent to spend capped their Christmas Day with homemade firecrackers that they made by blowing up hog bladders, tying them tight, and popping them in the flames of a fire.

Big firecrackers were commonly known as "baby-wakers," but the heavy artillery of Christmas noise throughout the South was provided by cannons and the colorful custom of "firing anvils." On Christmas Day, backwoodsmen would take the blacksmith's enormously heavy anvil, frequently placing it on a wheelbarrow for mobility, and pour black gunpowder into a hole in it.

# A Noisy, Old-Fashioned Christmas

Over the hole they would place a huge rock or even another anvil, and then lay a crude fuse of black powder a short distance away from the anvil. Meanwhile, someone would put a wire on the end of a long pole and get it red hot in a fire. He would touch the hot wire to the fuse and everyone would run like the devil. It was said you could hear the blast for miles.

During a Christmas in the 1880s, young men and boys collected six hundred barrels of wood for a bonfire in a Savannah, Georgia, park. The mayor contributed a hogshead of resin and a wagonload of fireworks.

With such bonfires, and with gunpowder providing fiery explosions of every description, it was inevitable that more than just fireworks occasionally took fire. During a pyrotechnic display in Macon, Georgia, on Christmas evening in 1871, a fireball was thrown into a store, igniting a large stock of fireworks. In the explosion that followed, four stores were burned.

On December 24, 1903, in Shaws, Mississippi, a black farmhand began his celebration of Christmas by exploding Roman candles and firecrackers. The fire he accidentally started swept down Main Street, burning two grocery stores, a livery stable, the post office, a general merchandise store, a dozen smaller stores, a real estate office, and several residences, including the large home of the town's doctor. By the end of Christmas Eve, all that was left of the town was a few houses and a couple of stores.

North of the Mason-Dixon Line, southwestern Pennsylvania wholeheartedly shared the South's affinity for the noise and smell of firecrackers at Christmas. In 1831 in

# A Noisy, Old-Fashioned Christmas

Pittsburgh, a band played while "splendid exhibits of Artificial Fireworks and Phantasmagoria" were given several times during Christmas Day and evening. The Pittsburgh *Daily Commercial Journal* of December 27, 1848, describes a firecracker Christmas in the City of Steel:

> We are in the midst of the Holidays. . . . "Juvenile artillerists" shake the streets with small thunder; and firecrackers emulate the spluttering of musketry, while the screams of alarmed ladies, as some young rogue discharges his firecrackers at their feet, would prove annoying, were it not for the peals of merry laughter that invariably followed the fright.

The following Christmas, a Pittsburgh storekeeper advertised the arrival of a small arsenal of 350,000 firecrackers, rockets, and Roman candles. Other ads for firecrackers were from a bakery and a saloon.

In Philadelphia horns were the chief noisemakers. As early as the 1820s, Philadelphia newspapers were reporting the sleep of citizens being interrupted on Christmas Eve by tin-horn-playing revelers. By 1861 an annual carnival of horns began about eight in the evening. By ten o'clock the center of the city was pandemonium. Tin horns and penny whistles were the basic instruments, supplemented by sailors' hornpipes, handbells, sleighbells, and spoons to drum on tin and iron kettles. Above the cacophony rose the atrocious noise of "horse fiddles," instruments improvised from a wooden dry-goods case, resin, and a long rail. When the rails were drawn across these "fiddles," the discordant sounds were loud

# A NOISY, OLD-FASHIONED CHRISTMAS

enough to make the hair stand up on the backs of the necks of all those within half a block. While most of the crowds vacated the streets before midnight, some of the amateur musicians never went home until morning. The remarkable noise kept enough people awake that in 1868 the parading and playing of horns on Christmas Eve was banned in Philadelphia. Following a brief revival of the custom in the late 1870s, such celebrating was again banned in 1881.

While the Philadelphia horn carnival was the principal example of the noisy phenomenon, horns of every size, shape, and description, especially tin fish-shaped "fish horns," were an indispensable part of nineteenth-century Christmases in many parts of the country. An observer in Jersey City wrote one Christmas morning that every child on the streets of the city seemed to be supplied with a horn. In New York City, early on Christmas morning, shortly after the gun of sunrise had sounded from the harbor fort, shrill whistles and rattling drums made their appearance in the streets. Where so many noisy boys had come from was a mystery. Every mother would certify that none of her children had left the house before breakfast, but every household could testify that boy after boy, groups and gangs of them, passed and repassed their houses with ear-shattering whistles, loud drums, and ear-rasping tin trumpets hours before breakfast. The noise continued day and night—more especially night—until irascible old gentlemen who slept, or rather, tried to sleep, in rooms fronting on the street cried out in desperation, "Blast 'em! Blast the horns!"

In 1891 the tin-horn mania was noted in the White House of Benjamin Harrison. The tooting of a tin horn in a series of more or less musical notes was the signal for the beginning of the celebrations on Christmas morning. Smiling faces appeared at every door in the corridor upstairs, and soon all the members of the presidential family had assembled in a laughing procession led by the President, Master Benjamin, and little Mary McKee. A stream of light shone from the library where, in a corner, glistening like a thousand stars, was the Chistmas tree.

For many years it was the custom in Grammar School number 3, at Grove and Hudson streets in New York City, to have what the pupils termed a Christmas "racket." In 1892 it took place on December 23 in the school's prettily decorated assembly rooms. Anyone who passed the school at three o'clock would have thought that a hundred calliopes were being played within. Every boy in the school—about seven hundred— was armed with a tin horn. At a given signal from the normally stern principal, B. D. L. Southerland (himself armed with a tin horn four feet long), they all gave a blast. The din was terrible, but everyone seemed to enjoy it, especially the boys. The more noise, the more fun.

Another old custom of the school was the reading of letters from old graduates to the present pupils. Many men who had graduated twenty or thirty years before never forgot to send a Christmas greeting to their old principal and his scholars.

# A NOISY, OLD-FASHIONED CHRISTMAS

The "racket" wound up with Christmas carols and recitations, short speeches by the ward trustees, a final toot
on the tin horns, and a hearty three cheers for old number 3.

Around New York City, the martial music of parading
target-shooting companies and the noise of their shooting matches was also a part of old-fashioned Christmas
Days. Almost regardless of the weather, Christmas
mornings from the 1840s till the end of the century found
uniformed, quasi-military shooting clubs marching
through the city, each led by a brass band or, at the very
least, a kettle drummer. Bearing names such as "The
Eagle Guards," "The American Rifles," "The Northern
Liberties Guards," and "The Van Dyke Cadets," they
presented a soldierly appearance while making all the
show they could. Most would make their way to some
suburban place by railroad or horsecars (almost every
village for miles about the city was visited on Christmas
Day by one or more target companies) and spend the
day in trying their skill in shooting and drinking beer in
staggering quantities. Wherever their line of march took
them, they were invariably followed by companies of
small boys marching with new toy rifles and snare
drums.

Many companies went target practicing on both Christmas and New Year's Day. Although we do not know
whether "The Packing-House Guards" were in action on
Christmas, they were on January 1, 1850, according to
*The New York Tribune:*

# A NOISY, OLD-FASHIONED CHRISTMAS

*The Packing-House Guards,* led by Capt. J. Dorian, composed of men in the employ of the West Street Beef and Pork packers, made a fine turn-out yesterday. They paraded in their working dresses, and bore a target emblematic of their business—in the shape of a hog. They went to Five-Mile House, where several fine prizes, presented by their employers, were contended for. We observed that they also bore a beautiful token of female regard in the form of a fine wreath of flowers.

Another troop sponsored by a proud employer made its debut in 1853. Since Christmas fell on Sunday that year, "The Terhune & Martin Guard," composed of employees of a cooperage in Manhattan, went on their first annual excursion on Monday, December 26, to Fordham, New York. They mustered eighty-nine officers and privates and contended skillfully and noisily for prizes ranging from five to eighty dollars, presented by the first-ward flour merchants. The company returned home in the evening highly delighted with the day's pleasure, and after nine hearty cheers for "Messrs. T. & M.," adjourned to meet again the following Christmas.

In the decade following the Civil War, veterans swelled the ranks of old target companies and formed countless new ones. The Christmas of 1867 found legions of uniformed men tramping with rhythmic tread toward the place where targets were slaughtered. Squads, companies, battalions, regiments, almost entire armies were parading the city and making their excursions to uptown and out-of-town parks and to the hills and plains of New Jersey. They were dressed in every conceivable costume

# A Noisy, Old-Fashioned Christmas

—Revolutionary War cocked hats, Zouave's fezzes, red shirts, red jackets, blue jackets, green jackets, no jackets at all, Scottish kilts, long-tailed and short-tailed coats, high boots, and low shoes with white stockings—and were accompanied by music of every description. Companies of Englishmen, Irishmen, Frenchmen, Germans, and mixed nationalities were all out.

As they returned to the city, many of the targets borne in triumph showed pretty fair shooting. In one company, prizes of cabbages and turnips were worn about the necks of the victors, creating considerable amusement among the spectators along the streets. Most of the target company members, after their return from the parade, were joined by their wives and sweethearts, and there was feasting and dancing until a late hour.

Target companies weren't the only ones firing guns around New York on Christmas Day. In the shooting rooms up and down the Bowery, the German section of the city, Teutonic sportsmen were aiming at fantastically shaped targets for three cents a shot. The gunsmoke and the noise must have been enough to satisfy the boy in every man.

Out in country places in northern New York State, in western Pennsylvania, and out West, first-rate marksmanship could be seen each Christmas Day at turkey-shooting matches. Generally, on Christmas afternoon round some country tavern, groups of men, each with his rifle, would assemble. The tavern keeper usually furnished the turkeys for the occasion. Each marksman paid so much a shot, and the man who killed the turkey

# A NOISY, OLD-FASHIONED CHRISTMAS

won him. It was usual to tie the bird to a blackened tree stump one hundred yards or more away, to make it more difficult to "draw a bead" on him.

No roundup of old-fashioned Christmas noisemakers would be complete without mention of two relatively late accessories, the Christmas "cracker" and the tin cricket. Both contributed a great deal of noisy fun to turn-of-the-century Christmases.

Today we think of crackers, the popping, confetti-filled party favors, only in relation to birthdays. In Victorian days, crackers filled with miniature toys were an inseparable part of children's Christmas parties. With a mixed look of fear and expectation, children waited for their cracker to "bang" and then how they scrambled for the surprise—a paper cap, a false face, a pipe, a bottle of "gin" (as intoxicating as the label that read "One Million Overproof"), a baby doll's bottle, a false moustache, and whatnot.

The Christmas cracker originated in France as a bag of bonbons in a paper covering that had to be tugged hard by two children before it burst open to release its contents. About 1860 a company in London created the "Christmas cracker," which produced a minute explosion at the moment the two parts split asunder. For the children of the rich, stores sold crackers three feet long that spewed forth multiple prizes with a tremendous bang.

During the last decade of the nineteenth century and the first of the twentieth, any store that claimed to be Santa's headquarters gave away a tin "cricket" to small

# A NOISY, OLD-FASHIONED CHRISTMAS

boys who went in before Christmas. It usually had a picture of Santa Claus as well as the store name prominently displayed. The little noisemaker, named for the sound it emitted, was stamped from tin in an elongated saucer shape, the hollow side of which had a piece of spring steel riveted to it. When one pressed the spring, it clicked, and when released, it clicked again. With a cricket and practically no effort, a boy could drive his sisters crazy. Crickets were a harbinger of Christmas—by the number of crickets you heard, you could tell how close Christmas was.

## Chapter 4

## A TIME OF GIFTS

**I**t seems
to me that the great
metropolis has resolved itself
into a vast bazaar,"
huffed a well-fed, avuncular
clubman given to noonday
breakfasts and afternoon promenades as he struggled
through the river of brown-bundle-bearing humanity
flowing between the storefronts and hawkers' stands
that lined the sidewalks on New York's Fourteenth
Street, a few afternoons before Christmas in 1881. "One-
half the populace seems possessed of a wild desire to purchase all the things the other half has for sale."

Not many years before—indeed, within the memory of
people who had not yet begun to go gray—the day had
been observed by only two or three religious denominations, but no one, not even the juvenile members, had received gifts. By the mid-nineteenth century, due largely

to the influx of immigrants from the Teutonic countries, the habit of giving Christmas presents began to be observed.

From one end of the country to the other, the growth of gift-giving was so rapid that there is nothing to compare with it in the whole field of popular customs. Suddenly there were December rivers of diamonds in big-city jewelers' windows; the philanthropic mill owner ordered a thousand turkeys for his employees; and in New York the baker left a present of a Dutch cookie with his loaves on Christmas morning. Beginning spontaneously in the 1850s, by the 1880s a Christmas gift-selling and gift-buying mania had seized upon all classes of the American population.

It is often erroneously stated that George Washington gave toys to his five-year-old stepson, Jackie, and his three-year-old stepdaughter, Patsy, on Christmas Day in 1759. He did not. The myth apparently began only in recent times. The fact is, Washington sent a letter in September 1759 to his agent in London ordering a number of toys, but, the mails being what they were in those days, they arrived—right on time—in March 1760 from a toy shop with the engaging name of Unwin and Wigglesworth. There were more than a dozen toys, including a miniature grocer's shop for Master Custis and a wax doll for his sister.

The English colonists in America were not accustomed to giving Christmas gifts, even to children, although servants and the poor were commonly provided for at Christmas as part of Christian piety, commonplace since the Middle Ages. In colonial New York, ladies had new dresses made for their female servants each Christmas, and in the South, too, the slaves were usually given new outfits at this season. Mrs. Mary S. Helm, who visited New Orleans on Christmas Day in 1828, found the blacks in Sunday finery:

> I never at one time had seen so many nice dresses, and was told they were cast-off dresses of their owners of the previous year, and that quite a rivalry existed as to whose slaves should be best dressed during the holidays. The men equalled, if they did not excel the women, in their shining broadcloth and stove pipe hats.

Many masters gave their slaves gifts at Christmas, such as cheap jewelry, pocketknives, pipes, and special rations like coffee and molasses. Often the gifts were given in a traditional surprise game played Christmas morning. Master and slave, meeting for the first time that day, tried to be the quickest to say "Christmas gift!" The winner earned the right to some small present from the vanquished. Custom, invariably, made the blacks the fastest to deliver their gleeful "Christmus gif'." A version of the game was played in the slave cabins as well. Among those with more spirit than worldly goods to give, the loser, after protesting comically, happily paid a forfeit such as a handful of nuts or a chicken. In the rural South, among blacks and whites alike, the institution of

"Christmas gift" with its smiling demand survived well into the present century.

In the antebellum South, as well as the North the association of Christmastime gifts with servants and slaves played a major role in holding back more widespread gift giving. In 1856, while commenting on the changing fashion, *The New York Herald* told its readers:

> Many years ago it was the custom in this city and Albany for the servants of gentlemen, particularly if they were blacks, to go around among their master's friends to receive Christmas boxes, and this practice led genteel families not to give or receive presents themselves on that day.

In Europe the tradition of Christmas presents dates back at least as far as the sixteenth century. Before that, people exchanged gifts at New Year's, and scholars believe that the custom originated in the Roman Empire. In 1564 Endress Imhoff, a wealthy Nuremberger, entered expenses for gifts in his housekeeping record book before Christmas, while in all former years his entries had been made after Christmas, suggesting that he had begun to give Christmas presents. Evidently, the tradition was not long in catching on. In 1616 in the same city, a priest complained that he couldn't hold an afternoon service on December 22 because all his congregation was shopping for gifts for children. And in 1679 Professor Johann Christophe de Wagenseil commented on the sur-

# A TIME OF GIFTS

prising diligence of Nuremberg schoolchildren in December. In Germany in the seventeenth century, children's Christmas gifts were called "Christ-bundles." They are recorded to have contained candy, cookies, apples, nuts, dolls, toys, useful things like clothing, and things "that belong to teaching obedience and discipline." Thus a rod was often attached as a reminder for good behavior.

The oldest record of Christmas gifts in America was set down on December 25, 1745, in the diary of the communal settlement of German-speaking Moravians at Bethlehem, Pennsylvania. "Some received scarves, some a handkerchief, some a hat, some neckerchiefs, and some a few apples."

For the Christmas of 1779, Henry M. Muhlenberg, a German Lutheran pastor working with German immigrants in the Philadelphia area, noted in his journal the fact that he'd received "gifts" of a turkey, soup, wheat flour and bran, sausages, two newly caned chairs, and a length of rope.

On Christmas Day in 1805, in the wilderness of the present-day state of Washington, Captain William Clark of the Lewis and Clark expedition recorded in his journal that he had received a present of "fleece hosiery, shirt, drawers, and socks" from Captain Meriwether Lewis.

Christmas presents were advertised in New York and Philadelphia newspapers in the 1820s, although such references were few and far between. For half a century thereafter, mentions of New Year's gifts or generic "holiday gifts" heavily outnumbered those of Christmas gifts.

# A Time of Gifts

One of the oldest literary references to Santa Claus in America, and the oldest reference to the gift-filled stocking, appeared in 1821 in a children's book, *A New Year's Present,* published in New York.

Edward Everett Hale, who was born in Boston in 1822, recalled in 1893 his richest childhood Christmas memory for a reporter for *The New York Herald*:

> The first present I ever had was a Noah's ark. It was given me by J. Van C. Thropp, a distinguished engraver, a cousin of my father. It was explained to me—a child of three or four—that he was of Dutch family and had lived in New York, that his customs were therefore Dutch, and that this was the reason why he gave his presents on Christmas Day instead of New Year's.

During the nineteenth century, the idea of giving holiday gifts was furthered by ladies' fairs for charitable and religious causes. If the pulpit needed refitting, the church repainting, the minister's salary increasing, the poor of the parish feeding, the Sunday School a library, the ladies were sure to get up a holiday fair.

The 1850s found merchants still only in the first stages of their joyful commercial exploitation of Christmas sentiment, but they were learning fast. In 1853 New York storekeepers were reported to have decked their windows and wreathed their doorposts with garlands of evergreen and to have set holly branches about their premises. The following Christmas, thirty-one-year-old Matthew B. Brady, the future photographer of Lincoln

# A TIME OF GIFTS

and the Civil War, offered miniature photographs set in lockets, pins, and rings from his Broadway studio.

In 1866, a few days before Christmas, a reporter for *The New York Times* noted the gas-lit windows of one dry-goods store displaying shining silks, glossy furs, and bright-colored, expensive robes ticketed with the new motto SUITABLE FOR CHRISTMAS PRESENTS. Among the crowd of richly dressed women gazing at the wonders in the windows was a ragged, muddy urchin whose implements of trade were normally a shoe brush and a box of blacking. In view of the approaching holidays, the lad had invested his spare capital in a string of toy watches and a dozen jumping jacks, all of which he assured the ladies were offered at "less than cost."

At a nearby street corner, a near-frozen Irishman had set up a small stand displaying cigars and imitation meerschaum pipes. Around the corner, an Italian who spoke no English offered a choice of plaster images: heads of Washington, busts of Franklin and Napoleon, and chilly Venuses. An enterprising Frenchman hovered over a group of toy donkeys and goats whose heads shook continuously as if in disapproval of some neighboring turtles, busy dodging their heads into and out of their shells and wiggling their legs and tails. An extemporized candy store spread out on a window shutter was doing a good business in all manner of confections: peppermint log cabins with lemon candy chimneys, a wintergreen man sitting on a vanilla chair, churches, sugar dogs and cats, and large chocolate bugs, dear to the hearts of the German population. Across the street, a black-bearded man

# A Time of Gifts

was drawing a large crowd of women to his open-air toy store. His cross-legged stands contained ten-pin alleys, churches, cows, horses, pigs, poultry, jack-in-the-boxes and jack-in-hoops, and soldiers on speckled horses. But his largest stock was dolls: china dolls, pine dolls, India rubber dolls, dolls with eyes and dolls without eyes, dolls that cried and dolls that didn't, rag dolls stuffed with sawdust, dressed dolls and undressed dolls, any doll any little girl could possibly want. A portion of the peanut stand on the corner was devoted to whistles, penny trumpets, and candy, enough to satisfy a regiment of children. Even the little apple girl who visited the newspaper offices regularly several times a day had extended her business operations and loaded her basket with a small but carefully selected assortment of toys calculated to seduce the lone penny from some breeches pocket.

Perhaps the most visible sign of the holiday season was the placard bearing the magic announcement HOLIDAY PRESENTS. The favorite form of lettering seemed to be old English, and the favorite colors purple and gold. Such signs were used indiscriminately in shoe shops, jewelry stores, millinery establishments, and toy emporiums. In one thoroughfare, a sign encircled by flaming gasjets informed the public of "A Holiday Hat," though it looked no different from a gentleman's everyday stovepipe hat. Everybody in every trade was making an extra Christmas splurge, and the streets were crowded with eager purchasers anxious to secure a suitable present for some loved one at home.

George Templeton Strong, the New York lawyer

whose diary is an almost unparalleled record of upper-class life in nineteenth-century America, first mentioned giving Christmas presents in 1853. On December 23, 1869, he got carried away at Tiffany's:

> Walked uptown this afternoon Christmassing. Broadway thronged with folk on the same errand. Was weak enough to stop at Tiffany's, resolving to be parsimonious this year and spend not more than $20 on a present for Ellie. But I was inflamed by a pretty cameo brooch, and involved myself to the extent of near $200, which was sensible of me, especially as I had been obliged to subtract a little *more* capital from the Trust Co. this morning to pay current bills. Never mind. I won't do so again, and I think Ellie will be much pleased with this bit of wampum, and then she has earned a nice Christmas present. She had already gotten herself certain gimcrackeries which she insisted should be her Christmas present, but I could not let Christmas Eve go by without producing something new. I should not have felt right all through the year. . . .

By mid-December 1872, the toy store of Strasburger, Fritz & Pfinffer was heavily stocked and customers were six deep at all its counters. The shelves and counters of F.A.O. Schwarz's four stores—one in New York, one in Boston, and two in Philadelphia—were gay with toys from many parts of the world: intricate toys made by deft Swiss hands; toys with lively French clockwork movements; and toys from little German hamlets where long winter hours had been spent fashioning them. But F.A.O. Schwarz also offered toys that proudly exhibited

"Yankee ingenuity." There was also always a crowd in front of the windows of L. P. Tibbals, where ingenious swings, little puffing railway trains that dashed furiously around circular tracks, and many other mechanical toys were displayed. At Maillard's elegant confectionery shop at the Fifth Avenue Hotel, there were over one hundred and fifty kinds of chocolates and petits fours of infinite variety, as well as toys, cigars, tiny bottles of champagne, little animals with hidden cavities for candy and miniature dolls, jumping jacks, and other gifts for little people.

At the palatial three-floor store of Ball, Black and Company, millionaires and the merely rich shopped for marbles, bronzes, silver, paintings, and jewelry. One could buy an exquisite silver celery bowl with mermaids for handles or a huge boat-shaped ice bowl of silver, with parts heavily frosted and a handle in the shape of an Eskimo and his dogs attacking a silver bear. While a reporter watched, a joyful rubicund fellow purchased a shell-shaped silver tureen lined with gleaming gold and ornamented with an Eskimo spearing a seal. He paid $550 cash from a wad of bills that was barely diminished by his outlay. Other holiday gifts for the rich were a silver grape dish with a crafty gold fox peering over the rim, with a matching pair of grape scissors, and a massive silver punch bowl in the shape of a ship for holiday wassail, with rudder, anchor, ropes, chains, and oars of solid silver. It went for $625, easily $20,000 in today's money. Fashion of the day decreed a passion for the bronzes and magnificent artistic specimens that had arrived from Paris: Perseus and Andromeda represented in a large golden bronze statuette, at the moment of his rescuing her from the sea monster; a life-size statue of Eros, bending to grasp a butterfly that flies at his feet; Psyche crouched on a base of rose-colored marble, holding a lamp to behold her mysterious husband; a superb Undine standing in the midst of water lilies on a revolving pedestal. There were busts of Dürer and Rembrandt, and oil paintings, including one of tourists in a German inn by Kindler, and another of a landscape with sheep by Eugene Verboeckhoven, valued at $700 each. Four still lifes with fruit by George Hall, an American, cost $300 apiece.

The increased popularity of Christmas shopping was in no small measure attributable to the new plan for selling everything, from fabrics to toothbrushes to jewelry, under one roof: the dry-goods store. As one store manager put it, "A great many people come in to buy one thing and see the tempting displays of all varieties of goods, some of which prove irresistible."

At Roland Macy's ever-expanding store on the corner of Fourteenth Street and Sixth Avenue, the pre-Christmas scene resembled a world's fair. Women who found their way in stayed a good part of the day. So varied were the articles Mr. Macy stocked that he advertised that people had little need to go elsewhere. In his twelve departments, shoppers could find counters covered with toys and dolls, shelves piled with games, larger toys scattered around the floor, French and German fancy goods, silverware, china, house furnishings, books, stationery, watches and clocks, children's suits and dresses, water-proof cloaks, grosgrain ribbons, artificial flowers, milli-nery, laces, veils, velvets and velveteens, satins and trim-ming silks, private-label hoop skirts, French percale and linen underwear, Berlin worsteds, silk ties, soaps and perfumes, candy, and hundreds of other articles.

While women were giving their husbands ebony smoking stands, some costing $200, with ornate recepta-cles for cigars, tobacco, pipes, matches, and ashes, and with burning-oil wicks for lighting cigars, many men were giving their wives large gifts for the home. Pianos, organs, and library tables were favorites. Steinway and Sons had trouble turning out their instruments fast enough to supply the holiday demand. Even by keeping their New York manufactory, with its thousand work-men, running until eight o'clock every evening, they still couldn't keep up. A popular new smaller present for the home was a sewing machine, both a curiosity and a use-ful gift. The motive power was a small crank, which could be easily turned by a child.

Macy's, Adam's, B. Altman, the stately "warehouse" of Brooks Brothers, A. T. Stewart's huge eight-floor cast-iron dry-goods palace, Lord & Taylor, Arnold Constable, Ehrich Brothers, O'Neill's, and W. & J. Sloane—all the principal retail establishments were open until ten or eleven o'clock at night in order to accommodate the thousands of busy people who couldn't find time to choose holiday gifts during the regular hours of business. Broadway, uptown from Union Square, and all the store-lined uptown avenues presented a brilliant scene in the evening hours. Ladies who at any other season would not on any account have been on the streets after dark were now seen in couples "meandering at late hours through the crowds selecting what pleases their fancy." The streetcars and ferryboats were filled until after ten o'clock with well-dressed ample-skirted women whose arms were full of parcels.

At 5:27 P.M. on December 20, 1880, the fashionable shopping district was crowded with thousands gazing into the glistening, flickering gas-jet-illuminated show windows. Few persons apparently remembered that at half-past five new electric streetlights were to be lighted for three-quarters of a mile along Broadway, from Fourteenth to Twenty-sixth streets. As the tall lamps went on all at once, almost in unison the people turned their eyes from the shops to the rows of lights high up on a level with the mansard rooftops. Exclamations of admiration and approval were heard on all sides along with some conjectures about the financial effect on the gas companies. Horses, streetcars, omnibuses, and passing pedestrians were lighted up with a brilliancy that, though by no means equal to "the light of day" to which many favorably compared it, was sufficiently strong to see signs on the stores at a great distance, and a newspaper could be read a hundred feet from the bases of the corrugated iron light poles. Artistic effects of strong contrasts in light and shade were everywhere. A pair of white horses attached to an elegant private carriage outside Tiffany's was brightly spotlighted against the deep black silhouettes of the carriages beyond. The great white outlines of the marble stores, the mazes of telegraph wires overhead, and the throng of vehicles all were plainly visible.

In 1882, Saturday, December 23, was the last day purchases could be made unless people chose to transgress the Sunday law and risk arrest. The vanguard of a vast army of shoppers made its appearance as early as nine o'clock in the morning and increased hourly until three in the afternoon, when it was almost impossible to walk on the west side of Broadway at other than a snail's pace. At every cross street, human traffic was stopped by the traffic of horse-drawn vehicles. Frantic policemen did what they could to pilot ladies from curb to curb. At every shop door, the collision of those coming out and those going in (fat women always came off with flying colors), caused wild confusion.

The average man carried home three packages, the average woman five. Of ten men who entered a Broadway horsecar at Thirteenth Street, five carried skates, two had books, two had pictures, and one had a huge sled. In other seasons, bundle-carrying was confined to "the gentle sex"; men as a rule sent packages home by messenger. But this week men without bundles were more conspicuous than men with them. Men with little wagons, men with shaggy bears and dolls and make-believe stables moved along the chilled pavements warmed by thoughts of children's pleasure.

A unique aspect of the street crowds at Christmastime was the brightness of most of the faces, the cheerfulness of the voices, and the merry laughter of the children. Goodwill was widespread. One gentleman was hurrying up Broadway and another was hurrying down. Both carried bundles as they dodged along through the crowds. At Twenty-second Street they collided violently. Their top hats toppled off and their bundles fell to the ground.

"Sir," said the gentleman going downtown, "if I ran into you I tender my apologies. If you ran into me, don't mention it. I have no time to argue."

"Sir," responded the gentleman going uptown, "there is no need of argument. May you live long and prosper."

Then they picked up their hats and bundles, said, "Good day, sir," and disappeared.

A reporter, even one for a staid daily paper like the *Times,* could not fail to be struck by the very large proportion of pretty young women marching past him in angelic revue. Every type of young American girl was on Broadway, from the bright-eyed little schoolgirl buying presents for her papa and mama, to the rose-cheeked woman just out of her teens, newly arrived at the dignity of a wedding ring and wondering whether to buy her husband a dressing gown and pretend she had made it herself or to purchase him a shaving case. There was a pale but gay little shopgirl who had denied herself food to save up enough money to remember her best friend on Christmas Day. And there were white-capped, rosy-cheeked Belgian nurses with children in tow. Other observers noted half-starved little unfortunates, blowing on their fingers to warm them, gazing wistfully into the store windows. A man from the countryside, bewildered by the tumult and confusion about him, kept his hands in his pockets in deadly fear of the terrible pickpockets he'd read about in his weekly papers and looked as if he wished he were back in his stable with animals, which he could understand. There was a nervous woman who kept dropping her bundles, forming a rift in the human tide when she stooped to recover them, and a gay blade with a pretty young thing on his arm, who stopped abruptly whenever a show window attracted his attention, with no thought of the crowd about him, and who was stepped on and spun about until he fell into line again. Blue- and gray-uniformed messenger boys ran this way and that. Clusters of brightly colored balloons showed at intervals above the heads of the crowd as their vendors moved along with the tide. Crouched close to a building, an old woman in tattered black rags turned a tuneless hand organ with imploring glances into the faces of those who hurried past in sealskins, satins, and velvets. Of all the hundreds who noticed the huddled form and heard the single copper rattle in her battered cup, just one threw a coin to keep it company, a blond mechanic on his way home with his dinner pail. A young woman in widow's weeds was telling a pitiful story of destitution to a youthful out-of-town clergyman, until a detective informed her that if she tried that "racket" on his beat again he'd pull her in, at which she swore so enthusiastically that the clergyman turned as white as his collar. All types went whirling around and around like corks in a huge pool, and hotel guests looked from their windows in amazement at the scene.

Despite the objections of the proprietors of stores and shops, street peddlers still did a lively trade in Christmas knickknacks and were generally unmolested by the police. "The poor devils," said one policeman, "what is the use of clubbing them off the street? I know they are disobeying the law, but holiday license lets us out. It is the one chance in the year that the wretches make a decent living and it would be an act of inhumanity to disturb them."

One peddler had a tray of rubber monkeys. When he pressed his finger on their stomachs, they squeaked, and children laughed in delight. He gathered in half-dollars at a wonderful rate, and though he cried continually, "Only a few more lef'," he managed to keep his tray more than half-full all the time. A little boy sold children's books from a basket, and black-haired, pale-faced Italian children sold matches and shoestrings. A man wearing a larger man's overcoat had a dozen puppies for sale; they whimpered and shivered with cold, and mercifully even the runt of the lot was on his way to a new home for Christmas within half an hour. Other peddlers offered baby rabbits and kittens and beribboned puppies of diverse breeds—solemn balls of fur from which bright, appealing eyes looked out upon the holiday world.

Express wagons dashed by with their freight of holiday goods; the horsecars clattered, their drivers shouting; the elevated trains roared overhead; and iron stagecoach tires rattled on stone-paved streets. Private carriages were driven carefully through the press by liveried coachmen, and the curbstones were lined with glossy, lacquered, silk-lined equipages with tufted leather seats and fur lap robes. Voluminous-skirted

# A TIME OF GIFTS

women and rosy-cheeked children passed in and out of the carriages from sidewalks so crowded that the largest stores employed stout porters to force a passage through for women customers.

Conductors on the crowded horsecars were driven to distraction. Many passengers had huge purchases, and everyone seemed to put everything on the seats. A small messenger boy, wrapped in a large scarf until only his eyes were visible, illustrated the prevailing spirit by placing beside himself a huge turkey and carefully hanging the dead fowl's ungainly feet down from the seat.

Let us have a look into one big store for a moment. The heavy mahogany and plate-glass door is thrown open by a uniformed small boy. Inside, there is the aroma of oiled wood; the fragrance of numberless perfumes; the scent of new wood recently fashioned into toys; and the rich smell of good leather stitched into portmanteau traveling bags, satchels, and pocketbooks. Above the tumult of the crowd, the shrill cries of cash boys sound like the rattle of musketry—"one out of five," "five out of ten"—as they hand money and bills to the cashier and hurry to and fro like aides-de-camp on a battlefield. The aisles are arched over with holly and bright-colored ribbons, giving a fairlike atmosphere. The scraps of conversation overheard as people pass all turn on one subject: "Well, I've just bought him the loveliest smoking jacket"; "I'm sure I hope she'll like the pin. I couldn't think of anything else she needed"; "Mary, for the love of mercy, tell me what I can get for Aunt Anne. She has everything in the world already." A round-faced man is squeezing a "crybaby" with awkward hands to see that it works all right; over in one corner a couple are discussing whether they can pay seventy-five cents for a Noah's ark, which they had hoped to buy for fifty. A pleasant-looking young man with a red nose and a rather shy, careworn expression says to the girl on the other side of the counter, "Please give me two yards of your best ribbon." "What color and what style, sir?" she asks. "I don't know, only give me something nice." "Do you mean sash ribbon?" she queries. "Oh, yes, that's it, sash ribbon." And his whole face lights up with an expression of pleasure and relief. "Please give me two yards of your best." He puts the prettily folded package carefully into the pocket of his threadbare black overcoat and walks triumphantly out of the store, as do we.

By no means all the holiday trade that evening was confined to the stylish shopping districts above Fourteenth Street. For the poor, the center of the holiday trade was Grand Street, east of the Bowery, where a nightly bazaar had been in progress for several weeks. "Pullers-in" stood in front of every kind of store, urging the passing strangers to buy their wares in a babble of German, French, Polish, Portuguese, and Italian, mixed with English. "A fine toy here for five cents!" "Five, five, five!" Boys' voices, half a dozen crying in unison, rang out sharp and clear in contrast to the deep ones of bearded men, all telling of the marvels inside the shops. There were sawdust-stuffed dolls, tops, toy wagons, wooden puzzles, walking canes, shoe blacking, cups and saucers, and tack hammers, at prices from one to fifty cents. Outside one store, a Laplander, dressed in native attire, offered a large collection of curiosities from the arctic regions and attracted such a crowd that a policeman was needed to keep the sidewalk partially passable. Hobby horses lined the sidewalks. Toy bird whistles that "sang" only in the mouths of those who sold them and stuffed animals delighted the juvenile fancy on all sides. Here and there the contents of a toy shop were emptied onto the sidewalk, presenting a medley of velocipedes, sleds, wagons, toy pistols, guns, and dolls, some lying stiffly in boxes like mummies in cases, others ignominiously hung by the neck. Muslin stockings full of popcorn and candy peeped out of one sidewalk booth overflowing with piles of lady apples and candy cats and dogs. At another stall, lighted by a naphtha lamp that flared and spluttered, rows of striped peppermint canes hung from wires strung above the hawker's head, and yet another was overflowing with nuts and raisins, grapes, and oranges. Upon a great hook hung a soft tan mass of molasses taffy, which a bare-armed man was pulling and rolling temptingly, while his son cut off huge chunks and sold them at ten cents a chunk. At the corner, a gnome-like man in a snuff-colored coat produced fresh layers of hot chestnuts from a little sheet-iron roaster. The smell of scorched holly and roasting chestnuts hung deliciously on the frosty air, and even the most garish objects seemed desirable in the flickering light.

Along the length and breadth of Little Germany on the east side, dimes counted as dollars, and small Christmas trees were being sold on nearly every corner. German was spoken everywhere, and all the toys and fancy articles had been imported directly from the *Vaterland*. There were wreaths of artificial flowers, such as were worn at German picnics, walnuts covered with gold leaf, toy bears that swallowed great slices of meat without so much as a single chew, little pianos with only four keys, little men made out of prunes, and figures of the Christ-child done in candy. Here too, as on Broadway and Grand streets, there was a joyous feeling abroad that was altogether contagious. The crowd, in rough homely clothes, bustled about like ants till the hours waxed late and the hubbub of the booths and streets died out in the quiet of the Sabbath morning.

Julius Bauman, the proprietor of a confectionary store on Sixth Avenue, was arrested later that morning for having his store open and goods exposed for sale on Sunday. To Justice Ford, at the Jefferson Market Police Court, the prisoner stated that he had simply opened the door to admit the milkman and didn't have time to close it before the policeman popped in. It being Christmas Eve, he was released on a hundred dollars' bail.

With each passing year, Christmas became ever more important. Nonetheless, as late as 1875, in many parts of the country it was still business as usual when Christmas fell on any day except Sunday. That year in many cities, merchants took classified ads to announce their intention to close their stores on Christmas Day, for the first time, in order to give their employees a day of rest.

A suggestion of the joy and astonishment that accompanied the still-new idea of Christmas-present giving

# A Time of Gifts

among adults was captured in a social item published in a Pennsylvania weekly newspaper for the Christmas of 1881:

> One of the happiest Christmas parties of the season was given on Saturday Evening by Mr. and Mrs. H. M. Reed.
>
> After dinner the Rev. L. Reed and wife, now verging well on Eighty, invited the party into the sitting room, where he had clandestinely deposited in baskets and boxes a large store of presents for his children and grandchildren. The old folks were in turn surprised and made recipients of some elegant presents from their children, as well as many surprises from one to another of valuable and appropriate presents.

For the Christmas of 1884, the postmaster of New York reported a larger number of packages than usual, and trainmen told *The New York Tribune* that passengers had never before carried home so many bundles. The following year, the New York Post Office handled twice as many Christmas packages as the year before, and a store manager explained the astonishing growth in Christmas shopping like this:

> People are making smaller presents to more persons. Where a man would come in years ago and say, "Give me twenty-five yards of $4 silk," and send it to his favorite maiden aunt for a present, he'll buy twenty $5 presents for all his sisters and cousins as well as his aunts.

About the only people who did not enjoy the new pastime that was beginning to be called "Christmas shopping" were the legions of weary store clerks, many of them women, who for several weeks before Christmas were on their feet from seven-forty-five in the morning until nine, ten, even twelve o'clock at night. For them, Christmas was a time of extra work and additional hours at no additional pay. In the 1870s salesclerks started at three to four dollars a week, with no commissions, and most worked six days a week, from 7:45 A.M. to 7:00 P.M. Fourteen-year-old cash girls worked the same long hours for a dollar fifty a week. Only by the turn of the century had a salesclerk's stipend risen to eight to ten dollars a week.

Two nights before Christmas in 1870, a number of young men, later alleged to be members of The Dry Goods Clerk's Early Closing Association, gathered in front of the Sugden & Bradbury store in the Bowery, which was brightly lighted and doing a good business. The gang hurled stones, breaking two large plate-glass show windows. That evening, there were several similar disturbances at other stores nearby. Frock-coated policemen broke up the demonstrations and arrested one of the miscreants. Messrs. Sugden and Bradbury had been keeping their store open later than usual to accommodate the holiday trade, despite the fact that, a few days before, they had been visited by a protest committee from the clerks' association. Their indifference to the eight-year-old organization's request for shorter hours was the cause of the bitter remonstrance.

Store clerks, though often as agile as acrobats, were frequently unequal to the overwhelming demand for

# A TIME OF GIFTS

merchandise, and firms' dignified owners and floorwalk-
ers were obliged to pitch in. Closing time saw the staff—
girls, women, men, and boys—disheveled and white-
faced from the long day's struggle. By the late years of
the century, wise merchants went to considerable expense to fortify their employees against exhaustion with
proper food. Many stores began to give twenty- to forty-
minute meal breaks and to pay "supper money" in order
to assure a warm meal. A few, such as H. O'Neill and
Company, fed their employees a hearty spread. Every
person employed by Mr. O'Neill sat down to dinner in relays every evening during the holiday season.

Uptown, at Bloomingdale Brothers', a substantial supper was served to over two thousand employees. Long
tables, each accommodating forty people, were set up in
a large storeroom on the fourth floor, and twenty-five
waiters were employed. Dinners began at five o'clock
and ended at seven-thirty, with clerks and cash girls eating in relays of four hundred. Each sitting lasted twenty
minutes. Soup, fish, roast meats, vegetables, dessert, and
tea were provided in unlimited amounts. The food was
far better than many would have gotten at home, and
the room was invariably abuzz with happy conversation.
The meal and the few minutes' rest were miraculous in
their restorative powers.

At Macy's, supper money was provided. Years later,
one of the earliest recollections of an old employee was
the sight of Abiel LaForge, Macy's partner, shepherding
an animated crowd of uniformed cash girls to a neigh-

boring restaurant, as was his custom during the holiday season.

When the great street doors were closed, new regiments began to "dress stock," as the task of restoring order among the tumbled wares was called. Through the night, men were busy wrapping packages and piling them onto the waiting delivery wagons. It was close to midnight before the flickering gas jets and the sputtering arc lights were turned down. Many of the clerks had to work on into the early hours, and some of the men finished the rest of the night sleeping on counters with bolts of cloth for pillows.

The husky young drivers of delivery wagons and their little assistants had especially hard work during the holiday season. Many slept in the stables, as it could be three o'clock in the morning before some of them would get home, and despite their late hours they were obliged to be up again before daylight. Even in the best weather, the work was, in the words of one expressman, "Like trying to sweep the ocean back with a broom." Complicated by ice, snow, or freezing rain, the hardships on the expressmen were fearful. In 1902 a boy froze to death because he was too tired to go home after he finished his deliveries at one in the morning and went to sleep in a wagon. Owners of horses and delivery wagons had a rich harvest at Christmas, as anything even resembling a vehicle was engaged by storekeepers. On Christmas night in 1886, New York Police Superintendent Murray was appealed to to allow the express companies to deliver parcels the following day, even though it was Sunday.

The shipments of Christmas packages from all parts of the country had been so overwhelming that half of them, a million parcels or so, remained to be delivered. So many of the goods were perishable that a tremendous loss would have ensued if the express wagons were stopped at midnight. Superintendent Murray decided that the Sunday law might be stretched far enough to save fruit, flowers, and other perishable items.

On Christmas Eve in 1879, a traffic jam on Broadway lasted five hours. The principal congestion, in the neighborhood of Wall Street, covered a distance of nearly a mile for the better part of the afternoon. The jam of vehicles extended from curb to curb, and the teams crowded each other so closely that shafts, chains, poles, wheels, and rungs became interlocked. For a while the mess seemed inextricable. One observer noted that several double and four-horse teams drawing heavy merchandise took three hours to move two short blocks. Caught in the massive jam were single and double teams, hacks, coupés, dray-wagons, jewelers' and fancy hucksters' wagons, two-wheeled dogcarts, furniture carts, fancy-goods dealers' light delivery wagons, and several advertising vans with filmy transparent canvas sides to allow illumination at night. Belgian horses capable of moving a three-ton load jostled against and crushed the slender, quick-stepping colts and ponies attached to the lighter vehicles. Thin wheels and gleaming bodies of coaches and lighter wagons were twisted and dented by the wheels and hubs of stagecoaches and warehouse trucks that threatened at intervals to crush them into kindling wood. After two ladies in a coupé had been trapped for an hour, they decided to get out and walk. But they could not open the doors of their vehicle, for on one side was a wagon loaded with hops in bales, to a height of fifteen feet, and on the other side were the wheels of a stage within a few inches of the door panel. As the mass of vehicles moved a few feet, the coupé, the stage, and the hops wagon moved also, and their relative position remained unchanged. The two ladies found they were truly trapped.

A furniture wagon with a set of parlor furniture for delivery to the Lehigh Valley Railroad was in the line for three hours, and at six o'clock the driver said he was too late to deliver the goods to the depot. He was waiting for a chance to turn into a side street and get back to the warehouse. Unless his chance came soon, he thought, the warehouse would be closed up and he would be obliged to drive the load to some place and hire storage for the night. Broadway policemen on the force for fifteen or twenty years said they had never seen such a "blockade." It was five-thirty before there were any signs of its breaking up and a truck or carriage was able to get out here or there. A quarter of an hour later, a dozen or more turned into side streets; a few minutes later, a dozen more. Then the mass began to move up and down Broadway slowly, and within twenty minutes, with a rush, a plunge, a splash, the cracking of whips, the shrieks of pedestrians, the swearing of drivers, and the commands of police, the lines of traffic moved. There was a terrible rushing of wheels and a clatter of hoofs, and in a miraculously short time the ordinary night quiet of the lower end of Broadway set in.

The delivery of many smaller packages was accomplished by ever-multiplying legions of delivery boys employed by stores or by the express and telegraph companies. Twelve hundred blue-uniformed American District Telegraph boys were kept at a lively gait all day and evening collecting packages and bringing them to their offices for distribution by express wagons.

The rush of express business led to seasonal shortcuts. In 1886, three days before Christmas, a man with a basket neatly bound with a piece of stout cord was one of a crowd laden with packages of various shapes and sizes who stood before the long counter of the Adams Express Company on Broadway. A row of clerks behind the counter took the packages and gave receipts for them as fast as they could write. A reporter wondered at the training and experience that enabled them, the moment they glanced at the address, to tell the express charge, whether it was going to Maine or California. In other months, the clerk would spend about ten minutes looking over his book of rates and five minutes weighing the package before the charge was stated.

When it came to be the turn of the man with the corded basket, he plumped it down on the counter.

"One dollar," yelled the clerk as he glanced at the address on the tag, which read BOYCE, VIRGINIA.

"Thunder-n-lightnin'," replied the owner of the basket. "I've sent a dozen baskets of the same weight to the same place within a month and never paid over sixty cents. There must be a mistake."

"One dollar," repeated the clerk.

The man demanded the return of his basket. It was shoved across the counter to him, and seizing it he fell out of line.

"This is a swindle," he remarked to the reporter. The latter advised him to go to the superintendent in the back part of the room, and he did so.

"Have express rates to the South gone up?" he asked.

"No," was the reply.

"Why is it then that I am charged nearly double what I usually pay?" And he explained the circumstances.

"Ah, yes, the fact is, you see, that at this time, when we are handling thousands of packages where we usually handle hundreds, we haven't time to weigh and look up the correct charges and the clerks estimate them. Probably the clerk in your case has made a mistake. I will look and see."

The superintendent weighed the basket: just twenty pounds. Then he looked up the fixed rate to Boyce, Virginia, and reported that the charge should have been sixty cents. The man handed over his six dimes and took a receipt.

"I am sorry you had so much trouble," said the superintendent.

All the while, the clerks were estimating the packages of hundreds of other shippers at the rate of five packages a minute.

In December 1902, seeking to lessen the usual crush of

# A TIME OF GIFTS

business during the week before Christmas, some express companies sent out circulars asking their customers to send in their packages of Christmas presents early. That year, the Wells-Fargo Company supplied printed labels reading DO NOT OPEN UNTIL CHRISTMAS, which were pasted on packages shipped early. In smaller towns, requests that packages be held at express offices and delivered Christmas morning were still observed, but the tremendous volume for delivery in larger cities was fast making the custom out of the question. Wells-Fargo's idea stuck and the DO NOT OPEN UNTIL CHRISTMAS label became a part of the American Christmas.

While the express companies were coping with every type of holiday goods, including live geese and turkeys that stuck their long necks out of their barred crates and gobbled excitedly as if they were directing their own deliveries, the General Post Office in New York was the scene of a veritable maelstrom of parcels. Almost without exception, beginning in the late 1870s, each year's holiday volume of business eclipsed the record set the previous December. "Holiday week" required day clerks to remain at their posts at first part and then all of each night, and night clerks worked straight through the day. The federal employees received neither extra pay for extra work nor the five-dollar bonuses that several of the express companies were beginning to give their employees each Christmas. No small share of the burden of additional work fell upon the letter carriers. The packs of the gray-coated public servants overflowed with parcels as they went their rounds. Little except the addition of white whiskers would have been needed to make any of them into a presentable Santa Claus. Children were not slow to notice the resemblance. On Christmas Eve in 1886, in a great throng on Fourteenth Street, a little girl's excited voice was heard saying, "Oh, Mamma, there goes Santa Claus. Let's hurry home before he gets there." Those who turned in the direction she pointed smiled as they saw only an overburdened postman.

In 1874 Macy's, long noted for its Christmas showing of ten thousand dollars' worth of fine French, German, Swiss, Bohemian, and Austrian dolls, exhibited a window display of dolls in the form of a tableau. Although it may not have been the first effort of that sort, it marked the beginning of a beloved tradition for New Yorkers. The hour for seeing the holiday windows in their greatest splendor was after dinner. Merchants understood that to secure attention at this season was to secure customers. Therefore the glories of the windows, lighted by hundreds of gas jets, were not allowed to pale so long as the citizens were out of their beds. In 1876, the nation's centennial year, in the window next to the main entrance of Macy's on Fourteenth Street was an exhibition of dolls elegantly dressed in colonial costumes and representing a tea party in 1776. In the big center window was a beautiful doll-size representation of life in a French home in New York in 1876. The corner window was a scene from a Paris park, with richly dressed equestrians and pedestrians. All the dolls and furniture had been specially imported for the exhibit.

In 1878 so many people collected on the steps leading to the elevated station in Fourteenth Street to look at the miniature "Pinafore" in Macy's window that passengers could not get up or down. The elevated company was compelled to put muslin at the side of the staircase to hide the view.

Each year found store window scenes more elaborate. In 1880 the entire window of one establishment was devoted to the representation of Niagara Falls, with finely dressed dolls standing and sitting upon the surrounding shores. A cascade of real water delighted the crowds that gathered daily and nightly before the window. The stage of a theater and the story of Cinderella filled the windows of another store, and children were brought from Brooklyn, Jersey City, and even more distant points to see the spectacles.

In 1883, apparently for the first time, Macy's windows featured moving figures operated by steam power. Soon the windows involved hundreds of mechanical figures. The week before Christmas in 1889, it was almost impossible to push through the crowds outside Macy's windows gazing with rapt attention at a panorama of scenes from *Uncle Tom's Cabin*. As they watched, the persecuted young Eliza with her child moved deliberately down Fourteenth Street, making her escape across paper ice from the bloodhounds of the cruel overseer. She disappeared around the corner, only to appear again in a minute and escape again. Each evening it was after eleven o'clock before the corner was clear.

By the 1880s a score or so of establishments employed men or women beginning to be known as "window dressers," whose sole or chief business was windows. In 1881 window dressers were reported to be liberally paid, receiving salaries of $2,500 to $3,000 a year. The work, under the supervision of the general manager, was generally done by young, usually unmarried, men who either volunteered or were asked to work overtime. By the end of the century, Christmas decorations were usually in place about the first week of December, but for two months before that, preparations had been going on. In one store where a crystal shower was part of the decoration scheme, thousands upon thousands of beads had to be tied in place. Each morning, before the rush of customers, fifty of the younger boys and girls in the shop were detailed upstairs for an hour or so of stringing beads. In the large dry-goods shops, installing the Christmas decorations took as much as a week of night work, and the decorators were given a day or two off, after the Christmas rush, to rest up.

Often, thousands of feet of evergreen ropes, huge wreaths, and forests of Christmas trees, sometimes of enormous size, were part of the decorative schemes. In 1898, at one o'clock on the morning of December 17, a Christmas tree sixty feet high at Bloomingdale Brothers', on Fifty-ninth Street and Third Avenue, took fire, causing damages estimated at five thousand dollars. The tree had stood in the center of the building in an atrium that

## A Time of Gifts

ran from the ground floor to the roof. A watchman discovered the blaze and turned in the alarm. The store may well have been saved by the actions of the scrub women at work on various floors who emptied their pails of water on the blazing tree, keeping at it until policemen ordered them out. The first alarm was followed by eight calls for additional fire patrol wagons because of the perishable nature of the stock. The remains of the charred tree were taken down, and the store opened for business as usual that morning only a few minutes late. Two days later the Bloomingdale brothers sent a check for one hundred dollars to the Fire Commissioner as a mark of their appreciation for prompt and efficient services.

Throughout the 1890s the teeming crowds of Christmas shoppers seemed to get bigger every year. The suburban population was increasing annually, and from that source came much of the New York merchants' revenue. The city was a holiday Mecca for many, including congressmen and cabinet members and their families from Western states who did not have enough time to return to home for the holidays. Eastern college students and groups of chaperoned schoolgirls from New England and the South also spent Christmas in the city. At some of the hotels, there were family reunions as parents came by railroad from distant cities to be with their children. Others journeyed from afar, exclusively to shop. On

# A TIME OF GIFTS

December 23, 1887, an excursion train in three sections with nine sleeping cars and twenty-one passenger coaches arrived in New York carrying twelve hundred people. The train had originated in Rochester and had picked up passengers along the line as far east as Oswego, Round-trip coach tickets from Rochester to New York were four dollars.

Just before the Christmas of 1895, the manager of the Waldorf Hotel said, "If you could see the hundreds and hundreds of bundles that are daily delivered at the desk for guests of the house, you would think they were buying out every store in New York. We keep an army of boys busy sorting and distributing these purchases."

Large numbers of the affluent shoppers found all they wanted at Messrs. Merwin, Hulbert and Company, at 26 West Twenty-third Street. Chiefly noted for its firearms and ammunition, the store sold useful presents of every sort: cutlery, from small penknives to large and handsome carving sets; fishing tackle of every variety; gymnasium equipment; skates of all types and sizes for winter, alongside hammocks for summer; and music boxes, complete photographic apparatus, picnic baskets, saddles of every kind, hunting shoes and outfits, and polo goods. Bicycles and tricycles ranged from $25 to $135, those for ladies having a wire screen on the back wheel to prevent skirts from getting tangled. Another specialty of the store was boats—from dingies to canoes to a $3,000 yacht or a $6,000 steam launch. For expensive presents, it was one of the best stores in New York.

Tiffany and Company was another aristocratic store

that met the demand for elegant and novel presents. For the Christmas of 1895, the store introduced silver-plated bicycles. Everything on the latest standard models for men, including the pedals, had been heavily plated with gleaming silver. The frame and all the joints were plated and chased in a style used by European gunsmiths on the finest hunting rifles. The handlebars were ivory, partly encased in chased silver. On the "saddle" was delicate hand-tooled silver ornamentation with shell scrollwork in the style of Louis Quinze. A "searchlight lantern" was ornamented with chased silver. A ladies' model with a jeweled lantern was still in preparation, but orders for Christmas delivery were invited. The bicycles were offered, a spokesman for the store said, "for the benefit of the smart set, who had long been desirous of having something better than the standard product."

But a man did not have to shop at Tiffany's to find unique and fashionable ideas for his wife's present. In Macy's, just before the Christmas of 1888, one man noticed how often lady customers seemed to look at the handles of their umbrellas. A salesclerk explained that one of the latest fads for the fashionable was putting watches in umbrella or parasol knobs. This added twenty to two hundred dollars to the cost of an ordinary silk umbrella. Women were said to find them extraordinarily useful on their shopping excursions.

No sooner were there Christmas presents to look forward to than some people grew as concerned with what they got as with what they gave. In Philadelphia, the Christmas of 1895, a lady shopper saw her husband examining pocketbooks at a showcase in another part of the store. When he had gone she approached the saleswoman in that department.

"Did he get the one I wanted?"

"Yes, the one with the silver horseshoe. I told him it was the best and would just suit."

"You're a jewel. I feared he would get something I didn't want. Thank you ever so much."

The husband had gone to his favorite drugstore where he asked, "Has my wife been here?"

"Yes," said the clerk with a grin.

"Did she get a toothbrush or a box of cigars for my Christmas present?"

"She looked at cigars."

"Ha! I know the brand—$2 a hundred. Well, if she buys a box, change them to my regular brand and I'll pay the difference—see?"

And the druggist saw.

The tremendous Christmastime hubbub in the stores and streets was fast becoming too much for many women who were wealthy enough not to have to do anything they didn't totally enjoy. Thus, for other women Christmas shopping rose from a pastime to a profession. By the 1890s in New York, several thousand women were paid a percentage by the big stores for spending other people's money. During the holiday rush season and just before the summer exodus from the city, professional shoppers were reported to have made as much as two hundred dollars a week.

By 1890 it had become a custom, among people whose means enabled them to make gifts of money, to apply to the Sub-Treasury or to their banks a few days before Christmas for brand new bills or gold pieces. That year, the new Treasury notes were in great demand. On December 23 alone, $300,000 worth of them, mostly in ones, twos, fives, and tens were paid out at the Sub-Treasury. A large proportion of the applications for new money for Christmas purposes came from the proprietors of stores. It was a matter of pride to return to their customers nothing but new money in change, whether it was bills or small coins.

Two-dollar gold pieces were extremely popular gifts for children, since the present encouraged saving, a paramount virtue. A woman who grew up in Ohio around 1915 recalls, "Each of the children in our family always got a gold piece from Grandfather Bannen. But we were never allowed to keep it. Or spend it. It had to go right into the bank. The day after Christmas, when the bank was open again, Grandfather Bannen would make a big issue of driving up to the house with the best carriage or sleigh and the best horses. All the children would pile into the back and we'd trot down to the bank. With great formality, the gold pieces would be deposited in our accounts.

"Grandfather Bannen was most strict about that. That's what the children should do with their gold pieces."

# A Time of Gifts

For every Christmas present that was "store bought" in the old days, hundreds were homemade. The lengthening evenings of November and December found adults and children alike busy as bees, their minds brimful of the happy business of planning and making presents.

Children were on the receiving end of a lot of clothing. In the 1870s, as Christmas approached, in New York City the five children of Leopold and Helene Damrosch were invited, one by one, to their mother's bedroom, blindfolded, and materials and patterns held against them for cutting. Sometimes, if the children kept their eyes focused on their toes, despite the blindfold they could see the cuttings on the floor and learn the clothing's color.

And parents made homemade toys. Around 1880 one parent wrote, "This Christmas I made a lot of the children's things. . . . Six-year-old Joe was very pleased with a brown canton flannel pony all saddled and bridled with shoe buttons for eyes and old-fashioned straight clothespins, put in with knob end down, for legs." A Scottish immigrant in Utah took blocks of rubber, known in those days as "guttapercha," and cut them into animal shapes with a sharp knife. His daughter's special favorite was a pig whose curly tail could be pulled straight and, when she let go, would curl up again.

Popular magazines were full of ideas of gifts for children to make for adults, many with copious instructions, calling for extraordinary craftsmanship, and presuming that any little girl of four could crochet, tat, and appliqué. Bookmarkers of perforated cardboard, with ribbon backing, fringe and cross-stitching; quilted satin watch-

# A TIME OF GIFTS

pockets; tasseled flycatchers; decorative pincushions; needlebooks; and pen wipers were a few of the articles frequently recommended. The Christmas of 1870, an editor of *The New York Tribune* complained of receiving nine pen wipers, even though they were each of a different design.

Many elaborate pieces of work exhibited the worst excesses of Victorian fancywork. Imagine the difficulty of saying, "Just what I wanted," when presented with a huge slipper-shaped holder for a feather duster; a picture easel made from the lid of a cardboard box and laboriously covered in silk and embroidered; a cross-stitched silk hanging case for pens and pencils; or an ornamented piece of cloth-covered cardboard in the shape of a little horn, which was intended to be hung from a projecting bracket near an invalid's bed, to hold a cup of milk or water or a vase of flowers. Too many to count were the men who annually were presented with one or more pairs of slippers crocheted by their female relations.

Before the 1880s gifts were usually tied unwrapped to the Christmas tree or else set openly on the table or floor beneath its boughs. But it was beginning to be thought that an attractive gift was doubly attractive if done up in a pretty and dainty package. Presents bought in fancy stores were delivered in boxes tied with bright ribbons and tinsel cords. Gifts made at home were usually wrapped in white paper held together with sealing wax or straight pins. It was a good many years before either decorative wrapping paper or Scotch tape were invented.

A typical old-fashioned Christmas parcel arriving from

relatives afar by express wagon or the postman would be in a rough pine box that had once held soap or dried codfish or candles at a grocer's, but that was now filled with a homemade fruitcake. The corners of the box might be packed with such articles as a smoking cap, slippers, a bottle of perfume, or store-bought soap.

From city Victorians of means came presents in trompe l'oeil packages manufactured primarily in France and Germany. Some of the prettiest of these boxes were in the form of apples, pears, oranges, and other fruits and vegetables. Realistically reproduced in cardboard and wax were opera glasses, trumpets, piles of plates with menus on top, balls of twine, slices and loaves of bread, rolls, cakes, roast turkeys, lifelike dogs, and enormous beetles, bees, and grasshoppers. Tiny gifts, from bonbons to diamonds, were concealed in imitation champagne corks, cigars, and spools of thread.

By the first years of the new century, fancy-goods shops and dry-goods stores (beginning to be known as "department stores") sold all sizes and shapes of boxes covered with holly-printed papers. But those who were clever at pasting could make their own boxes, which were daintier than anything offered for sale. In the words of one reporter, it took "only a little work, careful cutting, and neat pasting with library paste." After a box had been covered with remnants of flowered or striped wallpaper and left to dry thoroughly, two pieces of white tissue paper were pasted along the top edge of the box. Then four pieces of ribbon were pasted in for ties, and the finishing touch, for a lady's present, was paper lace placed around the inside.

Today it is forgotten that the German Christmas tree was originally a gift-bearing rival to the earlier Christmas stocking. But in 1883, while advocating the stocking of his own youth, a curmudgeonly editor of *The New York Times* called the Christmas tree "a rootless and lifeless corpse—never worthy of the day." He gleefully predicted that the Christmas tree had had its day and was being replaced by a return to the Christmas stocking. The stocking-versus-tree debate continued into the early years of the present century, resolved only when the average American family happily adopted both customs. In 1893 a Brooklyn woman of breeding and refinement was asked, "How do you celebrate Christmas? With a Christmas tree, or do the children hang up their stockings?"

"My husband's people always have a tree," was the reply, "but I was brought up to celebrate in the other fashion, and so we hang up ah–er—We hang up our hosiery."

In today's world, it is interesting and a little sad to realize that the President of the United States used to be able to enjoy Christmas shopping as spontaneously as an ordinary citizen. When Ulysses S. Grant was President, he used to find keen enjoyment during the holiday season in a stroll along Pennsylvania Avenue in Washington. In a single afternoon, one might see him mingling with a crowd of shoppers; further on, Amos Ackerman, his attorney general, bearing away in his arms some holiday gift too precious to be entrusted to a messenger; Hamilton Fish, his able secretary of state, in a bookstore gloating over fine bindings and engravings; and George Maxwell Robeson, the secretary of the navy, his jolly red face beaming on everybody, dropping dimes into the grimy hands of crossing sweepers.

On the morning before Christmas at the White House in 1888, Mrs. Grover Cleveland went "down town" in search of a few things forgotten until the last moment. In the afternoon it was so pleasant that she convinced the President to accompany her to the stores, and they drove out in the victoria. Mrs. Cleveland was reported by indefatigable reporters to have looked especially pretty and girlish in her Directoire coat of mahogany cloth, bordered with black astrakhan and a line of silver braid.

On Christmas Eve in 1909, as dusk fell, President William Howard Taft, looking not unlike Santa Claus himself with his rotund figure, round red cheeks, and white moustache, went shopping on foot in Washington. He wandered from shop to shop, taking a hearty interest in the store windows and good-naturedly returning the jostling of the crowds that fairly jammed the sidewalks. Captain Archibald Butt, his military aide, walked with him, and immediately behind him were two vigilant Secret Service men. Remarkably, only a small number of people recognized him. He raised his hat to those who saluted him, but he was not forced to do this more than a dozen times.

The President remained for some time in a jeweler's shop, selecting a present for Mrs. Taft and for his daughter, Helen. He next walked to a leather-goods store on F

# A Time of Gifts

Street, where Captain Butt halted him on the sidewalk before the window.

"That's just the thing," Captain Butt said, pointing with his walking stick to an elaborate traveling bag of deep red Russian leather, which was normally used for book-binding.

"You're right!" exclaimed the President, shoving the officer ahead of him good-naturedly. "Let's get a closer view."

There was a commotion in the crowded store when the President and his party entered. They remained more than a quarter of an hour and arranged to have several packages sent to the White House by messenger. They went next to a bookstore, where President Taft purchased a number of volumes. One of them, which he wanted to mail that night, he turned over to Captain Butt. "Here, Butt, you can take care of this," he said smilingly. "I've got all I can do to take care of myself."

Captain Butt put the package under his arm, and the party returned to the jeweler's shop, where the President's purchases were ready. A Secret Service man was left behind to see that the packages reached the White House safely, and the party started up Pennsylvania Avenue. As they passed a hotel on Fifteenth Street, the revolving door of the bar was spinning merrily. Four bibulous celebrants of the holiday season emerged. On varying degrees of rubber legs, they gained the sidewalk, laughing effusively and wishing one another the compliments of the season, when one sighted the Chief

Executive. "Merry Chrishmus, Misser Preshident," he cried, "Merry Chrishmus!"

All four managed to raise their hats. The President looked them over and then, with a broad grin, lifted his hat.

"Thank you, gentlemen," he said, "let me wish you the same."

The President's party returned to the White House, after an absence of about an hour and a half.

One afternoon in 1914, a week before Christmas, President Woodrow Wilson went out in his limousine to do his Christmas shopping. The President spent some time in a large department store where he was recognized by many of the shoppers, but nobody bothered him or showed any offensive curiosity as to his purchases. One woman who appeared to know him shook hands and talked to him for a moment. The President was in excellent spirits. The shopping tour kept him away from the White House for two hours.

On an upper floor of a big New York department store, there was a large auditorium devoted for eleven months of the year to fashion shows, concerts, and lectures by homemaking experts. In December, Santa Claus and children took over the room. In perfecting "the Christmas show," no trouble was too great, and no expense was spared. In 1912 all the entertainment was imported, very painstakingly and very expensively, from Ger-

# A TIME OF GIFTS

many. A mechanical circus, as lifelike as anything made of wood and sawdust and "clockworks" could be, was set up in the cavernous hall. On the Saturday afternoon before Christmas, between five or six thousand children turned out to watch clowns and acrobats, dancing dogs and trained seals, dancing elephants and lions that roared, and camels against a background of sand hills and Arab tents. The circus was only part of the fun. In a quaint toy German village, a fire kept breaking out, and countless mechanical figures of firemen and villagers fought the flames. When fire burst anew through the blackened rafters of the burning house, the fire chief gave directions to his good men, while lazy firemen and old men sought refreshment from a flowing beer barrel in the town's square; with such realistic touches, it was easy to understand why grownups jostled children in their zest to see the village afire.

But probably the most magical effect of all was provided by eight life-size mechanical polar bears standing among icebergs in a polar sea. Nearby, supervising the fun, stood a real Santa Claus. After one child dropped a quarter into a slot, everyone watched with rapt attention as the first bear took a little package from a basket, handed it to the next bear, and he to the next, and so on down the line until it reached the paws of the last bear of all, from whom the child received it. The package was carefully wrapped and contained a toy—a toy that, if it had been bought downstairs in the toy department, would have cost just a quarter.

# A Time of Gifts

On Christmas morning of 1914, Theodore Edison, the sixteen-year-old son of Mr. and Mrs. Thomas Alva Edison of West Orange, New Jersey, found one of the most exciting Christmas gifts any boy ever received. On arising, the young man looked out of his window and saw drawn up at the coach entrance to their house a maroon, nickel-finished runabout automobile, a present from Henry Ford. The automobile maker had taken a liking to the lad when the Ford and Edison families had spent several weeks together the previous winter at Fort Meyer, Florida.

By the following year, autos were fast becoming popular Christmas presents. Dealers reported Christmas sales running 25 percent ahead of 1914. Most deliveries were requested for Christmas Eve or Christmas morning. Some of the buyers planned little dramas around their gift's arrival outside their homes. At a prearranged signal, such as three honks on the horn by the chauffeur, the father might deftly draw his family to the front window.

"Look at that new car out there," he would say. "I'll bet it's a Christmas gift for someone."

"Only wish it were ours!" some member of the family was sure to exclaim.

Then the little auto drama would be brought to a happy ending by the father's announcement that it was their car.

# A TIME OF GIFTS

The early twentieth century found a few merchants beginning to question whether long shopping hours during the last two weeks before Christmas were a necessity, and as a test they closed at their regular hour of six o'clock. Others shortened their holiday hours to nine o'clock. In New York in 1909, clerks were made happy by a spontaneous outcry on their behalf led by the ladies of the Consumers' League, who publicized the fact that most of the stores still paid no overtime. At the same time that they were attacking the long hours that Santa's retailing helpers worked, the ladies were also amazingly successful in a related campaign in which they sought to relieve the pressure put on store employees by last-minute shoppers. Socialites told reporters how they had finished their Christmas shopping as much as a month before Christmas, and they encouraged the public-spirited to "Shop Early."

By the following Christmas season, the practice of keeping the big stores open until late at night had been largely abandoned. Those merchants who closed early were reported to have suffered no loss in holiday revenue. The new trend spread rapidly to other cities. In 1912 in Cleveland, for example, after years of bidding for last-minute Christmas purchases until Christmas Eve turned into Christmas morning, retailers united in an agreement to close at six o'clock on December 24. For the first time, thousands of store employees enjoyed the night before Christmas at home.

## Chapter 5

## THE OLD, TRADITIONAL CHRISTMAS TIP

**I**n December
1898 in an apartment
building in uptown New York,
the black gentleman in charge
of the up-to-date
"traveling chair" had his own
way of notifying his patrons that Christmas was at hand.
On one side of his elevator, he had a little white box with
a capacious slit in the top. Above it was a large card
showing a snow-covered Santa Claus and the words
WISHING YOU A MERRY CHRISTMAS. According to one observer, his passengers generally took notice, and even
women could not resist dropping a coin or two into his
box.

No one knows exactly how old the custom of Christmas tipping is, or its exact origin. In England, the giving
of money to servants at Christmastime is recorded in the
time of Henry VIII, and Samuel Pepys's seventeenth-

century diary records him "dropping money" here and there at Christmastide. In London, particularly, the poor man's "Christmas box," which he carried through the streets, was so much in use on the day following Christmas that December 26 became known as "Boxing Day." Originally, gifts of money were made by the rich to persons in subordinate positions, such as servants, apprentices, tradesmen, and their assistants. Soon children and scavengers pretending to be "in the trades" took up the practice of soliciting tips. By the first half of the nineteenth century in England, gratuities were going to everybody of inferior rank and less-prosperous circumstances until, by midcentury, the custom became such a wholesale giving, independent of merit, regard, or service, and such a tax on people's time and purse, that private and public efforts were put forward to abate the nuisance. Boxing Day was described as "a grave social injustice and hardship." One gentleman was thoroughly perturbed when even his lawyer asked for a Christmas gratuity.

While America never adopted the exact tradition of Boxing Day there was a price list for "Merry Christmases" in the nineteenth century for those who lived on rungs above the midpoint on the social ladder. The following is a list for a lone New York bachelor in 1892:

Wishing the elevator boy at his apartment house a Merry Christmas, from $2 to $5; wishing the hall boy and the door boy the same; likewise the maid who took care of his rooms, the maid who served him breakfast in his rooms, the bell boy, the boy who cleaned his boots, and the washerwoman; wishing the six elevator boys at his office building Merry Christmas, another $6; his office boy, one extra week's salary; his stenographer, the same; the scrub woman, $3, and the janitor $10; wishing his waiters at his several luncheon places Merry Christmas, a gold piece each; his barber who shaved him and trimmed his hair, the same; saying Merry Christmas to the hostler who took care of his horse, $5; the stable foreman, one box of cigars, $2.50. There were three restaurants where he frequently dined in the evening and in each of them there were two or three waiters who had to be remembered, as well as the head waiters who were always attentive to him. More gold pieces. At every club he entered a Christmas list stared him in the face, and the old doorman, the call-boys, the coat-check boy, the two boys who set up his billiard and pool balls, and the clerk kept one eye on the list and the other on each entering member until he had added his autograph and a pledge to the growing collection. Then there was the cabman who stood near the corner of his favorite club. On rainy nights he had been his fare often enough so that the man expected a Christmas gift if he had to ride with him during Christmas week.

If a young man went to law school or medical school, he found the janitor waiting in the hall on the last night before Christmas recess with a subscription list tacked up by the door and a gas-lighter in his hand as a pointer with which to call attention to it.

There were, however, rewards for those paying the Christmas tax. Take a lawyer in a downtown skyscraper

# THE OLD, TRADITIONAL CHRISTMAS TIP

during the Christmas of 1900 as an example. About a week before Christmas, he noticed that the elevator boy took particular pains to shoot past him for seven or eight floors and then come all the way back, greet him with a cheery, "Good mornin', Sir, pleasant mornin', Sir, what, Sir?" then tip his hat before he let his passenger escape. Suddenly the lawyer's bootblack seemed to take so much pleasure in his work that he applied coat after coat of polish, snapping and flourishing his rag without the least sign of fatigue. And the lawyer's office boys each seemed to have sprouted the wings of Mercury.

Christmas was a gala day for mailmen. Christmas morning found them all on hand at the post office at 6:30 A.M. to deliver the last of the Christmas mail. Although it was strictly against the rules of the department for them to solicit from the people on their route, they were allowed to accept tips, and they were usually generously remembered by their friends. A carrier would rather take a baby carriage or a wagon to carry the extra mail on his route than have an extra man assigned to help him. This was one point on which they were all a little touchy; many had been known to take along their fathers, brothers, or sons to help tote the bundles rather than take the chance of having another carrier reap the benefits from their particular route.

Each year, Christmas presented the employees of the big New York hotels with bonanzas of tips from their wealthy patrons. On December 24, 1907, gifts rained on the staff of the new Plaza Hotel. Not only did the pages, bellboys, footmen, maids, and porters receive the expected gifts of money, but many of the guests gave presents of various sorts. One bright-eyed young page received a fountain pen, a gold watch, a dozen handkerchiefs, and more than $150 in cash. Mrs. H. C. Strong, the wife of a Pennsylvania entrepreneur who had been at the hotel for a week, presented gold watches to a dozen of her favorite servants. Alfred Gwynne Vanderbilt, who was living at the hotel, gave away a thousand dollars in ten- and five-dollar notes. On Christmas night, George J. Gould, who lived with his family at the Plaza, was still calling servants to his suite and rewarding them with eye-opening gifts of money. Christmas had caught Mr. Gould somewhat unprepared. His cash supply was not commensurate with his good intentions, and his frequent requisitions on the hotel's safe were causing a money shortage. Like some of the other guests, he sent down orders for hundreds of dollars at a time, and he was compelled, while it lasted, to disburse used money instead of new bills. Indeed, so great was the Christmas Day run on the safe that several of the hotel's guests were forced to postpone some of their donations until the banks reopened on the twenty-sixth. The thirty-four-year-old operatic tenor Enrico Caruso, who was staying at the Plaza, gave away cash as well as some of his tracings to employees that he wished to have personal souvenirs. He spent his leisure moments tracing drawings in illustrated magazines and then coloring his copies with crayons.

The largest Christmas tip on record was given by James Gordon Bennett, Jr., the bon-vivant millionaire publisher of his father's *New York Herald*. He had frequently breakfasted amidst the silver and crystal of the old Delmonico's. After his Christmas morning breakfast in 1876, he gave the waiter who always served him a small roll of bills. As soon as the man had the opportunity, he looked at the roll, and when he recovered his equilibrium he took it to Mr. Delmonico. There were six $1000 bills. The proprietor, sensing that a mistake had been made, put them in the safe. When the publisher next visited the cafe, Mr. Delmonico told him the waiter had turned the money in. He added that he would return it as Mr. Bennett departed.

"Why return it?" said the millionaire publisher. "Didn't I give it to him?"

"Yes, but, of course it was a mistake. You gave him $6,000."

"Mr. Delmonico," replied Bennett, rising to his full and considerable height, "you should know that James Gordon Bennett never makes a mistake."

In the 1880s it became common to see long lines of men lined up to receive turkeys or food baskets, tokens of their employers' gratitude, as they left the gates of factories on Christmas Eve. A decade earlier, New York financial institutions had begun to make news by giving their employees small bonuses each Christmas. In 1883 P. Lorilard's tobacco factory in Jersey City, pioneered a now-common practice when it gave one week's salary as a Christmas bonus.

# THE OLD, TRADITIONAL CHRISTMAS TIP

In 1889 expressions of occupational appreciation still worked two ways. On Christmas night in Erie, Pennsylvania, the employees of the Watson paper mill expressed their good will by presenting Mr. H. F. Watson with a valuable carriage robe and an elegant Mexican onyx cabinet that had been greatly admired for a week past in a downtown show window.

## Chapter 6

## THE HOLLY AND THE TREE

**I**n the days
before Christmas, around
the New York railroad stations,
in the markets and
on street corners, filling
the brisk December air with
their resinous fragrance, an abundance of old-fashioned
Christmas greens were offered for sale. Holly, ground
pine, and mistletoe sellers did a rushing business; most of
them carried their stock in trade slung over their shoulders or about their necks, though some ran stands.
Storefronts were elaborately festooned with ropes of cedar and laurel and hung with wreaths. Butchers' carts
were gay with greenery and mock flowers. Other specimens of evergreen flourished from horses' bridles,
peanut ovens, roast pigs' mouths, and the universal but-
tonhole.

At the mansions of millionaires, wreaths were hung in

all the windows, and one was put around the front door knocker. Inside, ropes of evergreen wound about the balustrade of the staircase, brightened by branches of imported English holly and red satin ribbon, and a generous pendant of English mistletoe hung from the chandelier in the hall, while smaller branches dangled from open doorways. The maid's domain in the kitchen was not forgotten, for her mistress had hung holly wreaths in her windows too, and a piece of mistletoe from the gas light. The prettiest and brightest piece of holly was saved for the culminating culinary *pièce de résistance* of the season—yes, even of the whole year: the Christmas pudding.

The great market for Christmas greens was in lower Manhattan, beside the Hudson River and at the nearby Washington Market. The busy streets in the vicinity could have been forest roads, so lined were they with spruce, balsam, pine, and cedar trees, standing upright or piled like cordwood along the sidewalk. The awning posts were twined with ropes of green. Green festoons hung from the windows, and against the dark green the scarlet berries of holly, bittersweet, or black alder glowed like bits of flame. Amid these groves, sturdy farmers from Maine, from the shadows of the Catskills up the river, from New Jersey and the valley of the Mohawk, all displayed their forest trophies and drove sharp bargains with city retailers. Wagons piled high with their Christmas loads rattled away to every corner of the city. Children clapped their hands and chased after them, and more gathered to watch the unloading and to catch any stray bit of the evergreen to carry home.

# THE HOLLY AND THE TREE

Around Washington Market, the street trade in greens was carried on chiefly by women. About two weeks before Christmas, by tradition, they were allowed to invade the territory of the market and to erect their temporary stands in any unoccupied place. Barrels were set in rows; from them rose frames resembling the latticework of an arbor. Soon they supported small thickets of forest greenery. In the chill gray dawn, women in shawls stood about rubbing their hands for warmth while awaiting the footsteps of the first customer.

The pioneering business venture in Christmas greens for the New York market was made about 1840. A farmer's wife from Monmouth County, New Jersey, gathered enough pine greens to fill a sheet tied together by the four corners, loaded it on a sloop at Keyport with her pork and poultry, and set sail for the city. Forty years later, her grandson was selling 80,000 yards of "rope" (as various kinds of greenery used for festooning and twining columns were known in the trade), and wholesale dealers handled as many as 125,000 yards of rope each Christmas.

A new business in "fancy greens" had developed rapidly following the Civil War. At Christmastime, Victorians kept the graves of their loved ones green with cemetery emblems. Stars, anchors, and crosses were considered especially appropriate for God's acre, but wreaths, crowns, lyres, triangles, and doves were also used in great numbers.

By the 1870s the steamboat *Matteawan* was arriving in New York every morning for about two weeks before

Christmas, loaded with huge coils of rope, great stacks of wreaths of varied designs, baskets made of mosses, and leaves of holly and rhododendron.

While most of the decorative greenery was still done in the same small district of New Jersey, by the 1880s the bulk of the raw material had to be imported. The ground pine, a moss that looked like a miniature four-inch-high hemlock tree, had been nearly exterminated from the New Jersey woods, and the same was true of another moss known as the "creeping vine." Immense quantities of them were then collected in Connecticut, Massachusetts, and northern New York and shipped to Monmouth County.

The wreaths most in favor were made from the sharp-pointed and glossy leaves of American holly, considered by true Anglo-Americans to be inferior to the "armed and varnished leaves" of the English holly that the English diarist John Evelyn had celebrated more than two centuries before. Besides holly, a great array of natural materials were used in the construction of formal designs. Twigs of rhododendron, boxwood, mountain laurel, hemlock, cedar (with its blue berries), myrtle, princess pine, brightly dyed grasses and corn husks, and the red berries of black alder and the orange and scarlet pods of bittersweet—all these, together with the moss that hung on the north side of old oaks, were arranged decoratively, sometimes with considerable taste and sometimes with very little.

The painstakingly made wreaths and ropes brought their makers only low prices, but since the work was

# THE HOLLY AND THE TREE

done by country folk after cornhusking at a season when there was little else to do, the profit was not inconsiderable. Altogether, Christmas greens furnished many suits of Sunday clothes and new bonnets for people whose labors helped brighten the holiday season in the city. The work began early in November. The country lads carried greens from the woods by the wagonload, and the lassies spent long evenings in old kitchens around great fireplaces, busily twisting and binding. A skillful worker could do thirty to forty yards in an evening. Eventually, the New Jersey greens-makers had competition from Staten Island, the Catskills, and as far away as Maine, but Keyport, New Jersey, remained celebrated as New York's principal supplier of Christmas greenery. And the little coast steamboat that carried the greens to the city was equally renowned.

When the *Magenta* loomed up out of the fog over the North River (as New Yorkers called the Hudson at that time) on the shortest day of the year in 1898, the woods of New Jersey appeared to have arrived in the city. Her two decks were piled high with holly, laurel, pine, and other evergreens, including 200,000 yards of rope and, in round numbers, 50,000 fancy pieces. Her cabin, hold, between-decks, and steerage were filled with wreaths, crosses, stars, horseshoes, diamonds, and other fancy pieces. When the "Evergreen Boat" docked at ten o'clock at the foot of Thirteenth Street, Captain Walling found the pier crowded with horse-drawn vehicles of all kinds, and people of all descriptions lined the water's edge. Business began with a rush. In the crowd were theatrical agents, department store representatives, delegations from hospitals and charitable institutions, wives of corner grocerymen, wholesalers, and florists. Women of the Flower and Fruit Mission had sent representatives who bought more than one hundred dollars' worth of decorations for city hospitals and asylums. Theatrical men bought horseshoes and stars for decorating their amusement houses, and florists piled their wagons high. Department stores bought, by actual measurement, forty miles of pine and laurel rope. Despite the hubbub, every seller knew his wares, had them piled around him, and conducted his sales in a businesslike manner. Standing arms akimbo, Captain Walling estimated for the reporter from the *Times* that the makers of greens carried back to New Jersey more than $20,000 for the season.

Holly, princess pine, arborvitae, and laurel were much more highly esteemed than ground pine, cedar, myrtle, and hemlock, though the latter were sold to families and churches with small budgets. Boxwood rope was an expensive decoration, rare even in the stock of florists whose customers were of the wealthiest class.

Among Americans at that period, mistletoe was still regarded more as a risqué curiosity than as an essential accessory to the Christmastime fireside activity. In 1855 Nathaniel Hawthorne, the author, serving as the American consul in Liverpool, was shocked to discover the prominence of the mistletoe custom in British life. On December 26, he wrote critically:

# The Holly and the Tree

On Christmas Eve, and yesterday, there were little branches of mistletoe hanging in several parts of our house, in the kitchen, the entries, the parlor, and the smoking room—suspended from the gas-fittings. The maids of the house did their utmost to entrap the gentlemen boarders, old and young, under these privileged places, and there to kiss them, after which they were expected to pay a shilling. It is very queer, being customarily so respectful, that they should assume this license now, absolutely trying to pull the gentlemen into the kitchen by main force, and kissing the harder and more abundantly, the more they were resisted. A little rosy-cheeked Scotch lass—at other times very modest—was the most active in this business. I doubt whether any gentleman but myself escaped. I heard old Mr. Smith parleying with the maids last evening, and pleading his age; but he seems to have met with no mercy; for there was the sound of prodigious smacking, immediately afterwards.

Still, no recently arrived Anglo-American household was considered prepared for the holidays without a sprig. Indeed, it was considered unlucky for an English home not to have some mistletoe hanging in it. According to British superstition, a young woman who was not kissed under the mistletoe would not be married during that year. Also, since a berry was always plucked off at every kiss, maidens in former times saw to it that the branches did not fail to have a plentiful supply of berries. To have the full virtue that the superstition attributed to it, mistletoe was supposed to have fed on English air. Thus, in Washington Market, English mistletoe was always twice as expensive as the American variety. Its leaf is long and graceful in shape, while that of the American is short and rounding, and its translucent, pearllike berries are generally larger, though they often arrived after the four-week sea voyage in such poor condition that some florists preferred the native growth. During the 1880s mistletoe came to New York mainly from England and France, though ever-increasing quantities were beginning to be received from Georgia, Florida, and other Southern states. The American species was usually gathered by agile young boys from elm, hickory and oak trees, where its parasitic roots hung deftly on.

English mistletoe arrived in Washington Market still in the clusters in which it had grown, sometimes to immense proportions. In 1896 one dealer offered a thirty-three-pound ball for sale. A giant ball of mistletoe assumed unique importance in the days when the worst fate to befall any woman was spinsterhood and getting a husband was the consuming preoccupation of polite society. When a family had a large number of young females to worry about, the result was genteel madness. A few Christmases before, a young reporter had questioned a sharp fellow selling a sphere that weighed, as they said in those days, a quarter of a hundredweight.

"Would one person ever buy so much?" the reporter asked.

"Oh, yes," the dealer replied with a grin. "Some people, you know, are pretty hard to take a hint, and if the father of nine marriageable daughters finds the young men too obtuse for patience, he is very apt to make the mistletoe hint so strong that he who is blind can see it."

"How much does such a hint cost him?"

The dealer sized him up shrewdly to make sure that he was not a father in disguise.

"Well," he said, "that depends on how anxious he is. I can generally tell by the number of crows' feet and the look in his eyes. If he is only so-so, he could get that bunch for ten dollars. If the young man has been calling a long time but won't say anything, I can generally get twelve for it. But the father of nine—and I can tell him every time—cannot get off for less than fifteen or twenty, according to the size of his pocketbook. A chap in this business has to be a sort of human weather sharp."

From Florida came large quantities of Spanish moss, which served a double purpose: first, as a soft and dry packing material for oranges, and second, as a decoration. Its cool grayish-green color contrasted well against the dark shades of northern greens.

During the latter quarter of the nineteenth century, a new Christmas decoration was briefly adopted: dried and dyed flowers and grasses. Imported from France and Germany, the quantity increased every year during the 1880s and 1890s, and the windows of the most elegant New York florists as well as those in the German neighborhoods were brilliant each Christmas with their rich and varied colors. Dried wreaths, crosses, and crowns hung next to those of living green. Small dried flowers known as *immortelles* or "everlastings," either in their natural pale yellow or dyed bright red, blue, green, or black, as well as paper roses of all colors of the rainbow, brightened evergreen wreaths and ropes. These sold largely to Germans and Scandinavians who wished to have the dark green of most evergreens relieved by dashes of color. The Italians, like native-born Americans, seemed to prefer solid masses of green.

If anyone desired to make their own designs, greens and dried flowers in pieces were sold in Washington Market too, for a few cents a pound. The churches were among the best customers, especially those of the Episcopal denomination. Among the raw greens were English, German, and domestic ivy. For those who wished to have more Biblical-looking decorations, huge palmetto leaves were shipped to the market each Christmas season.

Big churches used thousands of yards of the largest "ropes" to twine about pillars, festoon the gallery fronts, and trim the altar and chancel rail. Customarily they purchased a number of cartloads of greens, and young men and women of the parish assembled on the evenings preceding Christmas to make the decorations and deck the church. While fair hands nimbly wove garlands and emblems, and manly forms ventured high aloft to put them in place under the critical eyes of the elders, not infrequently friendships formed that soon merged into closer bonds.

It was not unusual for great New York churches such as Trinity, St. Thomas's and St. George's, to be decorated with greens that had cost several hundred dollars, a lot of money in those days, in an effort to have the most gor-

# THE HOLLY AND THE TREE

geous display in the city. And each Christmas the decorations grew more elaborate. With the annual greens competition among New York's major churches being keenly followed by the public, the old amateur method of decorating became impractical and went out of fashion. Typically, by the 1880s it took a florist and sixty employees several days to put a single church in readiness.

On Christmas morning in 1883, the interior of the snow-covered brownstone St. George's Church on Stuyvesant Square was decorated with festoons, wreaths, and solid masses of Christmas greens. Across the ceiling, 140 feet above the floor, was a huge festoon of green wreaths. The chancel was draped with greens, and a bower had been constructed to represent the stable at Bethlehem. In front of the chancel was a large star of gas jets bearing the motto COME YE TO BETHLEHEM. To the apple-cheeked worshipers entering from the brisk snow-filled air, the fragrance of evergreen was overwhelming.

On Christmas Day in 1895, St. George's Church was even more handsomely and extravagantly decorated than usual. The walls and ceiling were virtually concealed by evergreens and holly. The doors of each pew were covered with clusters of holly berries and pine sprigs. Over the pulpit was suspended a large star of laurel, studded with electric lights of various colors. The chancel was decorated with a large cross of laurel and holly, and the chancel rail was banked with evergreens at each end, while cut flowers and plants stood in the center. All the greens had been sprinkled, as if touched by frost, with glittering diamond dust, and although the weather outside was unseasonably warm and pleasant, the church interior presented an astonishingly wintry appearance.

To supply enough greens for the florists in the church- and store-decorating trade, numberless workers stood up to their elbows and shoulders in fragrant florists' workrooms, shaping festoons by the mile, from Thanksgiving until the dawn of Christmas Day. The rooms had to be cool, and the workers could usually see their breath when they talked. In the typical room, from twenty-five to thirty men and boys labored. A brisk *snip, snip, snip* sounded above the endless swish of boughs, the snapping of twigs, and the rattle of holly. The ropemakers swiftly cast a ball of thin wire around the foliage, which they clasped to a cord in the other hand. The thud of balls of wire falling upon long wooden tables was as rhythmic as the snipping of hurrying fingers.

By the latter 1880s, along upper Broadway, every florist and confectionary store, theater, and liquor store indulged its fancies in Christmas greens. Looking up the street, one noticed little save a succession of pine, fir, and cedar festoons. Stores on Broadway had their pavements roofed over with long ropes of greens reaching the curbs. Typical of their interior decoration in that golden era of Christmas greenery, before fire regulations restricted the use of real evergreens, was the main store of the Great American Tea Company near the evergreen mart at Washington Market. Each Christmas, arches of evergreen and ground pine reached from counter to

# THE HOLLY AND THE TREE

counter. At night, the arbor was lighted by gas lights and Chinese lanterns. The scents of the greenery mixed deliciously with the aromas of teas and coffees from distant parts. Police stations were trimmed with evergreens, inside and out, till the places looked like "vernal bowers."

In 1888 perhaps the most elaborately decorated place in the city was a restaurant on Sixth Avenue near Twenty-eighth Street. It departed a bit from the usual decorations, for poultry and game entered into the scheme. The façade, up to the cornice, was covered with festoons of greens, yard after yard, making it as green as a moss-covered ruin. At the top hung an enormous white turkey with chickens, ducks, and other wild game birds below, while above the restaurant's door reclined a tiny pig with a sprig of mistletoe in its mouth.

Many private residences were trimmed as thoroughly as this, outside and in. Gothic arches of greenery were constructed in parlors, and ropes blended of light green laurel and darker ground pine twined around door frames, looped under windows and cornices, and wrapped picture cords and even the long chains on gas chandeliers. In 1892 the editor of the social page of *The New York Tribune* offered advice on how to decorate simply:

> Have the gardener bring to the house a small load of greens; cut these into boughs small enough to be handled easily. Stick some behind the pictures by fastening two or three to the wall or back of a picture with a small tack; or tied to the picture wire, they make a sort of framework for others so that quite a large background

can be formed. Do the same over the doors. The entrance from the hall to the dining room can be made especially pretty by standing quite large branches at each side of the door frame, and building the green framework wider and higher, and forming a large arch over the door by fastening the greens here and there with little tacks and fine green twine. One will be surprised how the boughs hold one another in place and how few tacks have to be used. Among the greens stick bits of holly with its red berries.

At the same period, a huge variety of hothouse flowers, from red roses to the white bloom we now call the Easter lily, were common Christmas flowers in countless towns and cities. Around New York, bright, clear sunshine, even during the winter, rendered the raising of flowers a paying occupation. Within a radius of fifty miles of the city was a unique combination of the horticultural skills of many nations—French and German and Dutch, as well as the flower-loving British. If Christmas Eve and Christmas morning were warm, the florists were the happiest of men, because the thousands of boxes of Christmas flowers that had to be delivered on Christmas morning could go out without winter packing. In freezing weather, every flower had to be packed in cotton, doubling the labor and time necessary. Even with a mild Christmas, however, the employees in the big retail florist shops worked most or all of the night before Christmas, for at seven o'clock the delivery wagons started, and before noon all the fragile blooms had reached the wives and sweethearts for whom they had been purchased. At the turn of the century, 20,000 boxes of flowers were delivered every Christmas morning in New York City.

In 1902 it was reported that the "mixed box" of flowers ranged in price from three to fifty dollars. It was a "very modest" little box for the price—just half a dozen roses, a dozen carnations, and a bit of Christmas greens. In the fifty-dollar box, there were probably half a dozen American Beauties (selling that year at thirty-six dollars a dozen); half a dozen long-stemmed Liberty roses of the rich, velvety, deep crimson variety; some violets, lilies of the valley, mignonette to sweeten the whole box, perhaps some sweet peas and hyacinths or a bit of heliotrope, always some holly, and a red satin ribbon to tie it all up. Red was preeminently the Christmas color, and both red carnations and red roses were the favorite purchases.

About the same time, the poinsettia, sold in some elegant New York shops at Christmas since at least 1870, began its career as the traditional holiday flower. Its name honors the man who is customarily given the credit for introducing the plant to this country. Joel Roberts Poinsett, a botanist, congressman from South Carolina, and the first United States ambassador to Mexico. Between 1822 and 1830 he had been intrigued by a tropical plant, a flaming red star with a brilliant yellow center, and twice brought it home to his greenhouses in Charleston. It became a curiosity for his horticulturist and botanist friends to grow in their greenhouses. By the early 1830s Poinsett's plants were being grown in Philadelphia. In the early 1900s Albert Ecke and his sons, flower growers in Hollywood, California, were among the first to develop and popularize the potted Christmas poinsettia.

There were probably no Christmas trees, as we think of them, in colonial America. There is a traditional story that says that the Hessian soldiers who were surprised by Washington and his troops at Trenton on Christmas night in 1776 had been celebrating around a candle-lit Christmas tree. Today historians can find no documentary evidence for the story in diaries or letters left by either the German mercenaries or the Americans who were present at the battle. Despite this, there is the slim possibility that there might have been a Christmas tree in Trenton that night, since we know that there were a few decorated trees in the Hessians' homeland at that period.

The oldest known reference to the Christmas tree in America comes from the same German-speaking Moravians who gave the first Christmas presents in the New World. According to a diary, at the settlement of Bethlehem, Pennsylvania, on Christmas Day in 1747, "several small pyramids and one large pyramid of green brushwood had been prepared, all decorated with candles and the large one with apples and pretty verses." Strictly speaking, the pyramids were not actually Christmas trees, but constructions of evergreen boughs—a tradition (whose roots are lost in the mists of European Christmas

# THE HOLLY AND THE TREE

history) that merged with the evergreen tree to become the Christmas tree we know.

Three-quarters of a century later, in the vicinity of Germantown, Pennsylvania, the German artist John Lewis Krimmel sketched a small holly tree hung with cookies and surrounded by a tiny picket fence and toy animals. It was a centerpiece for the table of a German family. The earliest Christmas trees, regardless of the type of evergreen used, were all small table-size trees. In the years ahead, tree-rich America invented the tradition of the large floor-to-ceiling tree.

Christmas trees were originally present-bearers, decorated largely with gifts of toys and edibles. In 1836 the *Token and Atlantic Souvenir* printed a short story in which a German maid was persuaded by her mistress to decorate a tree after the custom of her homeland:

> The sturdiest branch drooped with its burden of books, chessmen, puzzles, etc., for Julius, a stripling of 13; dolls, birds, beasts, and boxes were hung on the lesser limbs. A regiment of soldiers had alighted on one bough, and Noah's ark was anchored to another, and to all the slender branches were attached cherries, plums, strawberries and fine peaches, as tempting and at least as sweet as the fruits of paradise.

Prior to 1850 there are only a few known references to Christmas trees in America, these recorded among Germans widely scattered through Pennsylvania, New York, Massachusetts, Ohio, Virginia, and the frontier territories of Illinois and Texas.

# THE HOLLY AND THE TREE

In 1833 Gustave Koerner was one of a group of German settlers in St. Clair County, Illinois. Since that county on the banks of the Mississippi had no evergreens, Koerner and his friends decorated a small sassafras tree with candles, apples, sweets, ribbons, bright paper, hazelnuts, hickory nuts, and polished red haws, the fruit of the hawthorne tree.

An illuminating glimpse of the popular appeal of the earliest Christmas trees is found in the autobiography of Charles H. Haswell, *Reminiscences of an Octogenarian of the City of New York*:

> It was about this period [the 1830s] that the German families had increased in number so that their custom of dressing a "Christmas tree" was observed. So novel was the exhibition that it evoked much comment. I have a vivid remembrance of my going over to Brooklyn of a very stormy night to witness the novelty.

By 1850 the Christmas tree was beginning to spread beyond families of purely German heritage. Young Harriet Beecher Stowe, the fourteen-year-old daughter of the novelist, wrote an excellent description in a letter to her father:

> Our Christmas tree was a fine spruce & when it set on the table it touched the wall & I made four gilt stars for the four top branches & ma dressed a little doll like a fairy in white gauze with spangles & a gilt band around her head & a star on her forehead & a long gilt wand with a star on the end & gauze wings spangled with gold. She was placed in the top of the tree with her wand

pointing to the presents on it & there was no end to the gilt apples & nuts &c, &c.

Although Christmas trees would have been few and far between in America at that period, there were probably more than those few that were recorded might lead us to believe. We know that Christmas trees were sold in Philadelphia markets in 1848, and a Catskill mountaineer named Mark Carr sold the first Christmas trees in New York's Washington Market in 1851. In 1861 an American woman, Catharina Bonney, the wife of a missionary, Samuel Bonney, who sailed for China in 1844, described their Christmas tree in Canton as if they'd always had one:

> The "Christmas Tree" with its emblematic evergreen, whose top reached the ceiling, has budded and blossomed. On December 25th, the fruit was all plucked from its heavily ladened branches, much to the gratification and delight of the little folks whose bright eyes often would turn wistfully toward the locked door, and long to peep. The secrecy and mystery of its preparation has been tantalizing for them.

A charming account of the growing custom appeared in *The New York Tribune* on Christmas Day in 1855 (although *The New York Times* continued to describe the Christmas tree as a purely German oddity as late as 1883):

There goes the bright looking, well dressed mechanic's wife, with a Christmas tree in her arms, followed by her eldest son—who, as a required assistant in the household mystery, is admitted to the maternal confidence—carrying a large basket of paper parcels, out of which peep queer devices, sugar animals, cheap toys, and paper flowers for its adornment.

Thus, in splendid parlors and in humble rooms, the tree of Yuletide was set up. Whether it was aflame with the soft light of countless candles and glittering with ornaments and heavily hung with gifts, or half lit with little tapers and imperfectly decked out with trifling bits of decoration and humble presents, the rejoicing around it was equally heartfelt. Three decades into the present century, Junius Quattelbaum, who had been a slave in South Carolina, retained and described his fond memories of a plantation Christmas tree:

> Christmas mornin', marster would call all de slaves to come to de Christmas tree. He made all de chillun set down close to de tree and de grown slaves jined hands and make a circle 'round all. Then marster and missus would give de chillun deir gifts, fust, then they would take presents from de tree and call one slave at a time to step out and git deirs. After all de presents was give out, missus would stand in de middle of de ring and raise her hand and bow her head in silent thanks to God. All de slaves done lak her done. After all dis, everybody was happy, singin' and laughin' all over de place. Go 'way from here, white man! Don't tell me dat wasn't de next step to heaven to de slaves on our plantation. I sees and dreams 'bout them good old times, back yonder, to dis day.

# THE HOLLY AND THE TREE

The Christmases of the 1870s saw the introduction of "store-bought" ornaments from Germany, made to be kept from year to year. Wonderful were the little animals, fowls, birdcages, fruits, sausages, hams, and cabbages to be hung on the tree that, when taken apart, disclosed delicious bonbons. Among the prettiest ornaments were boots, cornucopias, drums, and trumpets made of colored isinglass so that the sugarplums inside were plainly visible. Turning slowly in the draft created by the many burning candles were tin ornaments faceted like crystal to reflect the dancing candlelight. Then there were glass balls, glass eggs, glass teardrops, paper flowers, and satin mottoes with messages like "Merry Christmas" and *"Fröhliche Weihnachten,"* wax cherubs, and comical figures suspended by rubber strings. From many a tree's branches, float-lights burned in bright-colored glass cups.

A description of the magic of such trees was captured for us by John Lewis, an Englishman who spent the Christmas of 1875 with his son in Philadelphia:

> There all the people seem to resolve themselves into Children for the occasion. The usual arrangement in this country is to have two parlors—be it a large or small house—opening to each other by sliding doors, the first being for state occasions. As large & fine a tree as could be accommodated being procured and set up, it is covered with every conceivable shape into which coloured & gilt paper & card can be cut, and little pictures, glass balls, chains, garlands, etc., anything to make a gay and imposing display. This being finished it is placed mostly

in the sliding door way, which allows it to be seen 2 ways. All the light possible is thrown upon it, often by reflectors, the lattice blinds being thrown open & it is thus open to inspection by passersby. Where the taste and industry of the owner prompts it, other attractions are added as fancy dictates—at one place I visited, an old doctor's, there was a very handsome river steamboat, perfect, 3 feet long with about 50 passengers (these last small pictures cut out) all of white, colour & gilt card; also a beautiful fire hose carriage. When the show commences people go round with or without their children to see them & frequently knock at the door to be admitted to a closer inspection which is readily granted. I heard of one house where 75 were admitted in about two hours. Riding through the better class streets on the cars, the effect is novel & very fine as every 2nd or 3rd may be exhibitors. I believe some keep it up 2 or 3 weeks.

Holding a small table tree erect had been a simple matter of nailing a board or a cross made from two short pieces of lath to the base of the trunk. As Americans began to erect larger Christmas trees, the engineering problems of holding up an unwieldy ten-foot evergreen proved to be considerable. Originally, big trees were replanted in boxes and tubs filled with rocks and earth. In 1876 two Philadelphians, Hermann Albrecht and Abram C. Mott, received the first U.S. patents for tree stands. Both their three-legged iron holders resembled old-fashioned flag stands, a secondary use named in their applications. Within a few years, Albrecht had an even better idea, and in 1880 he got a second patent for his improved design; his new holder gripped the tree's trunk by means of three large iron cleats that could be adjusted to the dimension of the trunk and screwed tight with a big iron ring. His stands, like Mott's, were designed to be screwed to the floor or else to some larger base for greater stability. During the next quarter-century, many patents were granted to other Americans, most with German names like Langenbach, Merk, Pannster, Schoenthaler and Westphal, who continued to invent new ways to hold up a Christmas tree. In 1877 Johannes C. Eckardt, a resident of Stuttgart, Germany, was granted an American patent for his clockwork music-box tree stand. Like Albrecht, he couldn't stop tinkering with his idea, and he was subsequently granted three more patents. His revolving musical stands were immensely popular well into the present century. In 1899 Alfred Wagner of St. Louis patented the first electric revolving tree stand. At the same time, Wagner solved another problem by providing a metal cup to hold water, thus adding days to the life of the tree and lessening the danger from its candles.

Others had long been at work on the problem of safety in those years when virtually all Christmas trees were candle-lit. Beginning in 1867 a whole host of designs for clip-on and counterweighted candleholders earned patents. They each attempted, with varying degrees of success, to solve the very real problem of how to keep a burning candle upright on a flimsy, drying branch that was loaded with presents and ornaments as well. In 1887 John Barth, a German Methodist minister in Louisville, Kentucky, patented a tiny oil lamp with a protective

# THE HOLLY AND THE TREE

glass globe, designed to replace a candle with its open flame. Barth's Christmas-Tree Lamps were particularly recommended for trees in Sunday schools and schools. In 1882, only three years after Thomas Edison had given the world the light bulb, his co-workers hand blew small bulbs and wired the first electric Christmas tree— although it was not until 1903 that the first strings of electric Christmas tree lights were sold by General Electric. In the intervening years, only the rich could afford to have electricians (then known as "wiremen") tediously handwire electric lights for their trees.

The period from 1880 to 1905 was the golden age of the old-fashioned Christmas tree. The evergreens of that era were richly overloaded with toys and dolls and delicate ornaments possessing a miniature, toylike charm. An angel or star competed for the position at the top of the tree. The boughs held little silver and gilt cardboard images of every animal of the farm and forest, birds, fish, houses, dolls, bicycles, ice skates, slippers and high-button shoes, ships with sails full spread, carriages, chariots, sedan chairs, locomotives, and sleighs. Here also were Lilliputian pianos and every instrument of the orchestra, ballerinas in fluffy skirts of tissue paper, stars and half-moons and whole moons, tiny watches and clocks, and myriad other quaint and dainty devices. There were real-as-life artificial pears, cherries, and strawberries. Apples and tangerines were hung, together with soot-black chimney sweeps made of prunes. Walnuts were dipped in egg white, gold-leafed, and hung by threads. And there were sparkling chains of beads, and paper chains made by children, and strings of popcorn and cranberries. There were toothsome gingerbread men, gingerbread horsemen, and gingerbread women. And there were animal cookies and animals made from marzipan, and melted sugar that had been molded into human and animal forms; in fact, sweets ran rampant in a hundred shapes, chocolate taking precedence over all the rest and made into Santa Clauses and musical instruments and a veritable Noah's ark of animals. Probably the universal ornament of the Victorian Christmas tree was the cornucopia, the bright paper cone lined with a paper doily and holding nuts and sweets. (In 1876 Thomas L. Cornell of Birmingham, Connecticut, fulfilled the period's penchant for patents by patenting his design for novel cornucopias—flat-sided, pyramidal paper boxes having from three to eight sides.) But then, no tree was complete without an orange, either. Its color stood out well against the dark green tree, and generations of children carefully carved orange baskets from orange skins, then filled them with candied sections of orange and hung them by means of red ribbons.

Family trees were unveiled on Christmas Eve or Christmas morning. The halls were purposely kept dark so that the children would be dazzled when the big double parlor doors were finally thrown open and they burst into a room lit brilliantly by their Christmas tree.

In New York in 1895, at about five o'clock on Christmas morning, a Third Avenue elevated train was rolling uptown taking a handful of reporters and other night owls home. Suddenly their attention was drawn to a lighted room in a "flat" that was level with their train. The shades were up, light streamed out into the night, and everything in the humble room was revealed. They saw four children, clad in white nightshirts, troop into the room while their father and mother peeked at them through the door. In one corner stood the green tree. They could almost hear the little ones' delighted cries. The scene was gone in an instant, but the fairy that ordinarily peeks in on such joyous Christmas-scapes could have had no better view than those passengers.

In the 1890s it became the fashion for wealthy children to have Christmas tree parties in order to delight and amaze even their cosmopolitan little friends. An article in *The Atlantic Monthly* in 1894 described a party where the tree had been hidden behind a sheet. Before they could see the wonders of the tree, the children were treated to a magic lantern show projected on the sheet. Then a chorus of "Ah!"s was heard as the sheet was drawn aside, revealing a big tree aglow with candles and topped with an angel. The family gardener stood by with a bucket of water, just in case. The Christmas tree was loaded with baubles and little presents that were distributed all around. Then the room "resounded with joyful voices intermingled with the sound of crackers which were drawn with exclamations of surprised triumph; paper cups, and aprons, and bonnets, and mottoes in the most execrable verse that ever the wit of man devised. There was a due quota of penny whistles, trumpets and accordions. The oranges and bonbons from the tree were followed by slices of cake from the table."

# THE HOLLY AND THE TREE

Although the boughs of the trees of the socially prominent city child drooped under the weight of hundreds of
toys and hundreds of candles (a contemporary magazine
recommended four hundred candles for a twelve-foot
tree) or the weight of brilliant electric lights and some of
the most expensive and beautiful ornaments ever made,
it was not necessary to buy a single object to have a
child-pleasing tree. On the day following Christmas in
1898, *The New York Times* printed an account of a
farmer's Christmas tree in a rural district of Pennsylvania:

> Tinsel, spangles and colored glass have but little place
> on the country Christmas tree. Instead there are huge
> honey cakes, ginger cakes, cut into shapes representing
> great fat hogs, sheep, rabbits, cats, horses, cows and
> other farm life. Some of these animal cakes are several
> feet square and made attractive by sprinklings of red,
> white and blue sugars.
>
> Perched on the branches of the tree are stuffed squir-
> rels, chipmunks, and other trophies of the hunt and the
> country boy's skill with the shotgun, while grouped
> around the base of the tree are opossums, raccoons, and
> occasionally, a large red or gray fox. All are appropri-
> ately decorated with Christmas greens and brillant-hued
> ribbons. The tree is also laden with great chunks of
> home-made taffy, large red apples and Winter pears,
> with a sprinkling of shell barks, chestnuts and other pro-
> ductions of the farm.

# THE HOLLY AND THE TREE

In a small Eastern city, a grocer, clad in a sweater against the wintry cold, paused, notebook in hand, repeating an order: a dozen oranges, six grapefruit, Malaga grapes, one box of sardines, one Christmas tree. An hour later, the grocer's boy deposited a bag in the kitchen of the big brick house across the street from the Presbyterian church. He left the eleven-foot tree on the back porch.

At the turn of the century, it would have seemed like a dream to many Americans that someone could order a Christmas tree from a store. At the same time, in parts of the country where trees could be had for the cutting, it was hard to realize that in millions of homes there would be no Christmas tree because there were no evergreen trees to be had. In much of the Midwest and West, Christmas trees were known only by hearsay. Water willows and scrub oak could not make a Christmas tree.

On the prairies, Santa Claus had to hang his presents in stockings on the back of a chair, though in Kansas, tales are still told of children who decorated tumbleweed or dried sunflower Christmas trees, and in the high-dry plains country of eastern Colorado they tell about a family with six children, who once stared wide-eyed at a cottonwood sapling nailed to the floor of a two-room homesteader's shack; from the bare branches on red calico strings hung bags of hard candy and peanuts, a mouth organ, a top, and homemade red mittens for each child.

In 1900 the Forest Service estimated that one American family in five had a Christmas tree, though many other children enjoyed one at their school, church, or grange hall. Nine years later, that the custom was taking hold was reflected in the government's estimate that one family in four celebrated around a Christmas tree.

In the West, the growth of railroads was a major contributor to the spreading of the Christmas tree custom. In towns along the railroad lines, the arrival of the Christmas trees was second in importance only to the circus. Word flew around the town that the Christmas trees were coming, and down to the station everybody rushed. The rail car was shunted on the side track, a wagon arrived, strong-armed men tossed the trees on, and the driver rattled away to the store with small boys running along in its wake.

But in countless other places not blessed by a railroad, a man could live his whole life without ever seeing a Christmas tree. Suddenly, as the nineteenth century drew to a close, Sears, Roebuck and the U. S. Post Office made it easy for everyone to have a Christmas tree. All that the family on the solitary Nebraska farm had to do was to turn to the pink index pages of their mail-order catalog and look under the *C*'s.

"Ch—Chr—There it is! Christmas trees, artificial, page 727."

"Which tree shall we get?"

"Which one can we afford?"

"One is $1 and one is fifty cents. The $1 one has fifty-five limbs and the fifty cent one has thirty-three."

"Fifty cents more could buy the one with the fifty-five limbs."

# THE HOLLY AND THE TREE

"Son, fifty cents is a great deal of money out our way."

Six days later the wonderful tree arrived, the one with the fifty-five limbs, in a cardboard box wrapped in string.

Proof that the Christmas tree had become an indispensable part of the American Christmas was supplied in 1910 when the Canal Commission sent Christmas trees to the army of workers on the Panama Canal. To keep them as fresh as possible, the trees were sent on a ship that did not reach the isthmus until the last minute.

## Chapter 7

## THE RIGHT WEATHER FOR CHRISTMAS

The Christmas
morning of 1883 in
New York City was cold—
bracing but not biting.
Snow was in the air,
but it refrained from beginning
until people had gone to church. Then a few flakes began
to fall, at first timidly and hesitatingly, then faster and
faster, until shortly after noon, as the worshipers were
homeward bound, it was snowing determinedly. The
second snowstorm in three days, the third in a week, had
begun.

The flakes were large and heavy, and by one o'clock
the muddy, snow-covered streets, churned into choco-
late-colored slush by the heavy traffic the day before,
had been completely transformed by freshly fallen snow.
Suddenly from the side streets onto the avenues dashed
sleighs of every size, shape, and description, from the

costly eight-seated vehicle with four splendid horses, filled with the family of a solid banker or merchant, snug under fur lap robes, to the jaunty cutter with its single horse and gaily jangling bells, driven by the young clerk who was cheerfully spending the last of his savings to give his sweetheart a long-promised ride. Following these came the improvised bobsled, a straw-filled wooden box on wooden runners with crossed boards for seats, drawn by a horse whose regular occupation was pulling a produce cart. One such vehicle consisted only of a horse, traces, and a soapbox, driven by a red-faced man in a dirty yellow coat. As the soapbox was flying up the avenue, gentlemen in sleighs that tried to distance the shaggy brown mare had their eyes blinded with snow.

The soft silence of the snowstorm was broken only by the mirthful voices of people wishing everyone they met "a Merry Christmas." "I wish you the same, and many more of them" was the reply dancing from lip to lip. People were singing in some sleighs; children laughed and chattered in others; there was the swish of steel runners, the tinkle of harnesses, the muffled clip-clop of the horses' hoofs, and the staccato stamp of fast trotters' feet. The air sang with the wild, sweet music of sleighbells, silver and brass and iron and gold, every fresh turnout adding a new tone to the tingling, jangling chorus.

One continuous line of sleighs headed uptown toward Central Park, through the park, along the country roads of the northern end of the island, and back again. Between the park and McComb's Dam Bridge, at present-

# THE RIGHT WEATHER FOR CHRISTMAS

day 181st Street, and north along Jerome Avenue, hostelries were overflowing with reveling sleighers in search of "food and entertainment for man and beast," as one exuberant fellow put it as he stomped into a road-house, shaking the snow from his fur coat like a dog. "Rest y'rself, sah!" laughed the black stablehand, ever on duty. "What'll you have?" shouted the pudgy publican, "what'll you have?" Whiskey and hot rum were the order of the day. In the circuslike atmosphere of one of the taverns, a prize pig was being noisily and eagerly sought in a contest based on guessing its weight.

Outside, the snow continued to fall silently. The red and brown houses of Harlem were trimmed and capped with snow. Manhattanville, in its hollow, looked as though it were peeping from under a white coverlet. With a jingling of bells and a snapping of whips and a whizzing of runners and a flutter of hoofs, the whole bright procession of fleet sleighs swept on and on, up and down the wide boulevards, thundering over bridges, bumping, plunging, gliding, flying.

Central Park was a veritable wonderland. Each tree was a white candelabrum. Every bush wore a skullcap of snow. The Egyptian obelisk was a fleece-covered column, and snow piled itself deeply in fountains and on the heads and shoulders of statues. The KEEP OFF THE GRASS signs were scattered like castaways about a snowy ocean. The lanes were crowded with elegantly attired young sports sitting alone in their single cutters, passing and repassing each other in continual brushes along the snow-covered serpentine drives. Despite restrictions against speed in the park, light cutters with a single occupant were seen going so fast that their bells scarcely had time to jingle.

Famous people and famous horses were out, including Vanderbilts and other members of New York society, their sleek sleighs gleaming black, their high-stepping purebred horses gorgeous with bright-colored plumes and shining harnesses, streaming and glossy manes, and switching tails. With snow flying from the horses' hoofs, drivers hallooing, footmen muffled to the eyes in furs, whips fluttering with rainbow-hued ribbons, ladies in their latest fashion with snow-covered lap robes, huge overcoats, and fur caps, sealskin sacques, cheeks blushing, eyes sparkling, ears tingling, little gloved hands clinging, the sleighing parties flashed through the park, a Currier and Ives picture in the making. Frederick Vanderbilt drove his new mare, Nickel, nostrils spread and ears acock, the very incarnation of animal enthusiasm. Captain Jake Vanderbilt, under a peaked cap and covered with a sealskin robe and snow, sang "g'long" to his horse, Boston, and the bay answered the cry with a swish of his tail and renewed speed. Colonel Frederick Grant, son of the former President, was driving three Arabian horses that had been presented to his father by a sultan, now harnessed abreast and attached to a handsome Russian sleigh. By three o'clock the fast-falling snow had become too deep for good sleighing, and silence fell over the park as the sleighing parties departed.

Downtown, where the horse-drawn trolleys ran, ten-horse snowplows—lumbering, noisy contrivances—and their attendant sandcars were hard at work. They piled the snow in mountains alongside the tracks, over which tottering, puffing, rubber-booted pedestrians slowly climbed. The tops of women's umbrellas were capped with snow; soft epaulettes covered the shoulders of men's Norfolk coats. By three-thirty the snow was whirling down so rapidly that it obscured buildings half a block away, and the wind drove blinding clouds of snow around street corners and into the faces of red-nosed wayfarers. The snowflakes stuck wherever the wind blew them, and the fronts of stores and houses were frescoed in white. Although there were few people still abroad, there was little interruption in the horsecars' service, despite the storm. But the doubled and tripled teams—four and sometimes six horses, instead of two— slipped and floundered, struggled and toiled, as steam rose from their backs while their Irish drivers laid about them with their whips and hurled oaths. The drivers were a brusque and hardy lot. Snow fringed every angle of their thickly clothed figures and froze in masses on their crinkled beards. Their strong hands were enveloped in great shaggy gloves. Huge woolen comforters were ludicrously wound about their necks and heads, muffling their voices as they shouted "get up" and "whoa." "But," said a cynical car driver as he struggled violently with his brake, "it would not be Christmas without there was great plenty, and today there's plenty for all of us—plenty of snow." The horses were sheeted with congealed perspiration, and snow and icicles hung from their harnesses like gems until they looked like the

steeds of the ice king. Inside the plodding, creaking, wooden horsecars on the Lexington Avenue line, the few passengers sat huddled in the cozy warmth of the potbellied stoves. They seemed full of good humor, joking and chatting about the difficulties that beset them. The rattling windows were covered with ice and snow. Outside, red sparks flying from the cars' tin chimneys disappeared quickly in the falling snow.

With the exception of the sleighers, the weather induced most people to keep their celebrations indoors. That morning, the slush left over from the seven-inch snowfall two nights before had been enough to dampen the spirits of most of the target shooters, the bands of ragamuffins, and the other boisterous paraders who usually made Christmas Day noisy. Long before the snow began to fall, large numbers had courted the warmth of the corner saloons, many of which had assumed a Christmas look with tall trees of green outside and an abundance of greens within. The foundation for many holiday headaches was liberally laid in these establishments, where the sounds of singing and clinking glasses could be heard until a late hour.

In the afternoon, small boys uptown, who found the snow too deep even to take the paint off the runners of their new sleds, and small boys downtown, who had been lucky if Santa Claus brought them more than a mission society bag of candy, all amused themselves by "cutting out" icy slides in the gutters and occasionally on the sidewalks as well, much to the consternation of elderly citizens. It was a good snow for snowballs too, but few of a boy's favorite targets, little girls and silk top hats, were abroad in the storm. So here and there groups of boys competed in rolling gigantic snowballs six feet high.

Up and down Broadway the awnings were deep with snow; people went in single file along the sidewalks, speaking jocularly to one another from the depths of their bundling mufflers.

On the seven-month-old Brooklyn Bridge, travel was light. The snow clung to every rail, girder, and guy, completely transforming the appearance of the structure. A few sleighs crossed early in the afternoon, but most people took the railroad-car-like cable cars, though few were running in either direction. About two hundred pedestrians who braved the drifts and banks of snow encumbering the footwalk looked, in the words of a *New York Times* reporter, "like stage Santa Clauses." Below the bridge on the East River, the heavy snow hindered the ferryboats, just as a dense fog did. Fog bells guided the pilots to their slips, and the vessels' fog whistles were kept sounding in their deep mellifluous tones until the boats were finally forced out of service as night fell on the snowbound river.

Throughout the city the ironwork columns supporting the elevated steam railways, some of them wound with Christmas greens, were disguised with a fleecy mantle of white. Twenty feet above the street, spectral trains loomed, their normal clatter softened and almost absorbed by the snow, their headlights blazing from their diminutive engines. At the height of the storm, riders could barely see the world of second-story windows out-

# THE RIGHT WEATHER FOR CHRISTMAS

side. The stairs leading to and from the gas-lit platforms were slippery as banana peels. The result was inevitable and frequent. At one station, a stout man with red whiskers, a blue nose, and an amiable smile slipped on the top step and bumped all the others until he reached the ground. After a minute, he picked himself up and lumbered slowly away, looking like an arthritic bear. Some of the elevated railway employees, although they had to work while most people enjoyed a holiday, were reported to have been infected to a degree with Christmas spirit. In place of their usual ferocious scowls, they slammed their gates in the faces of late passengers with beaming grins.

The city was unnaturally beautiful seen through a veil of falling snow that looked like "the old woman in the sky shaking down goose-feathers." All that was unsightly had been silently snowed under. On the Lower East Side, miniature avalanches from the shelving roofs of the old houses were common, and more than one passerby had his Christmas hat smashed and his Christmas temper tried by the unexpected showers from above. In the tenement district, the red shawls of the workingmen's wives flashed like cardinals in the snow.

In the streets of the silent downtown business districts, there was not a footprint in the snow, presenting a picture that the following morning's traffic would entirely change. In the deserted neighborhood around Washington Market, cold gusts of wind carrying thick clouds of snow in whirling eddies swept along the street, beat against the doors, rattled shutters, howled along the housetops, and sent snow sifting through the heavily frosted windows. Everything wore a decidedly sub-zero appearance.

Indoors, as the afternoon wore away and it began to grow dark, Christmas dinners were served in the fashionable parts of the city. The laboring portion of the community and the poor had already eaten theirs, and now while smoke curled up from pipes or cigars, they sat with their friends and talked over good times gone or better times to come. In the Catholic churches, solemn vespers signaled the close of the religious observance of the day. Outside, while lamplighters were making their rounds through the snowstorm, the fashionable uptown brownstone neighborhoods along Fifth and Madison avenues were invaded by an army of downtown tenement immigrants armed with shovels. The early evening hours were filled with the din of clattering shovels and scrapers and the swosh-swosh of brooms, and the air was full of flying snow. Then silently the Italians and Irish departed joyfully with pockets, for once, jingling with coins.

Although Christmas night was usually a great occasion at the theaters, attendance that night was remarkably light. That evening, most New York society preferred the warmth of family and fireside.

At about seven-thirty the storm began to abate. By eight o'clock the snow had nearly stopped. The U. S. Signal Service weather station measured it at just under eight inches, at the observatory on the ten-story-high Equitable Building, the Empire State Building of the day. Manhattan island looked like a scene in a fairy tale—a glowing snow-white city between two black rivers. At midnight, as the last home lights blinked out and sleep came down on New York, the white Christmas of 1883 passed peacefully into history.

## Chapter 8

## THE WRONG WEATHER FOR CHRISTMAS

For Christmas weather, tradition calls for snow. It seems almost impossible to imagine an old-time Christmas without the mercury somewhere near zero, the ground covered with a heavy mantle of white, and the frosty air alive with the music of merry sleigh bells.

We are convinced that our weather in general and our Christmas weather in particular is not what it used to be. There may have been more snow in the nineteenth century, but the truth is that the weather was just as crazy in "the good old days" as it seems to us to be today. Even in New England, where we believe it always snowed punctually for the holidays, there were a good many green Christmases a century or so ago.

The legend of "Christmas weather" was popularized and sentimentalized in the last century by the literary

# THE WRONG WEATHER FOR CHRISTMAS

talents of Charles Dickens, the master Victorian story-teller, with an assist from Clement C. Moore. As Dickens told it, snow lay on the ground, icicles hung on the wall, and there was ice on the lake when Mr. Pickwick and his friends spent Christmas at Dingley Dell. Although illustrators and movie directors have long put snow on the streets of London for *A Christmas Carol,* it was actually only cold and foggy on that most famous of Christmases. However, when Scrooge accompanied the Ghost of Christmas Past, Dickens served up plenty of snow, so much that London householders were up shoveling off their roofs. Records show that snow fell in London on many of the Christmases of Dickens's youth. Thus it is understandable that he idealized a white Christmas. During the rest of his lifetime snow fell less frequently, but Victorians on both sides of the Atlantic embraced the idea of a white Christmas as Dickensian Christmas weather.

New York City, where Clement C. Moore was born in 1779, had a good many green Christmases, and several that were preternaturally warm, during his eighty-four-year lifetime, but he left behind an indelible poetic image of reindeer landing on snow-covered rooftops.

In the nineteenth century, a green Christmas was both disappointing and disconcerting to a great many people, English immigrants brought to America the old wives' tale that "a green Christmas brings a full churchyard." Mild weather at Christmas aroused superstitious fears that many people would die before spring. In 1876, a green Christmas in New York, *The New York Times* told its readers that while its editors could find no evidence, in a search of hospital and mortality records, to support the graveyard saying, the belief was so widely held that the expression would probably be repeated at Christmas forever. When the city experienced a warm Aprillike December again in 1881, a *Times* reporter, convinced that the weather wasn't what it used to be, wrote that the way things were going, people would have to change their notion of Santa Claus from one of him with frost in his beard, dashing over snow-covered roofs, to one of him splashing his way through muddy streets, half-hidden in a pair of rubber boots and a huge waterproof coat.

Two of the greenest Christmases of the last century occurred in 1888 and 1889. On Christmas afternoon in 1888 at Winona, Minnesota, a long procession of young gentlemen, each with a young lady at his side, marched from the post office to the dock of the Mississippi steamer *Van Gorden*, preceded by perspiring members of the Gate City Band. Each parader was armed with a fan and wore a linen duster and straw hat. To celebrate the fact that there was no ice on the Mississippi that day, a steamboat excursion described as "the most novel scene in half a century" began at four o'clock. The boat ran upriver to Fountain City, where the population turned out en masse to welcome the excursionists. "My stars alive!" exclaimed one man; "Great gingerbread and molasses!" said another, when they heard that even field glasses had failed to locate a mite of ice on the river. The steamer returned to Winona at six o'clock amid a display of fireworks.

Even at Sioux Falls, in the Dakota Territory, "genial weather" held sway. The day was bright, even sultry. Windows and doors were thrown open, and many people spent the afternoon with basket picnics in the groves along the river.

In Washington, D.C., where the entire month of December had been more like late spring than early winter, the rays of the afternoon sun became so warm that the crowds in the fashionable thoroughfares sought the shady side of the street.

The temperature on Christmas Day in 1889 was summerlike in much of the country. In Chicago a cool summer had been followed by a warm autumn. As December progressed, Lake Michigan, famous for its winter storms, remained placid and ice-free. Christmas Day was clear, sunny, and sixty degrees in the shade. Lake Michigan was calm as a millpond, and oarsmen were seen stripped to the waist. On shore, croquet parties dressed in summer clothes played in the parks on grass in which dandelions grew.

Toronto had its first green Christmas in fifty years, and a newspaper dispatch from Iowa said the thermometer registered seventy degrees for several hours in the middle of the day.

In Findlay, Ohio, on Christmas morning, Philip Smith killed a blacksnake that had been running along the road as lively as if it were June. In all the ponds about the city, the frogs were acting as though winter didn't exist. J. W.

# THE WRONG WEATHER FOR CHRISTMAS

Taylor picked a bunch of daisies in his yard on Christmas afternoon. He said he'd had pansies blooming out of doors ever since April. From all parts of that county came reports that fruit trees were putting forth buds, and in several instances pear trees had blossomed for Christmas. Wheat and grass were as luxuriant as they were in May.

At Niagara Falls, roses were in bloom.

In Schenectady, New York, the thermometer registered 102 degrees in the sun.

In Pittsburgh, the mercury reached eighty-five degrees, and many families ate Christmas dinner with the windows wide open.

Even in New England, New Haven's thermometer soared to sixty-eight degrees, and Boston registered sixty-five degrees.

To New Yorkers on Fifth Avenue that Christmas afternoon, a conspicuous figure in the holiday procession was a well-dressed gentleman carrying a branch of mistletoe in one hand and a sun umbrella in the other. Onlookers regarded him with mixed amusement and envy. Where they were walking, a thermometer registered eighty degrees. In Central Park an unusually large number of carriages were out, and the walks were overrun with pedestrians. Robins that had not gone south for the winter brightened the lawns. The men were afoot without topcoats, their silk hats glossy and their gloves brand new. The ladies, in their broad-brimmed and feathered hats, were a picture of health and beauty, wealth and splendor. Easter Sunday was eclipsed.

# THE WRONG WEATHER FOR CHRISTMAS

Two years later, in 1891, for the first time in half a century, Montreal celebrated a green Christmas. Neither frost nor snow had yet appeared that winter, the weather being as mild as June.

In 1900 on Christmas Eve, it was fifty degrees in New York City. It was a somewhat incongruous sight to see perspiring shoppers struggling up the stairs to the elevated railroads, overcoatless and with coats unbuttoned, with clipper sleds or ice skates under their arms.

In the department stores along Sixth Avenue, dusty ceiling fans were set abuzzing, and women shoppers flocked to the soda fountains where, fanning themselves with menu-cards, they spooned chipped ice into cups of hot chocolate or drank ice water. Outside, the electric trolley cars on the Sixth Avenue line were listing heavily to starboard or port. The heat, turned on a few days before, came from beneath the seats on one side only. As no manager had given a stop order for it, everybody wanted to get on the cool side. The Broadway line ran many open cars, and they did more than a fair share of the business.

The mild weather enabled many late shoppers to go about the shopping districts in open victorias and landaus. The prospect of no sleighing at their country estates had kept much of New York society in the city, and early in the afternoon many delivered gifts, driving from house to house with the front seat of their carriages laden with packages. Mrs. Henry Clews and Mrs. Herman Oelichs, two of "The Four Hundred," went out together in a landau to give out their presents; Mrs. Oelichs was reported to be wearing a dark red gown and a three-cornered hat of the same shade embroidered in gold braid, while despite the unseasonable warmth, Mrs. Clews wore soft gray furs.

Christmas morning dawned on four inches of freshly fallen snow in 1902. For New Yorkers, it was the first white Christmas in six long years. The great red and black and gray metropolis had been transformed into a city of glittering white. With sleds and sleighs and snowballs, old and young alike rejoiced in the return of "old-fashioned Christmas weather." That year, no one had to worry about the morbid superstition that would nonetheless continue to be heard on snowless Christmases for another quarter-century.

## Chapter 9

## THE MUSIC OF CHRISTMAS

**T**he clock bell
of "Old Trinity"
in New York
rang out the last stroke of
twelve on Christmas Eve in 1899.
After a pause, there burst
from the dark tower a flood of
bells pealing Christmas melodies that rolled through the
silent streets below. The joyous sound, heard as far as
five to ten miles away when the wind was right, was produced by a lone bell ringer, the church's organist, Victor
Baier. High up in the stone tower, working despite the
cold without his coat or vest, his score illuminated by the
flickering light of a couple of tallow candles, he pushed
mightily on nine wooden levers attached by ropes to the
clappers of nine bells thirty feet above in the dark belfry.

For nearly sixty years Trinity's chimes had rung in

# THE MUSIC OF CHRISTMAS

Christmas in New York. To General George Brinton McClellan, their sound stirred memories of his boyhood Christmases in Philadelphia in the 1830s. One Christmas Eve, as a youth grown almost to manhood, he had opened his bedroom window to listen to the bells, and directly beneath him he saw his father looking out of his window, too. "Hello!" cried the lad. "What are you doing; trying to catch cold!" "Hello, boy!" his father answered. "I always like to hear the Christmas bells, for I feel so grateful to our God that he made the day a possibility." For the rest of his life, he never forgot the crisp night air and the ringing of chimes and the reverent manner in which his father's remark was uttered.

As the last Christmas morning in the nineteenth century dawned, every organist in every church in the city was seeking to do his best to please not only the august ear that heard everything, but also the music-loving souls of congregation and pastor, parish and priest. The great bells rang, the mighty hand-pumped organs pealed thunderous notes of joy, and the voices of the choirs joined in the *Messiah,* the favorite music of the day: "For unto us a child is born, unto us a son is given. . . ."

Parts of Handel's *Messiah* were known in colonial America in 1770, two years before its first performance in the composer's native Germany. In England, late in the summer of 1741, George Frederick Handel composed the work in the incredibly short time of three weeks and three days. Afraid to trust the fate of his new oratorio to the London critics, he decided to open out of town, in Dublin. There, on Tuesday morning, April 13,

# THE MUSIC OF CHRISTMAS

1742, he conducted the first public performance of the music without which no modern Christmas would seem complete. The elite of the city flocked to hear it. At its first London performance, George II had a sudden impulse to stand during the "Hallelujah Chorus," which has been the fashion since.

In this country, extracts from the *Messiah* were heard for the first time on January 16, 1770, in the Music Room of the New York City Tavern, in a concert of sacred music performed for the benefit of William Tuckey, the emeritus choirmaster of Trinity Episcopal Church. Tuckey had left his position as vicar choral of Bristol Cathedral in England to become the singing master of the boys' charity school connected with Trinity Church. It is likely that the soloists and chorus on January 16 were chiefly men and boys drawn from the Trinity choir. While no account of the event has survived, we can be sure it had an elite and fashionable audience.

New Yorkers again heard parts of the *Messiah* at Trinity Church the following October at a benefit for the widows and children of Anglican clergymen in America, and again the following April. The airs and choruses of the oratorio became a feature of public and private concerts during the early years of the new republic.

Not until December 25, 1818, did the Handel and Hayden Society of Boston offer the first complete American performance of the *Messiah* in Boylston Hall. On November 18, 1831, the Sacred Music Society performed the first complete rendition in New York with Uriah C. Hill (later the founder of the New York Philharmonic Society) conducting an orchestra of thirty-eight men and a chorus of seventy-four voices before an enthusiastic audience in St. Paul's Chapel.

Today many think of the oratorio as a work primarily for large choirs. Originally it was nothing of the sort. In Dublin, Handel's chorus was fourteen men and six boys. (During his lifetime, boys sang the soprano and alto parts.) Even in London in 1754, his chorus included only eighteen or nineteen voices. But as the *Messiah* became the Victorians' oratorio of oratorios, public taste called for ever larger productions. At the Crystal Palace, London audiences of tens of thousands heard the work thundered by as many as four thousand voices. In America, following the Civil War, huge choruses rendered the *Messiah* each Christmas in a New York armory. Until recent times, perhaps the largest group ever to sing the oratorio in the United States was the chorus of two thousand voices conducted by Dr. Leopold Damrosch in New York City on May 7, 1881. In smaller cities, up-to-date Americans attempted to follow the fashion in the best way they could. There simply could not be too many voices. In Cincinnati's Music Hall, on Christmas Day in 1880, despite a raging snowstorm, six hundred stalwart singers and an orchestra of sixty gave a soul-stirring rendering before an audience of four thousand.

One of the most unusual performances of the *Messiah* in the present century took place in 1916. On the night after Christmas, an audience of five thousand was seated in New York's old Madison Square Garden as the one thousand members of the Community Chorus filed in, followed by an orchestra of ninety. That army of performers was followed by another as companies of Boy Scouts stirred the onlookers to applause as they counter-marched down the broad aisles before sitting campfire-fashion on the floor. The performance, under conductor Harry Barnhart, was the first attempt in a generation to perform the Christmas classic on so large a scale, but that was not its most unusual aspect. The solo parts were sung not by soloists, but by groups of trained voices, from one hundred tenors in "Every Valley Shall Be Ex-alted" to more than three hundred sopranos in "I Know That My Redeemer Liveth." During a pause midway in the oratorio, the conductor led his chorus in ringing ren-ditions of the Christmas hymns "O Come, All Ye Faith-ful," "Silent Night," and "Hark, the Herald Angels Sing."

Handel's *Messiah,* originally written for audiences of nobility and gentry, had unmistakably become the prop-erty of the common man.

In December 1908, while at work in his study, Henry Edward Krehbiel, music critic for *The New York Tribune,* found his attention arrested by the sound of a familiar air from the *Messiah* rising from the street below. Looking out his window, he was surprised to see an Italian shep-herd blowing his bagpipe, no doubt following the Christ-mastime custom of his native land, where shepherd pipers gathered in Rome to play before the shrines of the Virgin Mary and carpenter shops, and to collect coins from people whose hearts had been warmed by the sea-son. As a musicologist, Krehbiel was delighted to recog-nize the same centuries-old shepherd's tune that had

# THE MUSIC OF CHRISTMAS

provided Handel, who had traveled in Italy, the inspiration for the Pastoral Symphony in the *Messiah.*

Krehbiel had a great love for the old music of Christmas. Several years before, he had received a letter from a New York glee club, composed of young men born in England, who intended to sing carols early on Christmas morning before the homes of their friends, thus reviving in America an ancient English custom. The club wanted Krehbiel's advice on what to sing. It was the first of numerous inquiries that he would receive from individuals, Sunday schools, and musical publishers about carols suitable to be sung, particularly at church services. Such requests were very satisfying to Krehbiel who, together with other musical scholars and compilers of folk tunes, went on to help a nearly forgotten Yuletide custom win its way back into favor in America.

The origin of the word *carol* is obscure. In Chaucer's time, it meant dancing interspersed with singing. The Christmas song of joy or praise is believed to have evolved from the mystery plays staged in or outside medieval churches. Since few people could read Scripture, these plays dramatized stories from the Bible as a way of teaching the congregation. Carols were sung as processionals and musical interludes in the performances. While they were not exclusively about Christmas, the vast majority of those that have survived are devoted to Mary and the Christ Child, shepherds watching their flocks, and wassailing. So the word *carol* and Christmas have come to be closely linked. From the churches, the words and tunes were carried to homes, where they became the basis of the extensive carol repertory of Britain, Germany, France, and Hungary. From the fifteenth century to the early part of the seventeenth century, carols were at their zenith. Their decline was a result of both the Reformation, with its suppression of Christmas observances, and changing musical fashion that rendered the pure and simple songs the musical equivalent of an endangered species.

In America many Reformed churches allowed no music at all in worship and considered music connected with the licentious festival of Christmas to be a double abomination. On the other hand, the churches that encouraged sacred music favored works far more complicated, in both music and theology, than the simple carols, as did trained singers. As late as the 1860s, such advocates of congregational singing as Henry Ward Beecher were thought of as impractical innovators. Fortunately, outside the churches, carols continued to be sung.

On the cold, wet Christmas Day during the California gold rush in 1849, New Yorker Joseph McCloskey and his partners, out of food, were trudging along in search of a meal. At midafternoon, as they rested on a wooded hillside, they heard caroling from among the trees. Investigating, they found four young men from Boston singing *"Adeste Fideles,"* who invited them to join in a holiday feast of flapjacks, johnnycake baked on a shovel, and coffee.

In many parts of America, the cumulative song "The Twelve Days of Christmas," in which swans swim, maids milk, ladies dance, lords leap, pipers pipe, and drummers drum, was sung on Twelfth Night as a Christmas game of forfeits.The players sat in a row, the first one singing the first round of the song, the second the second, and so on until one made a mistake or named the wrong gift. That player payed a forfeit, usually some humorous task. The words varied from place to place, from eight deers a-running and nine wolves a-howling in Missouri, to eleven bears a-leaping in Vermont. But in general carols were fading from memory.

Just before it was almost too late, small groups of Victorians interested in preserving folk songs and customs gave carol singing a new lease on life. Old carols were published, first in England and then in America, and small groups of quaint street singers called "waits" wandered Dickens's London, ready to sing the old Christmas songs for a few pennies. Christmas carols began to be heard in American Sunday school rooms but, because of that association, the carols were often dismissed as child's play.

Nonetheless, on Christmas in 1898, *The New York World* reported a revival of caroling in the hamlet of Hackensack, New Jersey. Male and female members of the British American Society were conveyed about the town before the sun rose in a four-horse wagonette to sing in front of the homes of their countrymen. In 1912 *The New York Herald* found that in Burlington, one of the oldest New Jersey towns, the custom of Old English–style "waits" caroling on Christmas Eve went as far back as the most ancient resident could remember. The sing-

# THE MUSIC OF CHRISTMAS

ers were recruited from the choir of St. Mary's Church, one of the first Episcopal churches in New Jersey, dating from colonial times. Men and boys made up the band of "waits," including a boy soprano whose pure, fresh voice suggested to the imagination of the reporter "the angelic heralds of the holy birth."

Within a few short years, the revival of the caroling custom was well under way all over this continent. A 1918 survey by the National Bureau for the Advancement of Music found thirty cities with community carol singing. By 1928 more than two thousand were reported.

Even during the period when caroling almost disappeared on this side of the Atlantic, what eventually became several of our best-loved American carols were written. The text for one of the oldest, "It Came Upon a Midnight Clear," was originally written in 1849 by Edmund Hamilton Sears, a Unitarian minister in the small farming town of Wayland, Massachusetts. The tune we now associate with it was written the following year by Richard Storrs Willis, a New York organist, who simply called it "Study no. 23." Sometime later, Uzziah C. Burnap arranged Willis's music to fit Sears's words.

"O Little Town of Bethlehem" was the creation of an Episcopal rector, Phillips Brooks. In 1865 on a trip to the Holy Land, the young clergyman had sat on horseback and looked down upon Bethlehem on Christmas Eve and recorded the scene in poetry. Three Decembers later, at the Church of the Advent and Holy Trinity in Philadelphia, Brooks gave the five verses of his poem to his or-

# THE MUSIC OF CHRISTMAS

ganist and Sunday school superintendent, Lewis Redner, and asked him to write some music. Under great pressure from seasonal obligations, Redner struggled for a week and had still not satisfied himself as he went to bed on Christmas Eve. During the night he awoke with the melody in his mind. In future years, Redner always referred to the tune as his "gift from heaven." The children of the Sunday school sang the hymn each Christmas, but it was many years before it was widely published.

In 1863, during the Civil War, Henry Wadsworth Longfellow learned that his son, a lieutenant in the Army of the Potomac, had been seriously wounded. The news led him to write the poem that begins, "I heard the bells on Christmas Day," which was later joined to a tune written for an entirely different purpose.

"We Three Kings of Orient Are" is one of the few modern carols with words and music written by the same person. The Reverend John Henry Hopkins, Jr., rector of Christ's Church in Williamsport, Pennsylvania, wrote it about 1857. One year earlier, the Reverend John Pierpont, a Unitarian clergyman in Boston, wrote a simple piece of poetry and set it to music. Although his "Jingle Bells" is not a Christmas carol in any true sense, in the present century it has joined the roster of American carols.

As these examples show, the best-loved carols are not necessarily the work of renowned musicians. George William Warren's hymn "Rock of Ages" maintains its popularity to this day, but, despite the fact that he was one of the prime movers in reviving caroling, he failed in his attempt to contribute a popular carol to the ages. The words for his "Christmas Snowflakes," published in 1890, were written by Dr. Thomas Potts, the assistant rector of St. Thomas Church in New York, where Warren was the organist. The words began:

*Falling, falling, softly falling,*
*Tiny snow-flakes pure and white.*
*Tell us have you any message*
*That you bring this holy night?*
*Coming, coming, He is coming,*
*Surely, surely it is meet.*
*That we spread this spotless carpet*
*For the Stranger's feet.*

It never became a favorite. Neither did a modern carol that was composed by Leopold Stokowski and included in the *New Hymnal* of the Episcopal Church in 1919.

A similar fate befell "the great American Christmas Symphony." On December 24, 1853, William Henry Fry's *Santa Claus* Symphony premiered in New York City. Fry musically portrayed the activities of Christmas Eve, including a lullaby, a snowstorm with imitations of winds, the tolling of the hour of twelve, the coming of Santa Claus in his sleigh, and his gift distribution. Finally, to represent the children discovering their gifts on Christmas morning, the orchestra played a variety of children's trumpets, whistles, drums, and rattles. The work was loudly applauded and, notwithstanding its length, was given in its entirety as an encore.

Seven years earlier, Fry had written the first American

grand opera, *Leonora*. He was also music critic for Horace Greeley's *New York Tribune* and an articulate spokesman in the struggle for American musical independence. The conductor for the première of the *Santa Claus* Symphony was Louis Antoine Jullien, a Continental charlatan who had descended upon the culture-starved new republic with his "grand orchestra" earlier that year. He had soon found that conducting music by American composers was a good way to get an audience. He was also quick to realize that, as music critic for the *Tribune,* Fry was a good person to cultivate. In rapid succession, he conducted four of Fry's symphonies, the *Santa Claus* being the last. Its presentation inspired tremendous controversy in the New York press. Fellow critic Richard Storrs Willis (composer of the tune eventually used for "It Came Upon a Midnight Clear") dismissed the work as nothing more than "a kind of extravaganza which moves the audience to laughter, entertaining them seasonably with imitated snowstorms, trotting horses, sleighbells, cracking whips, etc." An angry exchange of letters followed, but eventually, Willis's judgment prevailed.

Christmas night was always a gala night at the opera. In 1909 a blizzard set in late on Christmas afternoon, causing a unique interpretation of *Rigoletto* at the Metropolitan Opera House. The orchestra of the company had taken part in the afternoon performance of *Hansel and*

# THE MUSIC OF CHRISTMAS

*Gretel* at the Brooklyn Academy of Music. At the close of the opera, the instruments were packed into a horse-drawn van to be carried back to the Metropolitan. On the way, the van became stalled in what the *Tribune*'s man described as "a blockade" caused by the storm and did not arrive until after nine o'clock. As a result, the first act was played with hurriedly collected instruments; as no French horns could be found, the horn players were forced to use tubas. The effect, according to one listener, was "remarkable!"

In New York City, the Christmas of 1915, candles were a signal associated with caroling. "If you want the children to sing carols at your door, just put a lighted taper in the window on Christmas Eve" went the word-of-mouth announcement that spread among the residents of quaint old Greenwich Village. At 7:00 P.M. on Christmas Eve, bands of small minstrels assembled on the streets, representing a church, a public school, a settlement house, and the library. As they zigzagged through the quiet streets, stopping to greet a flickering candle with "O Holy Night" or "The First Noel," adults joined in. Several of the pretty young women chaperons had so many bass voices to contend with that they hardly knew what to do. As the library carolers passed the MacDougal Street police station, Lieutenant McKay threw open the window and yelled, "Hello, kids! Don't I get a song?"

"Ah, where's yer candle in yer window?" asked one of

# THE MUSIC OF CHRISTMAS

the smallest of the youngsters, not awed in the least by the blue-coated boss of the station house. The lieutenant admitted he'd forgotten.

"Can we sing for him, anyway, Miss?"

"Let's sing for the cops."

And so with quavering voices they sang for Lieutenant McKay.

> " 'While shepherds watched their flocks by night,
> All seated on the ground.' "

And he told them they were all right.

Ed Sullivan, the late television personality, always remembered pumping an old-fashioned church organ during his boyhood in Port Chester, New York. His older sister, Helen, had been the organist at Our Lady of Mercy. The pump handle moved up and down in a narrow slot and had to be worked carefully lest it scrape the sides and squeak loudly. He had to stop the handle just before it came to the end of the slot, or a loud bump would be very audible. And if he didn't keep the bellows full of air, the music would come to a wheezing stop. At Christmas Eve midnight mass, after pumping extra hard with perfect rhythm, he'd leap from his station and run to the choir loft rail. For a few seconds he'd watch the congregation singing a Christmas hymn below, and then he'd run back to the organ and resume pumping.

# THE MUSIC OF CHRISTMAS

In Boston candles and caroling filled each Christmas Eve with extraordinary beauty. As the sun set on Beacon Hill in the newly washed windows of the round-fronted, red brick Federalist townhouses, rows and rows of candles stood along the sills, along the middle sash, in straight lines, curves, and triangles. Frequently there were as many as twenty candles to a row, or forty, or even more. These were not little Christmas tapers but stout white candles, and in some cases great church altar candles. Some houses displayed the fine old silver candlesticks of the past. From the basement to the garret, to the octagonal cupola on the roof, the candles were ready for the Christmas Eve observance.

Shortly after seven o'clock the illuminations began, candle by candle, window by window, house by house. Each of the old streets became a soft blaze of light, with reflections from the windows on one side to the windows opposite. At the same hour, Bostonians from near and far began to assemble on the steep streets of the old district. Enchanting glimpses could be had of the stately rooms, rich with mahogany, silver, and family portraits by Stuart or Copley. By eight o'clock, the streets were thronged, the crowd quiet, expectant. White and black ties and opera hats and long dresses mingled with bearskin coats. At last came the distant sound of singing. Nearer and nearer approached a caroling company, carrying in their hands or aloft on poles old-time watchman lanterns with candles burning inside. In the course

# THE MUSIC OF CHRISTMAS

of the evening, there would by any number of different companies. And until the last of the singers finished their rounds at about ten o'clock, the crowd lingered on.

Into this glimmering setting on Beacon Hill, one Christmas Eve around 1915, Dr. Richard Cabot, distinguished by his perfect pitch and his family's reputation for "speaking only to God," led fifteen or twenty well-swaddled carolers. As the group crossed Commonwealth Avenue, a horse-drawn cab on sleigh runners rounded the corner of Arlington Street at locomotive speed, hoofs fluttering, a white cloud of snow about it. On top was lashed a large Christmas tree. As the carolers clumsily sought safety by retreating into a deep snowdrift, the horse caught sight of them and, eyes wide, shied badly, his nostrils steaming like a dragon's. The Christmas tree slued toward the carolers and slapped one Alice Cary Williams smartly across her face, tumbling her and several of the others into a heap. In a moment the cab was gone. After the first shock, Alice recognized the heavy body on top of her by its basso profundo expletive. It was Amy Lowell, the cigar-smoking Boston poet. As they bustled to their feet, Alice explored a part of her anatomy and told Amy she thought she had stove in a rib. "Pooh," Amy replied, "think of the condition of my cigars!"

## Chapter 10

## THE EXCESS OF CHRISTMAS SPIRITS

**I**n 1785
George Washington had a
contract with his gardener,
Philip Bater. At Christmas,
four dollars were due Bater,
"with which he may be drunk
4 days and 4 nights." On December 21, Dr. Brown of Alexandria was sent for to attend Bater, causing some latter-day speculation on whether he had started his celebration early, or was indisposed and Washington felt he ought to be put back in good condition for his annual spree.

For a book published in Cincinnati in 1842, George Sample wrote an informative account of eggnog and good cheer in Ohio back in 1806, an era when unquenchable Yuletide thirsts overcame many settlers:

> There were fifteen to twenty cabins at Manchester, one of which was called a tavern. It was at least a grog

shop. There were about a dozen visitors at the tavern, and as the landlord was a heyday, wellmet tippler with the rest, they appointed me to assist the landlady in making eggnog. I was inexperienced in the art, but I made out to suit them very well. I put about a dozen eggs in a large bowl, and after beating or rather stirring the eggs up a little, I added about a pound of sugar and a little milk to this mass; then I filled the bowl up with whiskey, and set it on the table; and they sat around the table and supped it with spoons! Tumblers or glasses of any sort had not then come in fashion. They all began to cut up, and especially a professor of religion. I thought he ought to have set a better example. When I found out how the game was going, I resigned my commission and went to bed.

In 1826 at West Point, Superintendent Sylvanus Thayer, "the Father of the Military Academy," decreed the first dry Yule for his students. But the cadets had other ideas. Despite the efforts of lynx-eyed regular-army officers, enough rum, port, buckets of milk, sugar, eggs, and nutmeg were smuggled into the barracks to fuel several night-long parties on Christmas Eve. After taps, the fledgling generals gathered in several of the upstairs rooms of their barracks. The windows were well curtained with blankets. Every precaution was taken to prevent a surprise. Sentinels were posted to give the alarm should an officer appear. When discovered at 4:30 A.M., the holiday high spirits turned into riotous violence, including the attempted murder of an officer. The official inquiry into "the Eggnog Riot" established that seventy

# THE EXCESS OF CHRISTMAS SPIRITS

cadets had been involved. Six were allowed to resign. An army court-martial was convened to try nineteen others, many from socially and politically prominent families. Ultimately, eleven of the nineteen were dismissed.

On Christmas night in 1880, twenty-eight-year-old John Denkler of Brooklyn, while under the influence of liquor, was struck by the idea that he was Santa Claus and ought to be making his rounds over the housetops. He draped a blanket around his head and shoulders like a monk's cowl and sprang out of the second-story window of his house, landing on his head. Fortunately, his fall was cushioned by the snow on the ground, and Denkler recovered.

When it came to old-fashioned Christmas "elatin' and celebratin,' " there were a good many more inebriates in the good old days than there are today. Saloonkeepers commonly gave free drinks at Christmas, as well as "bottled stuff" to be taken home by their best customers. In Chicago, the Christmas of 1880, the police reported that there was more drunkenness among young men than had ever before been seen on the streets. Many were from a class who seldom drank, and their state that day was accounted for by the custom of bars providing free eggnog for all comers.

In his book *The Gay Nineties*, R. V. Culter described a typical scene when hot Tom and Jerrys were on the house on Christmas morning. "At Jake's place down on the corner the session usually lasted until somebody's Little Willie arrived with the message, 'Mamma says Papa is to come straight home—the turkey's on the table.' " And many a father went home zigzagging to his family dinner.

On Christmas Day, saloons' free lunches were often culinary delights. No prouder gobblers were carved than in the fancy saloons, and no crisper suckling pigs or better salads or more delicious cold cuts of beef and ham were served. Some of the layouts ran up into the hundreds of dollars, and everyone was permitted to fill his plate as often as he wished.

In humbler quarters, the lunches were less elaborate but no less generously given nor less enthusiastically received. On Christmas Day in 1889, one open-hearted saloonkeeper on New York's Bowery had out his Christmas sign:

FREE CHICKEN FRICASSEE WITH EVERY 5 CENT DRINK

Another publican wrote in soap letters on his show window:

MERRY CHRISTMAS
OUR FREE CHRISTMAS DINNER TO-DAY COMPRISES BONED TURKEY
AND CHICKEN SALAD. ALL WELCOME.

And all were.

Even when saloonkeepers weren't giving away their stock, "Christmas cheer" was cheap. In New England during the 1870s, a reformer complained that rum was so inexpensive that a day's wages could purchase three gallons. When it came to quality, most of the alcoholic beverages consumed by the poor were vile but heady brews. "Liquor" was often pure alcohol with some coloring added. Even beer had a higher alcoholic content in those days.

But probably more than anything else, most old-time Christmas drunkenness was the result of whiskey, rum, and gin, all imbibed in straight shots, something we rarely see today except in Western movies. Pure 100 proof spirits, drunk without ice, water, or mixer, had disastrous effects on many a human nervous system. While the results of Christmas intoxication, though occasionally unique to the day, were generally little different from those suffered on any ordinary day, the victims who filled city and town jails on the eve and night of Christmas were usually dealt with a little more kindly than they might otherwise have been.

In New York City, in the days when cops rode bikes instead of motorcycles, policeman "Ajax" Whitman of the bicycle squad usually had his hands full with Christmas inebriates. The Christmas of 1898 was no exception. On Sunday, December 25, at the risk of his own life and at the expense of some bad bruises, he had saved the life of a pedestrian who had absentmindedly wandered in front of an electric trolley car. He had himself patched up by a Bellevue Hospital ambulance surgeon and reported for duty as usual the next morning. Since Christmas had fallen on a Sunday, a majority of the city's largest stores and businesses remained closed on Monday. Things were quiet along Ajax's beat in the morning, but in the afternoon, as he was cycling along Second Avenue, he saw a southbound trolley car bearing down on a gentle-

## THE EXCESS OF CHRISTMAS SPIRITS

man who clearly had taken in too much liquid cheer. The man lurched right in its path and would probably have been killed had Ajax not pedaled past the trolley, reached out from his bike, and swung him off the track. The car ground by, its brakes spewing orange sparks. Many saw the rescue and cheered the policeman's courage.

Not long afterward, Ajax spied a man trying to turn somersaults on the sidewalk. At every attempt, the man landed on his face on the pavement. Since the celebrant would not stop at Ajax's suggestion, the policeman threw the man over his shoulder, jumped on his bicycle, and rode to the nearest station house. People all along the way stopped to watch the improvised patrol wagon.

## THE EXCESS OF CHRISTMAS SPIRITS

There's the story of a family in Pittsburgh, early in this century, one of whose older members always got drunk at Christmas. Every year without fail, he fell into the Christmas tree and knocked it over. Finally, in desperation, the family began to hang their tree from the ceiling, so, like a punching bag, no matter how many times he fell into it, it always righted itself and swung back into an upright position.

Country folk also had trouble with intoxicating spirits around the holidays. Ernest Buckler, born in Nova Scotia in 1908, recalls a boyhood neighbor who had had a little too much homemade beer, apple cider, and beet wine. On Christmas Day he led his cow straight through the kitchen door and into the dining room. "I thought she'd like to see the tree," he said.

Stories concerning bootlegged Christmas spirits during the era of Prohibition are legion. One will suffice here. On Christmas Eve in 1920, two New York State troopers, Corporal Hirsh Dyke and Trooper Henry Lewis, stopped a car containing two men and a woman in the town of White Plains, New York. Inside a dressed turkey, they found a two-quart bottle of whiskey, and in a head of lettuce and pineapple, two small bottles of grain alcohol, apparently destined for a Christmas feast. The threesome spent Christmas Eve in a federal court. It was not reported what happened to the turkey and fixings.

## Chapter 11

## THE IMMIGRANT'S CHRISTMAS

**O**n Christmas morning in 1890, there were nearly one hundred immigrants, men, women, and children of half a dozen nationalities, left in quarantine at the Barge Office in Castle Garden on New York's Battery, at that time the government's immigration depot. Because it was a holiday, the immigration inspectors were off somewhere having their turkey dinners and, perhaps, a dash of rum. The immigrants were a miserable and homesick lot until a commissioner of immigration, General James O'Beirne, invited them all to have a good Christmas dinner with him.

Every face wore a holiday grin as the new arrivals marched up State Street to the German Mission House, where a bountiful spread of turkey and plum pudding awaited. Even the proverbial churchmouse would have starved trying to make its Christmas dinner from what food was left. The feasters whooped in their several languages all the way back to the Barge Office with a vigor that made even nerveless New York car horses jump. The general distributed cigars and candy when his guests were back in the detention pen, and they played games and sang songs till sundown.

In 1892 the inadequate Castle Garden facilities were replaced by Ellis Island. On December 23, 1912, as snow fell on the island, obscuring New York City across the harbor, twelve hundred guests of Uncle Sam enjoyed their first Christmas celebration in the New World. Sadly, it was to be the last for some of those present, who would be deported when judged by the health inspectors to be too sick or mentally incompetent to be self supporting. But for most, it was a treat that would linger long in memory.

When the crowd filed into the vast dining hall, unmistakable joy was expressed in more than twenty languages at the sight of two very large Christmas trees bearing hundreds of presents and many candles. Simultaneously, three orchestras struck up "The Star Spangled Banner," and the several hundred voices of the New York German *Sangerbund* began to sing. The words of the anthem had been printed in many languages on slips of paper and passed out, and many who could not sing the words hummed the melody. As the strains of the music filled the great hall, far up beneath the roof two large American flags and two strings of smaller flags representing every nation on the globe fluttered in the breeze.

# THE IMMIGRANT'S CHRISTMAS

The eyes of those from overseas rested for a moment on the Stars and Stripes and then sought eagerly the flag of the country they'd left behind. At the end of the anthem, there was applause, and more than a few of the strangers wept, stirred by memories of Christmases in other lands.

Then came the Christmas presents: nothing elaborate, but little things to cheer the heart and show that America was friendly. There were dolls for the girls and mechanical toys for the boys, rubber balls for the smaller children and rattles for the smallest. For the women there were brushes and combs and small pieces of costume jewelry, and for the men pipes, a card of collar buttons, or a purse.

When the presents had been distributed, lunch was served: chicken sandwiches, jellies, candies, fruits, chocolate, coffee, tea, and milk. Stalks of celery puzzled most of the immigrants. The consensus of opinion seemed to be that they were boutonnieres. Several men seized the crisp stalks, broke off the leaves, and stuck them in their buttonholes, an example quickly followed by many of the newcomers.

Addresses were made in different languages by clergymen who looked after the interests of immigrants, and songs were sung, including "Hands Across the Sea," "All Hail the Power of Jesus' Name," and Christmas carols from many nations.

# THE IMMIGRANT'S CHRISTMAS

Beginning in the 1870s, each Christmas saw a tide of immigrants flowing back to Europe to spend Christmas in their homelands. Even today, the distance from the Pacific Northwest to Scandinavia seems a long way to go to spend the holidays, yet nineteenth-century Danes, Swedes, and Norwegians from farms in Washington and Oregon, and from the upper Midwest in particular, arrived back in the port of New York by railroad-car-loads for the trip overseas. In most cases the joyous nature of their trip and the comfort of the Pullman cars they could now afford seemed to shorten the long journey. Crossing the continent, there was a continual recounting of their experiences in America to all whom they met, and once on the steamers, it was one long day of anticipation until they saw their native shores again.

To the Scandinavians back home, "the holidays" constituted an extended season of festivities. The winters were long and cold, and the summers short. For seven months of the year, almost no agricultural pursuits could be followed. In the many months of relative leisure, kinfolk in America who could afford to return were welcome, both to help create and to enjoy the holiday merrymaking. The holidays were the chosen season in which to marry, for those who were sufficiently well-to-do, so the majority of those visiting were bachelors, and a large percentage of them would be accompanied by brides as they returned to their farms or trades in the Midwest or West or to their work in the factories of New England.

German and Italian immigrants were also particularly

# THE IMMIGRANT'S CHRISTMAS

home-loving people. After being here for a few years and accumulating a little money, they were drawn to return to visit and tell of their successes in America. In the late nineteenth century and the period preceding World War I, mass pilgrimages to the old countries were as regular as Christmas itself. By 1911 the November and December exodus of Italians had reached record proportions. On December 2, 1911, 6,525 of them sailed from New York, and another thousand were left standing with their bundles on the piers when the liners moved out.

The first vessel to sail that day was the American liner *St. Louis,* to land at Cherbourg. With 900 in her steerage, she was the only one to get away on time. The *St. Louis* left about 250 passengers on the pier. They were sent to Philadelphia by special train, and the *Dominion,* one of the ships leaving that port, was held until it arrived.

The *Koenig Albert,* of the North German Lloyd Line, left Hoboken, New Jersey, at 11:20 A.M., twenty minutes late, with 1,625 passengers bound for Naples and Palermo in her steerage, all she could accommodate. Between 200 and 300 were left behind. Many of them seized their bundles and rushed back to New York to attempt to get passage on the White Star liner *Adriatic,* which was to sail for Naples at noon.

At the White Star pier, a crowd had begun to arrive before nine o'clock. The few women and children were singled out by the staff and taken aside out of the crush. Some of the men carried bundles as large as trunks on each shoulder, in addition to paper valises of varied colors. It appeared to one reporter as if "every Italian was taught to carry a bundle as soon as he could walk, and the size of the bundle appeared to increase with his growth."

One worried-looking father left his wife and three small children sitting weeping beside the gangway at nine o'clock and went away, gesticulating wildly to himself as he ran down the pier. He returned close to noon with a fourth child and two bundles they had forgotten in the rush for the steamer.

The White Star staff had considerable difficulty keeping the steerage passengers in line. Searching the passengers for weapons caused further confusion and delay at the gangway. Any weapons found were thrown into a large basket, to be handed to the police at Palermo or Naples. In addition, all bottles of brandy, whiskey, gin, and rum were confiscated. The liquor would be thrown overboard when the ship got outside the harbor—so the crew said. At one o'clock, an hour after the *Adriatic's* sailing time, Chief Steward Gibson walked down the gangway and said there was room for eighteen more, which would make 2,100 in the steerage. After the eighteen had been selected, about four hundred frantic souls remained on the pier. Some were told to sail the next morning on the *Finland,* while others started for South Brooklyn in the hope of catching the Fabre Line's *Sant' Anna,* which was to sail at three o'clock that afternoon for Naples.

The Fabre Line pier was just as crowded as the others, and as the hour of the sailing of the *Sant' Anna* drew near, the noise and excitement became intense. Nine-

# THE IMMIGRANT'S CHRISTMAS

teen hundred were taken aboard. The remaining four hundred picked up their bundles and went off to find a place to spend the night before tackling the *Finland* the following morning. For the next week, all the steamships sailing for Mediterranean and Continental ports had full steerages.

An Italian banker estimated that an average of $200 in savings was taken away by each of the steerage passengers, who were mostly men with families in their native lands. This means that $1,305,000 in cash was taken to be spent abroad by the 6,525 Italians sailing on December 2 alone.

Immigrants remaining in this country sent small Christmas gifts to their relatives abroad in the form of money orders. On December 9, 1899, the steamer *Umbria* sailed with 23,401 such money orders, representing $271,223. Of this, $124,901 went to Great Britain and Ireland, $50,083 to Germany, $4,054 to Switzerland, $5,912 to Denmark, $766 to Holland, $14,234 to Italy, $13,714 to Norway, $40,606 to Sweden, $11,953 to Austria, and $4,907 to Hungary. The superintendent of the money order division of the New York Post Office estimated that the steamer *Lucania,* sailing a few days later, would carry $2,500,000.

Most of the donors were people of small means. At the post office, large numbers of servant girls waited in line with their money, accumulated through months of labor and self-denial. No matter how humble their circumstances, it was a matter of pride not to let a Christmas pass without sending a money order to those held dear, or to those who were dependent upon them in the land of their birth. Post office people knew men and women bought Christmas money orders when they themselves were in need of clothing or even food.

Many bought as many as eight or ten different money orders in sums as small as one or two dollars. Slightly larger gifts were handled through banks, and all over New York City in December little oblong signs appeared in the windows of banks that read:

DRAFTS FOR £1 AND UPWARD ON GREAT BRITAIN AND IRELAND. EXCHANGE ON ALL PARTS OF THE WORLD.

In other cities with large foreign populations, like Boston, Philadelphia, Cincinnati, Chicago, Milwaukee, and St. Louis, clerks in banks and post offices were also kept long after hours in order to balance their books. In German neighborhoods, a great deal of money was sent through private bankers. That same week in 1899, Henry Bischoff and Company sent drafts to Germany amounting to nearly $50,000 and expected to send nearly double that amount the next week. Banks, savings institutions, the great Wall Street houses, and, in fact, all fiduciary institutions profited from the holiday trade. Nevertheless, not a Christmas went by without august members of the financial community warning against the dangers of immigrants sending so much money out of the country, saying it adversely affected the rate of exchange and the shipment of securities.

# THE IMMIGRANT'S CHRISTMAS

Among the immigrants there were as many different ways to celebrate Christmas as there were different nationalities. For most, Christmas was a bittersweet period of mixed homesickness and joyful observance of old customs.

Each Christmas, reporters were amazed to observe how much of the old country had come over with the Germans. At midcentury, two of their customs, the Christmas present and the Christmas tree, were new to most Americans. In 1856 *The New York Times* gave its readers a humorous account of the Germans' love of Christmas gifts:

> Giving and receiving presents at Christmas time seems to be as necessary for the well being of German men, women, and children as a mustache for a male and a hoop for a female. At least, we never knew any German who could get along without presenting his friends and relations with something on Christmas Eve, and if he be so unfortunate as to have no one near enough to give to or receive from, why it is very simple, make yourself a present. And it is a fixed habit with plenty of German old maids and bachelors, that if they need anything within a month or two of Christmas, they wait till then, and when the appointed time draws near, purchasing it with great secrecy, give themselves a great surprise by their unexpected and beautiful present.

Although the Christchild and other old Germanic gift-bearers would soon be replaced by the American Santa Claus, identical old-country Christmases would be observed in German-American homes in all parts of this country until well into this century. But before the end of the nineteenth century, the idea of adults giving Christmas gifts to other adults would no longer seem strange and humorous to anyone, and the German Christmas tree would be well on its way to becoming a universal custom in America.

From teeming Eastern cities to lonely homesteaders' huts on the Great Plains, new Americans were willing to do anything to keep Christmas as their parents had in Europe.

One Christmas Eve early in this century, in Sheridan County, Montana, near the Canadian border, a blizzard was in the making. Pastor Severt J. Fretheim and his wife, Christine, were braving their way on horseback to conduct a church service, when they were overtaken by blinding snow, and in crossing the Big Muddy River lost their way. After several unsuccessful attempts to find the trail, they turned back. Eventually they found their way to the ten-by-twelve-foot tar paper-covered shack of a pair of Norwegian "homesteader girls," Tillie and Clara Lee .

It was the young women pioneers' first Christmas Eve away from their parents' home in North Dakota, and their thoughts had been far away that evening. They welcomed the wayfarers with open arms. Five thousand miles and a generation away from Norway, the two sisters fed their unexpected guests *lutefisk* (dried Norwegian codfish prepared by soaking the fish in a lye solution for several weeks before cooking) and *lefser* (a

# THE IMMIGRANT'S CHRISTMAS

thin, saucer-shaped holiday bread made of potatoes, cooked on an ungreased griddle and eaten buttered, sugared, and folded up like a pocket handkerchief) and other foods without which it wouldn't have been Christmas for Norwegians.

Their little home consisted of only two tiny rooms, but Clara and Tillie Lee made a bed on the floor in the kitchen for themselves and gave the pastor and his wife their bedroom. Their cow spent the night with the chickens, giving up her stall to the Fretheims' horses.

As the snow from the blizzard continued to fall Christmas morning, inside the tiny house on the trackless frontier prairie, it could just as well have been Christmas in Norway.

## Chapter 12

## ST. NICHOLAS AND HIS COUNTERPARTS

In 1897 a little
girl in New York City
had a child-size problem:
some of her friends said there
was no Santa Claus. When
she questioned her father,
a doctor, he suggested she write to the "Question and
Answer" editors of the *Sun*, the newspaper he perused
each evening. Thus she wrote:

Dear Editor:

I am 8 years old.
Some of my little friends say there is no Santa Claus.
Papa says "If you see it in 'The Sun' it's so." Please tell me
the truth, is there a Santa Claus?

Virginia O'Hanlon,
115 West 95th Street,
New York City.

# St. Nicholas and His Counterparts

The reply to her letter was written by a reporter turned editorial writer, Francis Pharcellus Church. It was not until the day after his death in 1906 that it became widely known that he had penned the most famous editorial response in history:

Virginia, your little friends are wrong. They have been affected by the skepticism of a skeptical age. They do not believe except they see. They think that nothing can be which is not comprehensible by their little minds. All minds, Virginia, whether they be men's or children's, are little. In this great universe of ours man is a mere insect, an ant, in his intellect as compared with the boundless world about him, as measured by the intelligence capable of grasping the whole of truth and knowledge.

Yes, Virginia, there is a Santa Claus. He exists as certainly as love and generosity and devotion exist, and you know that they abound and give to your life its highest beauty and joy. Alas! how dreary would be the world if there were no Santa Claus! It would be as dreary as if there were no Virginias. There would be no childlike faith, then, no poetry, no romance to make tolerable this existence. We should have no enjoyment except in sense and sight. The external light with which childhood fills the world would be extinguished.

Not believe in Santa Claus! You might as well not believe in fairies! You might get your papa to hire men to watch in all the chimneys on Christmas Eve to catch Santa Claus, but even if they did not see Santa Claus coming down, what would that prove? Nobody sees Santa Claus, but that is no sign that there is no Santa Claus. The most real things in the world are those that neither chil-

# St. Nicholas and His Counterparts

dren nor men can see. Did you ever see fairies dancing on the lawn? Of course not, but that's no proof that they are not there. Nobody can conceive or imagine all the wonders that are unseen or unseeable in the world.

You tear apart the baby's rattle to see what makes the noise inside, but there is a veil covering the unseen world which not the strongest man, not even the united strength of all the strongest men that ever lived can tear apart. Only faith, fancy, poetry, love, romance, can push aside that curtain and view and picture the supernal beauty and glory beyond. Is it all real? Ah, Virginia, in all this world there is nothing else real and abiding.

No Santa Claus! Thank God he lives, and he lives forever. A thousand years from now, Virginia, nay, ten times ten thousand years from now, he will continue to make glad the heart of childhood.

Francis Church, the son of a Baptist minister, was born in Rochester, New York, on February 22, 1839. He graduated from Columbia College in 1859 and began the study of law, which he put aside to write. He worked for *The New York Times* as a Civil War correspondent before joining the *Sun*. He died in New York City, married but childless, on April 11, 1906. An interesting description of him is found in *Memoirs of an Editor*, the autobiography of Edward P. Mitchell of the *Sun*, the man who suggested one day in 1897 that he write a reply to Virginia O'Hanlon, an assignment Mitchell recalled Church had not at first cherished.

For thirty-five years and until his death in 1906 Frank Church was a regular contributor to the *Sun*'s editorial page. His lifetime lasted for four years beyond the date when I became editor-in-chief and for that period he was my alternate. There was never a more delightful associate. Quick of perception of the interesting in every phase of human activity except politics (for which he cared little, bless his soul!), there was in his features something of gentlemanly pugnacity—a latent aggressiveness that marred neither the delicacy of his fancy nor the warmth of his sympathies.

The *Sun* reran Church's editorial to introduce the Christmas season each year until the newspaper's demise more than half a century later. The little girl grew up to become Virginia O'Hanlon Douglas, for forty-seven years a teacher in the New York City schools. She died in 1971 at the age of eighty-two. To the end, she modestly felt it was Francis Church who should be famous, and not she.

The roots of the legend Francis Church defended so eloquently go so far back in time that they are no longer entirely traceable. However, there is evidence linking our American Santa Claus to the old Teutonic gods Woden, who rode a white horse, and Thor, who drove a chariot pulled across the skies by two goats; to a profusion of terrifying devillike figures associated with the midwinter season in the Old World; and to St. Nicholas, Santa's direct ancestor. As late as the end of the nineteenth century, vestiges of Woden could still be seen in the garb of some Santa Claus figures. In 1869 an illustration on the front page of *Harper's Weekly* showed a Santa Claus dressed in a short-skirted tunic edged with

# St. Nicholas and His Counterparts

fur, his bare, muscular legs only partially covered by knee-length boots. Other old-fashioned pictures in books, merchants' trade cards, and advertisements, including one for Macy's as late 1897, portrayed him still dressed like the old warrior god. At the same period, American children were playing with a German clockwork toy portraying Santa Claus riding in Thor's chariot pulled by two reindeer. Another tin toy of the time had Santa Claus in his sleigh, but drawn by Thor's two goats. When the toy was wound, the goats moved up and down, giving the impression that they were flying before the sleigh.

Scholars know virtually nothing about the real man behind the St. Nicholas myth. In 1969, after years of deep historical investigation, a report by the Roman Catholic Church, approved by Pope Paul VI, disclosed doubt as to whether many of the Church's saints, Nicholas among them, were saints or simply revered legendary heroes.

Legend has Nicholas born approximately 270 years after Christ, about 350 miles northwest of Bethlehem on the shores of the Mediterranean in Lycia—today part of Turkey. According to legend, his parents were wealthy Greek Christians. When Nicholas was still a very young man, he was consecrated archbishop of Myra (now Kale), an ancient seaport in Asia Minor. He was imprisoned and tortured during the reign of the Roman Emperor Diocletian, when many Christians were persecuted. From his own period, not one single shred of historical evidence proving that he ever lived can be found. He was believed to have died in Myra on December 6, about 343.

Numerous stories gathered about his name. Tales of

his good, charitable life and miracle-working were passed by word of mouth until the earliest known written accounts were recorded by Methodius, the bishop of Constantinople from 842 to 846. From the thirteenth century until the Protestant Reformation in the sixteenth century, St. Nicholas was the foremost saint in Christendom. Throughout Europe, several thousand churches were dedicated to him. In England alone, there were 446, more than twice the 204 dedicated to St. George. St. Nicholas, a divine ombudsman, always ready to help those who were in need, became the patron of little children, as well as of maidens and students, and of such diverse tradespeople as merchants, bankers, grocers, apothecaries, bakers, cobblers, coopers, pawnbrokers, tailors, wood-turners, fishermen, sailors, and others. He was nearly as important in the scheme of things as Mary, the mother of Christ.

By the Middle Ages, the patron saint of children was indissolubly linked with Christmas. Today it is thought that the giving of gifts to children in his name originated in France, where nuns in the thirteenth century began leaving presents at the homes of the poor on the eve of his saint's day, December 6. The custom spread across Europe as, on the night of December 5, street parades were led by someone representing St. Nicholas mounted on a white horse.

During the Reformation all saints fell into disrepute in the parts of Europe that were becoming Protestant. The reformers tried zealously to erase the popular St. Nicholas from people's minds.

# St. Nicholas and His Counterparts

But despite their fanatical endeavors, they were never completely successful. Removed from the churches, St. Nicholas lived on in the streets and homes. In Germany the saint who had put nuts and apples in the shoes of children became disguised in many Protestant homes as the Christchild. In 1545 the children of Martin Luther received gifts from the "Holy Christchild," after previously receiving them from St. Nicholas. Both saint and Christchild were described as wanderers, generally said to travel afoot, by chariot or horseback, inspecting the deeds of mankind in general and children in particular, making sure that good behavior prevailed before scattering apples, nuts, and sweets behind them.

In due course, the gift-bearer's visit was used by parents to gain improved behavior from their offspring. Both St. Nicholas and the Christchild were depicted with switches for bad children. But more often than not, they were given a servant companion to perform the disciplinary duties. Particularly in German-speaking Europe, the visit was the occasion of a solemn, sometimes terrifying inquest into the behavior of the juveniles; a purgatory before a paradise. The servant was a frightening being given to ogrelike growls, the opposite of the gift-bearer's shining goodness. Widely known as *Ruprecht* or *Knecht Ruprecht*, the disorderly fellow was also known by other names, including *Hans Trapp, Krampus, Klaubauf*, and *Schwarze Peter*. If the shaggy, black-faced figure wasn't quite the devil, he was, at least, the bogeyman. In the manner of a medieval mystery play, the holy figure was made to seem even holier by comparison to and domination of an obviously wicked one. The degree of terror that dark figures like Ruprecht were allowed to spread naturally depended on individual families.

In 1869 Cosima von Bülow recorded in her diary an account of Christmas Eve with Richard Wagner's family. The German operatic composer and dramatist had spent the afternoon rehearsing the performances of the Christchild and his servant, who would visit them that evening. We can well imagine how professional the talent selected to play the roles for Wagner's children would have been. After dinner, Knecht Ruprecht burst in, roaring like a lion. His act ended as he scattered nuts on the floor for the children, and the Christchild, "illuminated," waving a small Christmas tree in one hand, distributed toys and mesmerized the small ones before departing.

No scholar has ever solved totally the mystery of the origins of another major German Christmas figure generally known as *Pelznickel* ("Nicholas in furs"). Seemingly the servant without the master, Pelznickel traveled alone. Children feared him but waited for him, wild with excitement, because they knew that he always brought them nuts and confections. Evidently, as a result of the Reformation, St. Nicholas underwent a lot of irreverent changes in Protestant homes to make him appear ridiculous and frightening to children. Dirty and disheveled furs, stout stick, and a sack were the emblems of his office. (More will shortly be heard of the Pelznickel in America.)

One last German Christmas figure deserves to be mentioned briefly because of his increasing prominence in the nineteenth century. Indeed, he has become the modern German Santa Claus. By the beginning of the last century, the *Weihnachtsmann,* a kindly, secular St. Nicholas, was also engaged in Christmas Eve travels. Like Pelznickel, the Weihnachtsmann traveled alone, on foot, a sack or basket filled with toys on his back. Though he was said to have a kindly disposition, in one hand he carried sticks or a staff to whip bad children, while in the other he carried a small Christmas tree. He was invariably pictured as a thin, stooped, heavily laden old man with a long white beard.

English immigrants brought yet another Old World Christmas folk figure to these shores: "Father Christmas." Quite different from the mannerly old gentleman who now sits in department stores, disguised in red robes and white whiskers, his ancestor was well known in medieval mummers' plays as a pagan spirit more concerned with wassail, mistletoe, and the yule log than with gifts for children.

Near the end of the last century, this venerable Christmas spirit was still kicking up his heels in the mountains of Tennessee. An old custom related to Father Christmas was recorded in one of Charles Egbert Craddock's books on life in the Tennessee mountains:

> The hour of midnight has arrived. The dancers range themselves in two parallel rows, facing each other. Then, amid a pronounced silence, the lights are put out and the fire partially covered. The host will usually say:

"My friends, Krismus have come and have stayed with we'uns all for jist four-and-twenty hours, and now hev been obliged to go back whar he come from. How shall he git outer thish yer house? Hit won't do to say that he kum up the chimney." The rest of the party will then chant in a sort of recitative:

*"In by the door he came,*
*Let him go out by the same."*

Somebody then opens the door and the two rows of dancers bow silently as though to a departing guest. The door is closed, the candles relighted, and the dancing resumed.

Europeans first brought St. Nicholas to the New World in the fifteenth century. On his first voyage, Columbus named a port in Haiti for St. Nicholas; and the Spaniards originally called Jacksonville, Florida, "St. Nicholas Ferry." The Dutch who settled New Amsterdam in 1624 undoubtedly were familiar with St. Nicholas. But at the same time, the Reformation was fiercely dividing the Netherlands, and very shortly thereafter a Protestant government assumed power. The city fathers of Amsterdam passed an ordinance banning the giving of cookies and cakes to children on the streets on St. Nicholas Eve, a custom that had been as entrenched as our own trick-or-treating on Halloween. While there is proof that St. Nicholas remained a popular, though underground, folk figure in Holland, among the Dutch settlers in the New World St. Nicholas apparently never gained wide popularity. Virtually all traces of him disappeared as seventeenth-century Dutch New Amsterdam was becoming eighteenth-century English New York. After years of research, Charles W. Jones, the preeminent Santa Claus scholar has been able to find only four pieces of evidence which show that St. Nicholas was known in eighteenth-century America. Simply stated, for all practical purposes, the old Dutch St. Nicholas disappeared from America until he was resurrected in early nineteenth-century literature and folklore.

At the same period that St. Nicholas was being rediscovered, a flood of German-speaking immigrants were bringing with them a positive attitude toward Christmas and introducing their own Christmas figures. In 1887 a newspaper in Pennsylvania printed the Reverend A. W. Kaufman's reminiscences of a Christmas three-quarters of a century before, when he was a seven-year-old hired lad on a Lancaster County farm. On Christmas Eve, the farmer told him to "set his basket," as the Christchild would come that night. He did as he was bidden, but instead of a large plate or decorative basket, commonly used in German households, he was given a large straw basket and told to put hay in it for the Christchild's mule. The next morning he had a well-filled basket containing, in Pennsylvania "Dutch" dialect, *snits* (dried slices of apple eaten by children as between-meal treats), *choosets* (candy), walnuts, and gingerbread.

Many German farmers used to leave hay in the barnyard on Christmas Eve for the Christchild's donkey. The next morning they fed it to their cattle. To the naïve mind, fed on folklore, hay left for the donkey would make the livestock prosper for another twelve months.

As those Pennsylvania Germans intermarried with their "English" neighbors, the dialect "Christ-kindle," from the proper German *Christkindlein,* became "Krist-kingle" or "Kriss-kingle." Eventually the term "Kriss Kringle" became attached to an entirely different Christmas figure. By the 1860s, due in large measure to two children's books, the holy child gift-bearer had turned, virtually within a generation, into a lookalike to Santa Claus. The two volumes were *Kriss Kringle's Book,* printed in Philadelphia in 1842, and *Kriss Kringle's Christmas Tree—A holiday present for boys and girls,* printed in Philadelphia in 1845 and 1847, and in New York in 1846. In neither book did the concept of the Pennsylvania Dutch Christ-kindle appear. Kriss Kringle was just another name for Santa Claus, except that he ignored stockings hung by the fireplace and hung his presents on the branches of a small Christmas tree that he brought with him.

By the latter half of the nineteenth century, Kriss Kringle was the most common Christmas gift-bearer in Pennsylvania. But at the same period, to numerous German-speaking children the Christmas figure was, instead, the menacing Old World Pelznickel—better known on this side of the water as "Belsnickel." He was usually portrayed by someone out for some fun by scaring children half to death, before changing character and giving them sweets.

While Belsnickels were most prevalent in eastern

## St. Nicholas and His Counterparts

Pennsylvania, where Christmas Eve found them out in force, there are nineteenth-century accounts of their visits to children in Maryland, Virginia, North Carolina, and even Nova Scotia. As Christmas approached, children were warned about his possible visit and told that he was as likely to deal out punishment as gifts. At the mere mention of him at the dinner table, tea went down a child's throat the wrong way. The Belsnickel invariably carried a whip, a rod, or sticks in the most menacing manner possible. Youngsters were acquainted with the fact that if they were bad, the Belsnickel might kidnap them and take them away. Where to was seldom said, but their own imaginations usually pictured a fate worse than anything the adults might suggest.

His visit was often announced by the sound of his sticks or staff raking across the windowpanes from outside. After several minutes passed to heighten the suspense, the door opened a crack and presently a handful of nuts rattled across the floor. Frightened, in some cases their hair literally standing on end, children cried and hid behind their mother's skirt. In a minute, with a rain of more nuts, the door opened wider and in strode a terrifying figure. His face was blackened, and his eyes were almost hidden by a battered hat. He generally wore a disheveled fur coat or a coat turned inside out, and old torn pants. Wise children tried to keep the table, or some other piece of furniture, between themselves and the Belsnickel as he questioned their behavior and asked them to sing, dance, or recite for him. One diary tells how the windows rattled as the Belsnickel laid about him with a horsewhip, wrapping it about the wrist of the first child to reach, without his permission, for some candy he had just scattered.

In some areas a group of jovial fellows led by a Belsnickel went from house to house collecting food and money to give to the poor. "Belsnickeling" survived well into the present century in Pennsylvania as a custom incorporating the activities of mummers and carolers.

There is evidence that both the gift-bearing Christchild and his Old World servants were well known among German children in New York. Meanwhile, six nineteenth-century New Yorkers of varied national backgrounds were primarily responsible for transforming the Old World St. Nicholas into the American Santa Claus.

The first was Washington Irving. In 1809 Irving published his first major work, *A History of New York from the Beginning of the World to the End of the Dutch Dynasty by Diedrich Knickerbocker.* It provided the first literary description of St. Nicholas to appear in America. The son of a Scottish merchant who had emigrated from the Orkney Islands to New York, Irving was a twenty-six-year-old lawyer turned journalist. His whimsical history, poking good fun at the Dutch founders of New York, contained numerous references to the Dutch patron saint. In later editions, Irving added an account of St. Nicholas bringing gifts:

—and lo, the good St. Nicholas came riding over the tops of the trees, in that self-same wagon wherein he brings his yearly presents to the children. . . . And he lit his pipe by the fire and sat himself down and smoked. . . . And when St. Nicholas had smoked his pipe, he twisted it in his hatband, and laying his finger beside his nose, gave the astonished Van Kortlandt a very significant look; then, mounting his wagon, he returned over the tree-tops and disappeared.

Irving was the original source of all the myths about St. Nicholas in New Amsterdam—of St. Nicholas as the patron saint of the city, of the emigrant ship *Goede Vrouw* with a figurehead of St. Nicholas at the prow, the descriptions of St. Nicholas Day in New Amsterdam, and the colony's first church dedicated to the saint—all sheer fictions produced by Irving, the father of American literature.

Irving's book was a best seller of the day, read not only in the drawing rooms of the city but in log huts on the frontier. After its publication in 1809, the St. Nicholas legend traveled fast.

One year later, Irving was at the first-anniversary dinner for St. Nicholas given by John Pintard and his friends at the New-York Historical Society. At that event, Pintard distributed a broadside he'd commissioned and engraved at his own expense. It included a poem, *"Sancte Claus Goed Heyligman!"* ("Santa Claus, Good Holy Man!"), adapted from an old Dutch song about the gift-bringer. A wood engraver, Alexander Anderson, created an illustration for the piece, the first known picture of the saint to be made in America. John Pintard was a merchant of Walloon Huguenot ancestry. A whirling dervish of energy, he started the first savings bank in New York and was also a politician, historian, editor, and philanthropist. Pintard was a principal force in the founding of the American Bible Society and the New-York Historical Society, as well as the recognition of Washington's birthday as a holiday. In 1793 Pintard mentioned the ancient Dutch patron saint in an almanac he published.

But it was in 1822 that Clement Clarke Moore provided the first definitive description of the Santa Claus we know today. Moore was from an old New York family. One of his ancestors had sailed over in 1609 with Henry Hudson aboard the *Half Moon*. Not long afterward, members of Moore's family emigrated from England and settled on Long Island and in Manhattan. His maternal grandmother's home, Chelsea House, the big 1750 farmhouse that he had inherited and made his home, stood on a hill in rolling countryside on present-day West Twenty-third Street. The estate of one hundred acres stretched from what is now Eighth Avenue to the Hudson River, and from Nineteenth to Twenty-fourth streets. In 1800 that part of Manhattan was all farms, apple orchards, cow paths, and country lanes, reminiscent of England. To Chelsea House, in 1813, Moore took his beautiful young bride, Eliza Taylor, a descendant of some of the Dutch settlers of New Amsterdam. There they raised nine children.

Moore was a gentle and talented man. He was devoted to his family and had a keen sense of humor. The son of the first Episcopal Bishop of New York, he was a devout churchman. Nonetheless, he exercised the courage of his own convictions in publicly disagreeing with his minister on the subject of slavery. In the eighteenth and the first half of the nineteenth century, slaveholding was far more widespread in New York, New Jersey, Ohio, and New England than is commonly remembered today. Like many of his contemporaries, young Clement Moore saw no inherent evil in the paternalistic relationship he enjoyed with the slaves that cared for his family. His substantial property holdings in New York City and upper New York State meant that, in the words of one biographer, "he was apparently at no time under the necessity of earning a living," and could pursue his natural inclinations as a scholar. He was fluent in German, French, and Italian, and he eventually became the professor of Greek literature and Biblical languages at the Episcopal seminary he helped to found by donating the land it stands on.

Moore also dabbled in architecture, urban planning, and versifying. He loved music and played the organ, poorly, in the estimation of an acquaintance, the diarist, George Templeton Strong. It is ironic, but at least an irony with a happy ending, that out of a lifetime of scholarly and philanthropic pursuits, one fifty-six-line poem, written solely to amuse his children, assured him of immortality. By penning the poem that begins, " 'Twas the night before Christmas . . ." Moore inadvertently Americanized the Old World St. Nicholas, turning him into "jolly St. Nick," a plump, happy-go-lucky elf with a sleigh full of toys and eight flying reindeer.

The reindeer seem to be an entirely American addition. The Christmas before Moore wrote his poem, William B. Gilley, a personal friend and onetime neighbor of the Moores, published a book titled *A New Year's Present for Little Ones from Five to Twelve*. In it, an anonymous poet describes Santa's sleigh as drawn by a lone reindeer. It seems reasonably certain that no one before Moore had conceived of a team of reindeer. Interestingly, not only his "miniature sleigh and eight tiny reindeer," but also their driver, have grown larger in people's minds over the years. The original illustrated editions of Moore's poem show an elf only three to four feet high driving reindeer only as large as collie dogs.

Probably Moore's model for jolly St. Nicholas was a short, pudgy, ruddy-faced Dutchman who served as a handyman and gardener in his neighborhood. New York City enjoyed a white Christmas in 1822, and the big old house surrounded by an immense lawn deep with snow would have offered appropriate surroundings for the author of a Christmas poem.

As best as the story can be reconstructed, Clement Moore allowed his verses to be copied by a relative in her album. She in turn allowed Harriet Butler, the daughter of his close friend the Reverend David Butler of St. Paul's Church in Troy, New York, to copy them. Miss Butler read the poem to her Sunday school class and then gave a copy to Orville Luther Holley, the editor of *The Troy Sentinel*. The following Christmas, the poem appeared in his newspaper, anonymously—apparently the poet did not wish to claim authorship. It was Holley, it seems, who gave the poem its title, *A Visit from St. Nicholas.* The Christmas of 1825, the poem was published in the New Brunswick (New Jersey) *Almanac* and shortly thereafter in newspapers in New York and Philadelphia. The public began to clamor for the name of the author. In 1829 Holley, who knew Clement Moore was the author, published the poem again, still anonymously but with a description of the author as "belonging by birth and residence to New York City." In 1830 the poem, this time illustrated, appeared again in Troy, as a "carrier's address," or a single page that *Sentinel* delivery boys handed out in hopes of receiving Christmas tips from their customers. The accompanying wood engraving was attributed to Myron B. King, a New York City resident, and it showed St. Nicholas in his tiny reindeer sleigh dashing over snow-covered Dutch-style rooftops. Only in 1837 did Clement Moore finally acknowledge his authorship by allowing his work to be included in *The New York Book of Poetry,* compiled by a friend and distinguished literary critic, Charles Fenno Hoffman.

It is always interesting to look for the sources of any work that becomes a classic and the influences upon its author. In 1821 the General Theological Seminary of New York opened its doors, and Clement Moore and the other members of its little faculty were in constant contact. By the Christmas of 1822, the seminary's professor of the evidences of revealed religion, Gulian Verplanck, and Moore were the closest of friends. Verplanck was an enthusiastic devotee of Irving's St. Nicholas. Historian Charles W. Jones believed Verplanck may well have been the one who placed the idea for a St. Nicholas poem in Moore's mind that year.

The first painting of St. Nicholas by an American artist was by Verplanck's friend and former colleague, Robert Walter Weir, professor of painting and drawing at the Military Academy at West Point. He taught future generals William T. Sherman and Thomas "Stonewall" Jackson, as well as the young James McNeill Whistler, in the time before cameras when military officers were expected to sketch fortifications and the new terrain they explored. In 1837 Weir did a painting of St. Nicholas.

Weir regarded this painting, which he exhibited at the National Academy that year and then apparently kept for himself, as one of the best things he had done. He was thirty-four years old at the time and would eventually gain some renown as one of the Hudson River school of painters. His picture, twenty-four by thirty inches, showed an elflike figure without a beard dressed in high Dutch boots, a brown suit, and a red cape. The Christmas saint, with an impish grin, was "laying his finger aside his nose" a moment before ducking into the fireplace on his way up the chimney. Into two wool stockings "hung by the chimney with care," he had placed presents, into a third only a switch, but in an apparent gesture of forgiveness, he had attached a jumping-jack to the toe. Weir's St. Nicholas wore a rosary, and what appears to some to be the end of a sword scabbard partially hidden behind one leg is just as likely to be the end of a large crucifix.

In 1844 friends persuaded Clement Moore to include his constantly reprinted and ever-more popular poem in a volume of his own poetry. Since that poem was atypical of his serious writing, he made a point of prefacing the verses with the remark that they were of no more significance than "a good, honest, hearty laugh which conceals no malice."

Through the years, many publishers have offered the poem as an illustrated book for children. The first was published in 1848 by Henry M. Onderdonk, a New York printer and bookseller, and a friend whose shop Clement Moore frequently visited. Onderdonk engaged Theodore C. Boyd, an elderly wood engraver who had a shop around the corner from his own, to do the illustrations. The small, eight-page pamphlet, prepared as "a present for good little boys and girls," had seven woodcuts depicting sleeping children, stockings hanging, the Christmas elf driving his miniature team through the streets and over the rooftops of a quaint old-fashioned Dutch New York, and other scenes familiar to every illustrated edition since. Legend has it that Boyd's model for St. Nicholas was the same rubicund Dutchman whom Moore had used for his model. Only two known copies of that paperback publication have survived.

Despite the immense popularity of his poem, Moore apparently never asked for or received a single penny in royalties. Like the man he wrote about in his poem, he received his reward in the happiness his work gave to others. He died on July 10, 1863, five days before his eighty-fourth birthday, and was buried in St. Luke's churchyard, now gone. In 1890, Moore's final intern-

# ST. NICHOLAS AND HIS COUNTERPARTS

ment was made in Trinity Cemetery at 155th Street and Broadway in New York City.

In 1915 the children of the Sunday school of the Episcopal church across the street decided to honor the author with a Christmas Eve graveside reading of his poem, beginning a tradition that continues to the present day.

Clement Moore had given the country a written description of the ideal St. Nicholas, or Santa Claus, as he came to be more generally known with every passing year, but it remained for illustrator Thomas Nast to develop the visual prototype. Nast was a political cartoonist; he created the Republican elephant and the Democratic donkey. His career would reach its peak with his successful attacks on corruption in Boss Tweed's ring in New York.

In 1863, however, Thomas Nast was a twenty-three-year-old German immigrant working as an assistant illustrator at Frank Leslie's Magazine. The Gregory Company of New York approached him with an offer to do the illustrations for a book of Christmas poems, including Moore's. Locating a copy of Moore's poem, Nast read it aloud, over and over, jotting down sketches of the character he saw in his mind. He sought to draw a warm, jolly old elf. When *Christmas Poems* appeared and was a success, Nast was able to get a better job, with *Harper's Weekly*, where he helped cover the Civil War and other leading news stories of the period. His first *Harper's* Santa Claus appeared as a small part of a large illustration titled "A Christmas Furlough" in the December 26, 1863, issue. The following year, his drawing showed

# St. Nicholas and His Counterparts

Santa arriving at a camp of Union soldiers in his reindeer sleigh, wearing a special suit decorated with the Stars and Stripes. These drawings inaugurated a long tradition at *Harper's Weekly*. Each Christmas, Thomas Nast set aside his regular news and political coverage to do a Santa Claus drawing. For twenty-three years Nast's drawings gave the country an intimate look at Santa's deeds and his workshop. Today it is hard to realize the tremendous effect these anxiously awaited, long and joyfully pored-over drawings had on Victorian children. Then, sadly for both the children and the illustrator, the paper changed from a leading newsweekly into a magazine for late nineteenth-century homemakers. Nast's political cartoons no longer fitted. Almost symbolically, his association ended as it had begun, with an illustration that appeared for the Christmas of 1886, showing a family of mice tucked snugly in their beds awaiting the arrival of St. Nick.

Even before Thomas Nast had begun to define the widely accepted idea of what Santa Claus looks like, children were dreaming about him, and some were even lucky enough to meet him in person. Although there are indications that a few children were visited by St. Nicholas before the literature of Washington Irving and Clement Moore resurrected the old Dutch custom, very few accounts of his visit can be found before the 1850s. One of the oldest and most illuminating is part of a memory of Christmases on a farm in western New York in the 1820s, recollected almost three-quarters of a century later by Theodore Ledyard Cuyler (1820–1909):

# ST. NICHOLAS AND HIS COUNTERPARTS

As the visits of Santa Claus in the night could only be through the chimney, we hung our stockings where they would be in full sight. Three score and ten years ago such modern contrivances as steam pipes, and those unpoetical holes in the floor called "hot-air registers," were entirely unknown in our rural regions. We had a genuine fire-place in our kitchen, big enough to contain an enormous back-log, and broad enough for eight or ten people to form "a circle wide" before it and enjoy the genial warmth.

The last process before going to bed was to suspend our stockings in the chimney jambs; and then we dreamed of Santa Claus, or if we awoke in the night, we listened for the jingling of his sleigh bells. At the peep of day we were aroused by the voice of my good grandfather, who planted himself in the stairway and shouted in a stentorian tone, "I wish you all a Merry Christmas!" The contest was as to who should give the salutation first, and the old gentleman determined to get the start on us by sounding the greeting to the family before we were out of our rooms. Then came a race for the chimney corner; all the stockings came down quicker than they had gone up. What could not be contained in them was disposed upon the mantelpiece, or elsewhere. I remember that I once received an autograph letter from Santa Claus, full of good counsels; and our coloured cook told me that she awoke in the night and, peeping into the kitchen, actually saw the veritable old visitor light a candle and sit down at the table and write it! I believed it all as implicitly as I believed the Ten Commandments, or the story of David and Goliath. . . .

# ST. NICHOLAS AND HIS COUNTERPARTS

Around Buffalo, New York, where a heavy concentration of Germans had immigrated around 1840, St. Nicholas used to call at homes on "Nicholas Eve" (December 5) to take orders for presents to be delivered on Christmas Eve. The custom lasted for sixty years, then disappeared. Late in the century in Dutch communities in New York, Michigan, and Iowa, St. Nicholas appeared at homes on his saint's day, bearing oranges and switches.

In New York City in 1865, at midnight on Christmas night, a St. Nicholas appeared at a ball in his honor. A reporter for *The New York Herald* described the honored guest as "appropriately rotund and bewhiskered." The good saint's tailor seemed to be well familiar with Weir's West Point portrait of the gentleman:

> His boots were buckskin, and of large proportions; his pants were of a fawn color, with a blue stripe. A vest of scarlet, with large brass buttons, encircled a truly aldermanic paunch. A coat of dark brown, over which was thrown an ample cloak of scarlet and gold completed his attire. He was laden with toys—they hung from his arms, round his neck, his waist, and his back was heavily freighted. Round the room he tripped good humoredly, chuckling to himself as he distributed his stock and trade to all.

However, because Clement Moore had described a fur-clad St. Nicholas, and bearskin and other fur coats and hats were common winter attire for men in the nineteenth century, when Santa Claus made a personal appearance, even well into this century, he was likely to be garbed in fur of one type or another. For example, on Christmas Eve of 1884, there were eight hundred wide-eyed youngsters from New York's Five Points Mission School in the mission hall, which was hung with flags and bunting, when Santa Claus made his entrance "wrapped in a great coat of Siberian wolf skins, over which his long beard hung down to his knees."

But Santa Claus was also frequently pictured, and occasionally made his rounds, in green clothes, or blue or black. In 1853 Mary Moore Ogden, a daughter of Clement Moore, created a calligraphic, illustrated version of her father's poem as a Christmas present for her husband. Mysteriously, despite her father's words, "dressed all in fur from his head to his foot," she painted a St. Nicholas in a long green coat.

The first edition of *A Visit from St. Nicholas* that showed him in a red cloth coat appeared around 1870. The name of the artist is still unknown. However, in 1866 young Thomas Nast had illustrated George P. Walker's verse story *Santa Claus And His Works* with a little gnomelike, rotund Santa who wore a fur suit of a red-brown color, trimmed in white ermine. The book was published by McLoughlin Brothers, the printers of the first American children's books using color lithography. There is little doubt that this enormously popular book, in its day, was a major contributor to the idea that Santa wore red. Walker's story also contributed to the legend of Santa Claus the fact that he lives at the North Pole.

Not until the early years of the present century did red

# ST. NICHOLAS AND HIS COUNTERPARTS

Santa Claus suits begin to proliferate and be sold by department stores and mail-order houses such as Sears, Roebuck. One man from Massachusetts indignantly objected in a letter to *The New York Times:*

> What Anarchist started the notion that Santa Claus should dress in red? When I was a boy Santa Claus, whether corporeally present at a Christmas tree or merely ideally described, always wore a fur coat, as is appropriate to his northern home and to the season, and, as stated in Moore's poem, "Twas the Night Before Christmas," which I was trained to regard as the standard book authority on Santa Claus. Who is responsible for rigging him out in red?
>
> One would think, as a resident of the North Pole, he should wear the white fur of polar animals; but in my memory he has the black or dark brown of the principal furs of the temperate zone—more practical for coming down a chimney without showing soot than either white or red.
>
> Stephen T. Byington<br>Ballard Vale, Mass.,<br>Dec. 11, 1913

By the middle of the nineteenth century, stores had begun designating themselves as "Santa Claus headquarters." The earliest known was J. W. Parkinson's in Philadelphia. On the day before Christmas in 1841, Mr. Parkinson saw to it that many a child's dream came true. Before the children's very eyes a real "Criscringle" descended a chimney above the door of the shop. Throughout the afternoon and into the evening, the man impersonating the jolly, bearded soul drew the attention of the youngsters from the bonbons in the windows. By 1846 Mr. Parkinson was advertising his store as "Kriss Kringle's Headquarters."

Despite the simplicity and attractiveness of the idea, it was almost forty years before James Edgar, owner of The Boston Store in Brockton, Massachusetts, became the father of the department store Santa Claus. Edgar, a Scottish immigrant, was tall, rolypoly, with a white beard, a warm voice, and a hearty laugh, and he was the perfect model for Santa Claus in more than just appearance: he loved children.

For the Christmas of 1890 he decided to have a Santa Claus suit made and to wear it in the store for the children in the late afternoon after school got out. But in a few days, his idea had proved so popular that there were long lines waiting outside the store, and he ordered a second suit for Jim Grant, his big floorwalker. Parents and children from Boston and as far away as Providence, Rhode Island, began arriving in Brockton by train, and news of a Santa Claus whose ears you could actually whisper into was heard all the way down in New York. Before the turn of the century, department stores in all parts of the country had added a throne for Santa Claus.

Even before most children ever dreamed of sitting on his knee, children had been dropping letters for Santa Claus into post boxes with bounteous faith. In 1874 a typical letter read: "Mr. Santa Claus, a big wagon—not so very big—four wheels, two packs pop-crackers, a Mother Hubbard book. Wilmer." By the 1890s post offices were inundated by Santa letters each December. There was considerable diversity in the way his name was spelled. "Sandy Claus" was one frequent variation and "Sandy Clows" and "Santy Klaws" were others. The clerks gravely stamped the letters with a certification that the addressee could not be found before forwarding them to the dead letter office in Washington. Many children, sure of the knowledge of postal officials, merely wrote "Santa Claus" on the envelope and trusted that somebody would do the rest. Many letters mistakenly gave the South Pole as his habitation, and others thought that his address was "Heaven," while a good many others thought he lived in New York City.

The week before Christmas in 1894, a letter written in a childish German hand to "Die WeinachtsMann" was displayed in the frame of the Yonkers post office window where letters with incomplete addresses were put. Two days before Christmas, it disappeared, and the postmaster said it had fallen into good hands.

Other typical letters of the period tell us a lot about the children who wrote them. For the Christmas of 1900, in New York City, a small boy dictated the following letter to his mother:

Dear Santa Claus: I hope you'll pay 'tention. I want a soldier hat and a sword and gun, and please don't fill up the toe of my stocking with peanuts as you did last year. If

you wouldn't mind leaving my things before I go to bed I'll be much obliged.

Allen Mr. Starr

One Christmas Eve, eight-year-old Edsel Ford, son of Henry and Clara Ford, and the future president of the Ford Motor Company, penned a Santa letter in Detroit:

Dear Santa Claus: I Havent Had Any Christmas Tree In 4 Years And I Have Broken My Trimmings And I Want A Pair of Roller Skates And A Book, I Cant Think Of Any Thing More. I Want You To Think Of Something More. Good By.

Edsel Ford

Just as Clement Moore had failed to give Santa Claus's address, causing some confusion among his young readers, he had given no information on another important point that gave rise to interesting speculation among children and adults alike. Was Santa married? Not until 1899 did Mrs. Santa Claus make her debut in *Goody Santa Claus on a Sleigh Ride*, one of thirty-two now-forgotten books by Katharine Lee Bates, who would achieve lasting fame as the composer of "America the Beautiful."

It is not known exactly when or how the tradition of leaving food for Santa Claus began. In 1908 *The New York Tribune* told its readers how children in one family left a little luncheon for Santa Claus, who would be tired after his hard work. The table was set, coffee was ground, and a few sandwiches and cakes were put covered on the table. All the children helped to get the luncheon ready, and they were very happy when the next morning the food was gone and they found a note pinned on the Christmas tree thanking them for their kindness and wishing them a "Merry, Merry Christmas."

While this custom continues to the present time, others have come and gone since the early years of the twentieth century. In addition to food for Santa, children used to leave carrots for his reindeer, and country children, knowing what animals needed, left piles of salt on their windowsills. The following morning it would be nearly gone, and tracks showed where their noses and tongues had been at work—evidence as plain to children as the crumbs on Santa's plate and their filled stockings that Santa Claus and his reindeer team had visited them while they slept.

A 1910 advertisement for Ivory Soap started another Christmas Eve custom that flourished and then disappeared. The ad showed a small boy in his nightshirt seated in front of a fireplace where two stockings hung. The lad was saying to himself, "Santa Claus will get very dirty coming down the chimney. I'll leave a bowl of water, a couple of towels and a cake of Ivory Soap in front of the fireplace—so he can wash up." Doing just as the ad said, the next morning children found a very dirty towel, and, as often as not in those days, the dirty gray water that he had washed in was frozen solid in the bowl.

Yet another old-fashioned custom, now lost, was practiced around many a fireplace on December evenings when letters to Santa Claus were "mailed" up the chimney. With careful parental guidance, letters on single sheets of paper were thrust into the updraft of a roaring fire. Before

St. NICHOLAS.
Dec. 6th   A.D. 343.

SANCTE CLAUS, goed heylig Man!
Trek uwe beste Tabaert aen,
Reis daer me'e na Amsterdam,
Van Amsterdam na 'Spanje,
Daer Appelen van Oranje,
Daer Appelen van granaten,
Die rollen door de Straaten.
SANCTE CLAUS, myn goede Vriend!
Ik heb U allen tyd gedient,
Wille U my nu wat geven,
Ik zal U dienen alle myn Leven.

SAINT NICHOLAS, good holy man!
Put on the Tabard,* best you can,
Go, clad therewith, to Amsterdam,
From Amsterdam to Hispanje,
Where apples *bright*† of Oranje,
And likewise those *granate*‡ surnam'd,
Roll through the streets, all free unclaim'd.
SAINT NICHOLAS, my dear good friend!
To serve you ever was my end,
If you will, now, me something give,
I'll serve you ever while I live.

*Kind of jacket.   † Oranges.   ‡ Pomegranates.

Alexander Anderson's St. Nicholas. 1810.

Thor.

Knecht Ruprecht.

Father Christmas.

The Christ child.

Robert W. Weir's St. Nicholas. 1837.

Theodore C. Boyd's Miniature Reindeer.

An 1845 Santa Claus.

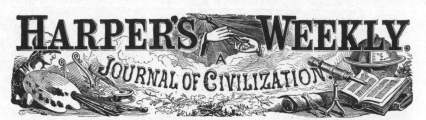

# HARPER'S WEEKLY.

## JOURNAL OF CIVILIZATION

VOL. XIII.—No. 627.]     NEW YORK, SATURDAY, JANUARY 2, 1869.     [ SINGLE COPIES, TEN CENTS. $4.00 PER YEAR IN ADVANCE.

Entered according to Act of Congress, in the Year 1868, by Harper & Brothers, in the Clerk's Office of the District Court of the United States, for the Southern District of New York.

A Thor-like Santa Claus in 1869.

the bright eyes of the children, they were carried swiftly up the chimney, down which they hoped their presents would soon come. With childlike faith, the youngsters imagined their requests being carried to the North Pole on breezes as fleet and dependable as a carrier pigeon.

As a rapidly changing America approached the twentieth century, writers and artists began to portray Santa Claus in numerous updated forms of transportation. On snowless Christmases he was first shown on a bicycle, and then, at the turn of the century, regardless of the weather, he landed on rooftops in a mind-boggling variety of balloons and futuristic airships.

In 1903 *The New York Tribune* printed a poem representative of another mode of modernized transportation:

> *'Twas the night before Christmas,*
> *in each little house*
> *The children were waiting*
> *As still as a mouse*
> *To hear the puff puff*
> *And the pish, chugg, and squeal*
> *Of good old St. Nicholas's*
> *Automobile?*

Finally, in 1912, he was seen for the first time actually dropping out of the sky in a thoroughly twentieth-century manner. There was no snow for his reindeer sleigh in San Francisco, so Santa Claus floated down from a brilliantly blue sky in his double-winged "aeroplane." He landed safely in Golden Gate Park on Christmas Day with candy and nuts and toys for ten thousand children.

## Chapter 13

## THE JOY OF STORE-BOUGHT TOYS

**M**ost children had only homemade toys until mass-manufactured ones appeared near the middle of the nineteenth century— indeed, toy shops were almost unknown before 1850. By the 1860s, however, December in cosmopolitan New York City was a children's bonanza. Shopkeepers piled high their counters and shelves with drums and horns, hoops and rocking horses, toy kitchens with real wood-burning stoves and grocery stores with tiny food packages, tall six-room brownstone dollhouses and dollhouse furniture, china sets, and lead knives and forks, doll beds, wooden soldiers, jacks, masks of every description, tin horses in hoops, little cows that rolled on wheels, and big wooden lions, tigers, and rhinoceroses.

Among the most popular toys were the venerable, indestructible wooden "Noah's arks." When their bright roofs were opened, out of cavernous depths came Noah and his family, together with a seemingly endless caravan of wild and domestic animals. Some arks held as many as three hundred beasts, birds, and insects. While such details as the differences of coloration between the sexes of a species were strictly observed in the little gessoed and painted figures, scale was another matter. Dogs were as large as horses, flies a size or two smaller than elephants, and grasshoppers half as large as monkeys. It made no difference in happy children's eyes as they arranged them, two by two, in a parade snaking across the parlor floor. In households where the keeping of the sabbath was strict, the ark's Biblical connections made it one of the few toys the children could play with on Sunday.

Kites were another favorite toy. On the day following Christmas in 1870, *The New York Tribune* reported:

> Notwithstanding the freezing atmosphere, there were hundreds of little fellows flying their kites upon the housetops. From Attic windows in the high portion of the island, infinite numbers of kites could be seen speckling the sky over every part of the city.

In the years following the Civil War, many playthings were made of India rubber, from the garden variety rubber ball to reversible dolls with two faces. Balloons of all shapes abounded, including a real-looking snake that could be blown up to the size of a boa constrictor and writhe about until it was finally deflated. Among the balloon toys that flew about on Christmas mornings were cows, elephants, roosters, and parrots; as their air escaped the cow mooed, the rooster crowed, and so on.

Motion and sound were two features children loved most in their toys, and the latter half of the nineteenth century saw an explosion of ingenious new toys, at prices for every pocketbook. The beloved jack-in-the-box and popgun were joined by whales that spouted water and cannons that fired peas. As early as 1854, New York newspapers mentioned doll babies that cried and dogs that barked at the slightest provocation. That year, a reporter happened to be present when a woman was about to purchase a "crying baby" from a street vendor. After examining it, she discovered that it didn't always cry. "So much the better, ma'am," said the vendor. "You know that babies oughtn't to cry always." The sale was effected.

In Europe generations of royalty had enjoyed intricate "clockwork" toys and music boxes. Now craftsmen made such wonders in quantities. In America one of the best places to admire them—and buy them if you could afford it—was the giant emporium of the Ehrich brothers on Eighth Avenue in New York City. Julius Ehrich presided over the lower floor where the toys were displayed, and though a young man, he seemed to have a sort of paternal regard for the children of his clientele. He took pains to secure the most extraordinary and varied collection of toys manufactured in Europe, as well as those by the fledgling American toy industry. One of the most fascinating toys of the 1875 Christmas season was a little lady in a bustled brown dress standing before a looking glass with a powder puff in her hand. As the machinery that controlled her movements was set in motion, she applied powder to her cheek with ladylike delicacy. She leaned forward, peered into the glass, and then with the aid of a hand mirror inspected her operations and their results. For the hosts of little girls in his store, young Mr. Ehrich set the figure going again and again, and she enchanted all beholders. Alas, she cost sixty dollars, a thumping sum in those days.

Other costly examples of the Old World toymakers' skill were an Oriental maiden being slowly fanned by a slave in time to music, a little ballerina dancing, and a woman playing a small piano. One little foot rested on a pedal as her hands glided over the keys. As her head moved from side to side, she bent toward the music in perfect harmony with the measure of the piece.

The perambulations of a life-size baby in a walker was also a source of delight. She could walk the length of a room with tiny tottering feet and cry, "Ma, Ma!" There was a little girl trundling a wheelbarrow filled with flowers, rabbits nibbling carrots, and gymnasts, and cakewalking minstrel-show figures, and a young equestrienne who rode a bay horse and applied her whip gracefully. And there was a pair of roosters that flew at each other with their spurs like real fighting cocks, of particular interest to young gentlemen inclined to sporting practices.

Each Christmas Mr. Ehrich added fascinating new examples of the French and German mechanical toymak-

# THE JOY OF STORE-BOUGHT TOYS

ers' art. One, in 1887, deserves special mention: a head of cabbage that made the ladies blush and say, "So sweet." When one touched the top of the cabbage, it flew off and a wax baby arose slowly from the interior, moved its arm to its mouth as if blowing a kiss, and went back into the cabbage again.

But there were less expensive marvels in Mr. Ehrich's toy department too, from a bubble-blower capable of blowing a bubble within a bubble, and another that made chains of six or eight bubbles, to cows that emitted loud "moos" when their heads were turned. His cows, offered in several sizes including a big six-dollar model, could be milked in a bright pail, once milk had been poured into a hidden opening in the back.

For little girls, the array of Christmas dolls was marvelous. Pink wax and eyes of beads were out of date. Mr. Ehrich's dolls of wax or bisque had lifelike complexions with exquisitely molded features, luxuriant real hair, brown, black, or violet-blue eyes with lids that closed, and flexible shapes allowing any sort of manipulation. For the dolls, there were all sorts of toilet necessities: sponges, hairpins, crimping pins, soaps, and brushes, as well as sealskin, cashmere, and velvet wraps, gloves, fans, parasols, and skates. Young gentlemen dolls were imported too, dressed in the latest fashion, with hair parted on one side and captivating moustaches.

Every little girl dreamed of having a doll like those crowding Mr. Ehrich's counters. But for most parents, even the least expensive represented a considerable investment. Thus necessity gave birth to the widespread tradition of having Santa secretly recondition and re-dress the same doll year after year. Many an elderly woman recalls to this day the frustration of looking for her doll that always mysteriously disappeared just before Christmas.

Some of the best-loved toys at old-fashioned Christ-mases were edible: giant icing-covered gingerbread cows and horses, and lions with "Lion" written on the side in icing to show that they were not cats, as well as gingerbread soldiers in bright uniforms of sugar.

Several weeks before Christmas, candy shops were transformed into veritable groves of candy canes; some were as big as walking sticks, and others were baby canes less than three inches long. Confectioners striped their canes according to flavor. Peppermint canes had one fat stripe of red and two thin ones. Clove canes had two large and one small, while sassafras had only one large. Thus the flavor could be identified at a glance. Most of the canes were red and white, but there were green-striped canes and black-striped canes.

Candy makers also molded "clear toys"—hard sugar candy in stained glass colors—in the shapes of animals, knights on horseback, ships in full sail, locomotives, two-pound lions, and other playthings, to use as tree decora-tions and stocking stuffers.

For Victorians who loved to mix pleasure with instruc-tion, magic lanterns were a favorite toy. Lucky was the child to whom Santa Claus brought a complete outfit in-cluding a four-wick oil lantern, a nine-foot square white cloth screen, and twenty-five views. Until the late years

# The Joy of Store-Bought Toys

of the century, when photographic slides became common, hand-painted slides were used, the image in a circle three inches in diameter on a glass plate.

An alcohol boat—a steam yacht about two and a half feet long, equipped with a boiler, engine, compass, and rigging, that could go across the lake in Central Park before needing a fresh supply of alcohol—delighted the boy fond of machinery. The water mill was another toy guaranteed to please. A mountain, valley, and stream of tin were painted with trees and tiny flowers. On top of the mountain was a reservoir. When the child put water in, it gushed down the incline in a shoot, making a real cascade that swelled the stream below and set the mill wheel going at a lively rate.

A capital new toy at R. H. Macy's to keep youngsters quiet—comparatively quiet—was the New Kindergarten Mechanical Speller. It looked something like a combination of a little typewriter and an upright piano. Pictures of a ship, a hand, a cow, a cat, and so forth, were on a roller that passed across the front of the machine. The child stopped turning the crank when he found a picture that pleased him. Below the pictures were little portholes through which the letters of the alphabet showed as the child thumped the keys. Also at Macy's was a big mechanical cow gaily decked out in yellow and blue ribbons and ridden by a lifelike doll dressed in bright red. The doll looked so real that youngsters begged their mothers, "Have the red girl get off and let me ride it, mamma."

There were yards of calico cats to attract the little girls in Hearn's dry-goods store. They were so fat and lifelike

# THE JOY OF STORE-BOUGHT TOYS

that in a dim light they might easily be mistaken for the real thing on the alert for mice. Mr. Hearn also sold cloth stamped with the cat design with directions for sewing and stuffing. "The calico cats are a vast improvement on the china ones," a fond father remarked. "The children can throw them at one another without hurting the cats or themselves."

Famous people and current events were quickly reflected in the world of toys. During the Civil War, there were sleds with General Grant's name on them, and during the Centennial year of 1876, there were iron banks in the shape of Independence Hall—with the bell, crack and all. With Theodore Roosevelt in the White House during the Christmas of 1906, one million "teddy bears" were reported to have been on sale in New York alone. As the holiday approached in 1909, Roosevelt was in Africa. The big-game-hunting ex-President took pains to prevent his movements from being reported in the press. Nonetheless, he was everywhere, both in the newspapers and in the toy stores. A "Teddy in Africa" game "went like hotcakes." It featured a little tin Roosevelt in shooting costume, able to perform remarkable gymnastic feats without losing his pith helmet or his spectacles.

The nineteenth-century boy's fascination with forms of transportation was reflected in tin and cast-iron locomotives, horsecars, and steamboats. As early as 1887, he could have been mesmerized by the sight of electric trains circling Christmas trees on high three-railed tracks, with flashes of blue sparks and a genuine railroad clack and clatter. The old-fashioned electric train gave off a scent of ozone from its motor that became as much a part of the holidays as the aroma of evergreen. There were also steam trains whose boilers generated real steam with the aid of naphtha lamps. One ran on a track of steel with wood "sleepers," half an hour at each firing, the locomotive puffing great white clouds of steam. Eight times around the track took one minute. Perfect in detail and workmanship, richly finished in steel, bronze, and polished brass, it appealed mightily to the boy in every man.

By the first years of the twentieth century, there were toy flying machines, submarines, and automobiles, as well as trains. Some of them cost $100 (easily $1500 to $2000 today), and toy dealers whispered that in a good many cases they were being bought by grownups for themselves. In New York a dignified judge, known to have a fondness for mechanical toys, bought an entire railway system of train, tracks and switches, stations, bridges, and a roundhouse, on the pretense that he was going to give it to his nephew for Christmas. He also bought a seventy-five-dollar toy automobile. He said it was "for the little son of a friend," but the merchant who sold them asserted his belief that they were both running about in the judge's uptown home for the amusement of that gentleman alone. In another shop, a Wall Street banker was said to purchase every new mechanical toy that made its appearance on the market, taking extraordinary pains to conceal the fact that he was buying them for himself.

On Christmas Day in 1902, a twenty-five-cent airship

# THE JOY OF STORE-BOUGHT TOYS

that looked like a torpedo was going around and around in countless homes, powered by an India rubber band and a propeller at the stern. After the little flying machine had been suspended from the ceiling by a thread, someone wound it up, and it began to circle and rise through centrifugal force. To the delight of the children, it would circle the room for many minutes.

In 1903 Mr. and Mrs. George Gould, Sr., bought six-year-old George, Jr., what was probably the biggest, if not the best, toy train ever built. Even in those days it cost five hundred dollars. The locomotive was large enough for the son of the railroad millionaire to seat himself in the cab, where he handled the throttle and brake lever. The coaches, parlor cars with staterooms and smoking compartments, dining car, and mail car were twenty inches high. The train huffed and puffed around its track, driven by a steam engine fueled by alcohol.

The best "submarine boat" cost six dollars and was made of brass in Germany. Operated by a steel spring wound with a key, when first placed in water it ran on the surface for a short distance, then plunged beneath the water as a weight inside shifted its position. After a submerged run of a few feet, the weight again shifted, this time toward the stern, bringing the boat to the surface, before it dove again. It could be operated indoors in a bathtub—not the size they make today, but a commodious old-fashioned tub.

Every Christmas, toys appeared to have reached the limit of ingenuity, only to be eclipsed the following year by those even more marvelous. For the Christmas of

# THE JOY OF STORE-BOUGHT TOYS

1903, Santa Claus pulled some extraordinary things out of his bag, from a three-foot-long battleship, the *Indiana,* to a battery-operated telephone with wire and equipment for telephoning from room to room, to a real bathtub for dolls that could be attached to the spigots of a big tub by rubber tubes and nickel-plated pipes. Made of porcelain, with adjustable curtains, the small tub could also be used for a shower.

To adults, it sometimes seemed like toys had become "too clever by half." In 1911 one caused a bear hunt in New York City. As dusk settled one afternoon shortly before Christmas, the screams of women brought a policeman running to Fifth Avenue and Sixty-second Street, near the wall of Central Park.

"A grizzly bear has escaped from the Park menagerie," the patrolman was told. Pressing his way through the circle of spectators, high-hatted and frock-coated men, and befurred women, he saw a bear on the sidewalk, rocking back and forth and growling ominously. The policeman leveled his revolver at the swaying form, and the crowd waited breathlessly. As if with a sigh, the growling ceased and the bear toppled over. The officer was nonplussed. Was it faking, or had a four-and-a-half-foot bear died from fright on Fifth Avenue after escaping from the zoo?

The patrolman summoned sufficient courage and poked the furry body with his club. It remained motionless.

"Dead?" inquired a score of voices.

"It never was alive," said the policeman. He held the

# THE JOY OF STORE-BOUGHT TOYS

bear aloft for the inspection of the crowd. Several women screamed.

"Don't be alarmed—it's only a big teddy bear," said the patrolman. A general inspection of the big toy began, and it was discovered that at the pull of a lever the bear could sit up, rock back and forth, and emit a low growl at regular intervals.

Hanging from a ribbon about its neck was a tag bearing the following: A MERRY CHRISTMAS FROM UNCLE TUT-TUT.

When it came to toys, never had Santa Claus offered more exciting Christmases.

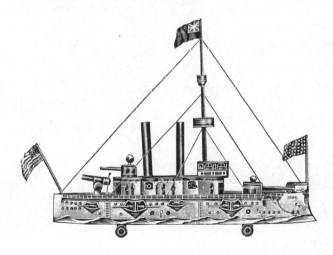

# PRANG'S CHRISTMAS CARDS

---

## Chapter 14

## REMEMBERING ONE'S FRIENDS
## AT CHRISTMAS

---

**S**omething startling and spectacular was happening early on Christmas morning in 1882 at the city post office in Washington. The rows of long tables that filled the gas-lit distributing room were piled ceiling high with mail. Like towering banks of snow, the envelopes lay in mountainous heaps and piles. It was a discouraging sight to the mail carriers, who had hoped to be home early for Christmas dinner with their families. The superintendent, J. E. Bell, who had already put on sixteen extra men, surveyed the extraordinary mail—cards ranging in size from calling cards to cigar box covers to washboards—and chatted with a reporter who had dropped by from the Washington *Star*. "I thought last year would be the end of the Christmas card mania," he grumbled, "but I don't think so now. Why four years ago a Christmas card was a rare thing. The public then got the mania and the business seems to be getting larger every year. I don't know what we will do if it keeps on."

Nonetheless, like snow under the rays of the sun, the paper piles began to melt under the energetic efforts of the agile, nimble-fingered mail carriers who sorted letters and packages with rapidity and threw each into its proper pouch or compartment with lightning precision. Eventually they shouldered their bags and crammed their pockets full. Each man carried a staggering load. One estimated the cards in his bag weighed a hundred pounds. By afternoon the entire mass of mail was distributed.

Behind the avalanche of cards taxing Superintendent Bell's men to their utmost was a German immigrant, Louis Prang, about whom more will be said shortly, and the age-old custom of exchanging New Year's greetings. In Europe the custom can be traced back to Roman times. In England written greetings, including the sentiment preferred by Lord Chesterfield, "the compliments of the season," as well as today's "merry Christmas and a happy New Year," can be found in late seventeenth-century correspondence. "About Christmas time there is a great plenty of good wishes sent about the kingdom," said Alexander Pope in 1736. By the nineteenth century, it had become the custom for Christmastime visitors to leave behind written greetings on their visiting cards.

The Christmas card was also foreshadowed by "Christmas pieces," school compositions embellished with birds, animals, and scrolls formed by the elaborate pen flourishes for which nineteenth-century writing masters had a remarkable attachment. At the approach of the holidays, schoolboys were accustomed to writing laboriously, in the copperplate-style script of the day, seasonal greetings to their parents, demonstrating the progress they had made in composition and penmanship.

The Christmas card proper can be traced to London in 1843, when Henry Cole—a gentleman of many interests and talents who later founded the Victoria and Albert Museum—found himself in a predicament as Christmas drew nigh. He owed letters but was too busy for seasonal letter writing. His impulsive solution was the first Christmas card. He commissioned an artist friend, John Calcott Horsley of the Royal Academy, to design a card to reflect seasonal sentiments. Then he had it printed by lithography and hand-colored by a professional water-colorist. Horsley's design consisted of a central scene and two side panels. In the center the artist drew a family party with three generations toasting the season by quaffing draughts of wine. The side panels illustrated an act of charity, with poor people being fed in one and a poor mother and child being given warm clothes in the other. Mr. Cole's greeting on the first Christmas card was the now-familiar "A Merry Christmas and a Happy New Year to you." His seemingly innocent card caused great wrath in temperance circles, and Cole apparently never attempted another.

In the years shortly thereafter, the idea of printing Christmas greetings seems to have occurred independently to several other Englishmen. Not until 1862, however, did the custom become popular, when a playing card manufacturer in London created attractive, inexpensive Christmas cards. Within a decade small, visiting-card-size Christmas cards were well established in England.

In America newsboys had presented their customers with New Year's "addresses" since the late eighteenth century. These were poems ending with thinly veiled requests for tips. By the 1840s references to Christmas were frequently included, and the news carriers no longer had a monopoly on printed New Year's greetings. Firemen, letter carriers, lamplighters, bill posters, waiters, and other servants of the public adopted the idea; eventually even the messengers of Western Union joined in.

The earliest known American Christmas card was a business greeting issued by Richard H. Pease, an engraver, lithographer, and merchant, in Albany, New York. His card, believed to have been printed about 1851, depicted a family celebrating a Dickensian Christmas with a punch bowl and a plum pudding. The drawing, done by an unknown artist, included Pease's store as well as Santa Claus. The message, "A Merry Christmas And A Happy New Year, To:———From:———," suggests that the entrepreneurial Mr. Pease probably gave them to his customers for their own use. It would not be the last time sentiment and business joined hands.

But the aforementioned German immigrant, Louis Prang, is the father of the American Christmas card; he single-handedly devised appropriately decorated cards and popularized the custom on this side of the Atlantic. Prang, a sixteen-year-old refugee from the German revolutions, arrived in New York in 1850 with a knowledge of printing gained as an apprentice and journeyman printer. After working as an artist for a time, he started a printing plant in Roxbury, Massachusetts, and pioneered in making reproductions of famous European paintings, which he sold for six dollars apiece. He constantly invented printed novelties, including battle maps during the Civil War. His first Christmas cards were sold in England in 1874 and were then offered in America in 1875.

The Civil War years had seen a development entirely necessary for the success of Prang's mass-produced cards. Without it, a Christmas greeting would hardly have aroused totally positive feelings. Before 1863, if one sent a letter to a friend, the recipient would have to either pay a carrier to deliver it or make his way to the post office to pick it up. That year, Congress, at the urging of Abraham Lincoln, a onetime postmaster of Salem, Illinois, who used to carry letters in his hat, authorized the postmaster general to establish free delivery in big cities. During the next decade, as the government hired more and more mail carriers, the stage was set for Prang's stunning success.

In the 1860s the tiny but ever-growing American demand for Christmas greetings was supplied from abroad. Originally, many of the cards, showing fairies and garlands and dressed-up animals, were similar to Victorian valentines made by the same English publishers. Indeed, the first Christmas cards produced were entirely floral designs. Prang had displayed his "chromolithography" at the Vienna exhibition of 1873, where he publicized his work by handing out business cards with lifelike flowers printed on them. The cards proved so popular that the wife of his London agent suggested he print holiday mottoes on the designs and sell them as Christmas greetings. When he saw how well they sold in England, Prang introduced similar cards in America showing a single blossom or a small bouquet of pansies, lilies, roses, or carnations with a ribbon that read MERRY CHRISTMAS or A HAPPY NEW YEAR. Prang's cards often depicted subjects such as seashells, butterflies, and insects that now seem unusual motifs for Christmas.

At the beginning the colorful cards were small, usually three and one-half by two inches or four by two and one-half inches, printed on only one side. By the end of the 1870s, Prang's elegant eight-color "chromos" had grown larger and the messages longer. At the same time, the pictures, mottoes, and verses began to represent more distinctive Christmas themes. Now there were Nativity scenes, Santas, little tots in snow, and little girls with dolls. A typical example, first published in 1878, portrayed a hoopskirted child holding her doll while a small boy in a sailor suit was trying to steal a kiss under the mistletoe. Other humorous cards showing animals in human garb and mishaps with hunters and ice skaters were popular. Once this product, which caught the enthusiasm for Christmas then building in America, became readily available, the Christmas card exploded into a fad.

In 1880 Prang held the first of a series of juried competitions for Christmas card art and offered prizes of $200, $300, $500, and $1000. That year, the entries were displayed at the Reichard's Gallery in New York, and the first prize went to a young woman, Rosina Emmett, whose painting had a center panel showing four little girls singing from songbooks while a fifth played a violin, and a decorative border with an angel appearing to a shepherd watching his flock by night. Prang, who well understood the value of publicity, saw to it that among the judges for his contests were famous artists, Samuel Coleman and John LaFarge, and architects, Stanford White and Richard Hunt. In 1882, by which time he was selling more than five million cards each Christmas, Prang increased the top prize to $2000. Each of the winning cards had the artist's name and the award printed on the back. Prang's generous prizes tempted some well-known painters, including Elihu Vedder, Thomas Moran, Will H. Low, and J. Alden Weir. In 1884 Weir's painting depicted a poor farmer or hunter seated in his rustic kitchen before an open fire, quite unconscious of the Christchild materializing in the smoky vapors. "Contentment is better than wealth" was the motto. Prang issued his cards in three forms: with silk fringe and tassels, beloved by Victorians; on heavy gilt-edged mounts; or plain.

An undated Prang card measuring about eight by five and one-half inches portrays Henry Wadsworth Longfellow sitting before a tiled fireplace. Gathered about him are three children listening as he tells them a bedtime story. In the lower left-hand corner are Longfellow's lines:

*Between the dark and the daylight,*
  *When the night is beginning to lower,*
*Comes a pause in the day's occupations*
  *That is known as the Children's Hour.*

On the reverse side, appropriately illustrated, is his poem "Christmas Bells."

For the Christmas of 1883, Isabella Maud Rittenhouse, of Cairo, Illinois, recorded in her journal the fact that she had received "about a peck of Christmas cards, the handsomest among them being one of Prang's, an immense thing, the back of which was imitation alligator-skin, and inside on one side a satin hand-painted sachet, on the other a dark rich painting with holly-berries all around it."

In 1893 the sight of shoppers gathered about the Christmas card counters of a bookstore in New York led a *Times* reporter to the office of L. Prang and Company in the same city. Mr. Kimball, one of the gentlemen in charge, smiled a little quizzically when asked if, as was reported, the use of Christmas cards was decreasing.

"Ten years ago," he said, "was the great boom in Christmas cards. At that time Prang and Company had the field practically to themselves in this country; now there are eight to ten competitors, and every one of us is doing a large business in these cards. That hardly seems like a decrease so much as a division, doesn't it? It is possible," he went on, "that the amount of the bill is re-

# REMEMBERING ONE'S FRIENDS AT CHRISTMAS

duced, but the country is getting as many cards. The price of them has much lessened. A former one-dollar one sells now for twenty-five cents, and a twenty-five cent one of a few years ago costs the buyer only five cents today.

"The system of prize cards has been given up, but every year sees more beautiful and artistic cards. Ten years ago, everybody bought fringed cards. Now one can't be given away. At that time, at our manufactory in Boston a hundred and eighty young women were employed doing nothing but putting fringe on the cards; today there is not one so engaged.

"Nothing has been more popular this year with us than violet and pansy calendars."

Also popular were die-cut booklets, shaped like such familiar objects as a watch, a banjo, or a candlestick. Among Prang designs were a Christmas mince pie and a plum pudding. "The shape booklets, as we call them, come chiefly from England and Germany," continued Mr. Kimball. "One of ours this year is this dipper," he said, showing a realistic tin drinking dipper whose bowl opened into the leaves of a poem, "The Old Tin Dipper." "And look at this pumpkin pie," he said merrily, showing the reporter that the triangular pieces were each little booklets containing Whittier's poem about that dish.

In Prang's chromolithographic process, the drawings were made on zinc plates instead of lithographic stones. Every tint used meant a separate drawing and a separate impression, and each color had to fit over the others "to a hair's nicety," as Prang's man put it, or the whole was spoiled. A book of color proofs showed the evolution of a design from the artist's sketch, through as many as twenty color printings, working from the lightest to the darkest colors, to the perfect finish.

As is often the case with excellence, Prang's cards were more expensive than those of his competition, much of it foreign. Popular taste being what it was, sales were often in inverse ratio to the cards' artistic merit. Within a few years, Prang, refusing to compromise his product, withdrew from the Christmas card business entirely. Today he is best remembered as a printmaker, a contemporary of Currier and Ives. Prang, using countless artists, including Winslow Homer, published more than two thousand different lithographs for the walls of Victorian homes. Among them were a number of Christmas prints, some used as premiums for the newspapers and magazines of the day. He is also remembered by a few oldsters as the manufacturer whose watercolors and crayons put art classes in public schools.

The Christmas card business was revolutionized by the postal card, a worldwide craze that can be traced in this country to Chicago's Columbian World's Fair in 1893. Since the postage required was one cent, a new Americanism entered the language. The "penny post card" was given a boost in 1898 by the introduction of Rural Free Delivery to isolated homes and farms across the country. In 1900 the half-tone photoengraving process, which had already created the illustrated newspaper, produced inexpensive photographic postcards. While Christmas and New Year's greetings printed on

# REMEMBERING ONE'S FRIENDS AT CHRISTMAS

government postals were as old as the 1870s, the idea did not apparently take the fancy of the public in those days. According to historian J. R. Burdick, postcard greetings were reborn in the middle 1890s, when people began to inscribe holiday sentiments on the new postal view cards. Publishers noted this and began to print such sentiments on their view cards, either as an overprint or as part of the design. Until World War I, the Christmas card trade was virtually monopolized by German postcard manufacturers.

Early in the new century, competition between postcard makers led to embossing, die-cut edges, and scented inks, as well as mechanical novelties. Little pull-tabs and revolving discs caused a Santa's head to shake or snow to fall. "Hold-to-light" cards made a Santa's eyes light up or his reindeer sleigh appear magically over snow-mantled chimney tops.

Large "installment post-card" pictures were mailed a card a day, until the recipients, usually children, had a complete picture of a Christmas tree or a St. Nicholas. Those being the days when the post office made deliveries on Christmas Day, grandfather could put the last card in the post box on Christmas Eve, and his grandchildren could put the final piece in place moments after the postman pulled the front doorbell on Christmas morning.

Another favorite type of card, allegedly invented to amuse children but probably equally appreciated by adults, was the "pop-up." When opened, it revealed a tableau that closely resembled a miniature stage, on which die-cut animals stood about the Holy Family, or a

frosty scene with children skating or amusing themselves about a snowman. One showed a fully detailed
chapel, complete with stained-glass windows, altar,
pews, and angels. Another publisher, striving to outdo all
the others, produced a three-inch-high Victorian Christmas tree with tiny wax candles that could actually be
burned—under parental supervision, we trust.

In 1909, after touring the world, Louis Prang passed
away at the age of eighty-five. The Christmas card, that
convenient conveyor of goodwill among men, was his
lasting gift to his adopted country.

By the turn of the century, with his simple push-button
camera and celluloid film, George Eastman had made
everybody a photographer. For the Christmas of 1902,
Eastman's Kodak Company shrewdly took advantage of
the postcard fad by offering postcard-stock photographic
paper on which amateur picture-snappers could print
their own negatives of their children grouped about the
Christmas tree. So popular was the idea that in 1906 Kodak advertised its own service of printing postcards from
its customers' negatives. The following year, when the
U.S. government liberalized the postal laws to allow the
inclusion of short messages on the address side of
postcards, the number of Christmas trees, stocking-hung
fireplaces, children, and toys that stood before father
and his camera increased again.

In those days, amateur photography was not without
its dangers. Magnesium flashpowder was a highly explo-
sive, dangerous substance that ignited in an instantane-
ous blast of brilliant light, and many accidents resulted

# REMEMBERING ONE'S FRIENDS AT CHRISTMAS

from its use. It also made candid pictures virtually impossible because of the glare, smoke, and smell it produced.

As with most other commodities, what was stylish in Christmas cards at one time could be out of fashion a few years later. Around 1915 there was a decline in personal photographic cards. At the same time, World War I abruptly cut off German postcard greetings, hastening a return to cards sent in envelopes. The majority of the new folder-type cards were printed in England or France, including the first boxes of cards that made their appearance about this time.

In the 1920s American greeting card companies recaptured the market. The ever-growing popularity of the custom continued, December after December, to increase the size of the avalanches of mail that the post office struggled to deliver in the last two weeks before Christmas—a fact to which subsequent generations of Superintendent Bells have testified.

## CHRISTMAS AT CHURCH

**T**he fires of
the old religious controversy
over Christmas observances
still burned high midway
through the nineteenth century.
For the Christmas of 1858,
John Udell, a Baptist born and raised in Connecticut, was
in New Mexico bound for California with other pioneers
in a pack train. On Christmas Eve in Albuquerque, he observed Mexicans performing a Nativity play in their
large Catholic Church. He found the idea of people
playing the parts of the Virgin Mary and the Apostles "ridiculous" and went on to record in his journal, "in the
eyes of us American Christians [Protestants], it was considered most blasphemous mockery."

Three years earlier, in 1855, Christmas Day fell on
Tuesday. The following day, *The New York Times* reported, "The churches of the Presbyterians, Baptists,

Methodists, &c., were not open. They do not accept the day as a holy one, but the Episcopal, Catholic and German churches were all open and decked with evergreens."

A sign that the denominational differences over Christmas could eventually be reconciled is found in the example of Dr. James Waddel Alexander, the son of a Presbyterian minister and himself pastor of the Fifth Avenue Presbyterian Church in New York City. On Christmas Day in 1838, he ventured to wish a correspondent a "Merry Christmas"—no small thing for a fervently pious Calvinist. Although his church was locked up tight on Christmas Day in 1851, the Reverend Dr. Alexander was drawn to explore those of the Christmas-keepers. The day, he wrote, "saw me in nine churches: St. Francis Xavier's, St. Patrick's Cathedral, St. Joseph's, St. Vincent de Paul, St. Somebody's (German), Bellows', Grace, Calvary, and Muhlenberg's Little Gothic Free Seat Chapel." The following year, his growing desire for some public observance of the day was openly expressed, only to be set aside in obedience to his ruling elders' orthodox Presbyterian tenets. It seems reasonable to assume that Dr. Alexander's aspirations played a part in the fact that on Christmas Day in 1854, 350 "urchins and urchinesses" assembled for cake and candy in a mission chapel of the Fifth Avenue Presbyterian Church.

Protestant Sunday schools adopted a lenient attitude toward the day earlier than the churches did. As early as 1846, the *Advocate,* a Philadelphia Methodist Sunday school publication, wished boys and girls a happy Christmas, but not, its editor warned, "a merry, foolish one devoted to mirth and trifling and mingled with sin." Even in the years after the Civil War, when the national Sunday school leadership generally countenanced the observance of Christmas, local opposition by the stricter Methodist brethren frequently had to be overcome.

In the Congregationalist denomination, each church had a large measure of independence. For instance, the First Congregational Church of Boston held a musical Christmas service in 1817. In 1859 the Congregational Church in Litchfield, Connecticut, ventured, not without protest from some members, to install Christmas greens. But the evergreen cross that some brave soul had placed above the pulpit had to come down before the service, although the rest of the decorations remained. When the minister attempted a Sunday school festival with a Christmas tree in his parsonage in 1867, the criticism was so strong that it was a decade before Litchfield was safe for Christmas again.

Very different was the state of affairs among the Episcopalians. It is claimed that the first Sunday school Christmas tree in this country was provided for a Christmas celebration at the Episcopal Church of the Holy Communion in New York City in 1847. According to Dr. Charles E. Tiffany's *History of the Protestant Episcopal Church,* Dr. William A. Muhlenberg initiated the children of his Sunday school into the joys of a Christmas tree loaded with gifts.

On the night after Christmas in 1884, a similar Christmas tree festival was held for the children of the Sunday school belonging to the First Reformed Episcopal Church in New York. There were tiny mites who could just lisp a few words; there were the usual irrepressible youths, clean and tidy for this occasion only; and there were pretty young girls of eighteen and twenty who were quite as interesting to many in the church.

"And now, my children," said the Reverend Thomas T. Sabine, who had been talking pleasantly and amusingly for some time, "dear Mr. Brown will talk to you for a little. I know he will have your ears and eyes, won't he, boys and girls?"

"Yes, sir," chirruped four hundred voices, and the Reverend O. F. Brown stood in front of the tree to speak, where the children could look at the tree and still appear to be regarding him. Mr. Brown told Hans Christian Andersen's story about a willful young tree that was discontented with its lot and envied the big fir trees. Then, when it became a big fir tree, it longed to develop into a Christmas tree. At last even this desirable condition was reached, but after a brief reign of glory it was stripped of its gifts and thrown into a garret to die miserably.

"That teaches us the lesson of contentment," said the reverend gentleman placidly. "It was very wrong to wish for so much, wasn't it, boys and girls?"

There was a pause, and a little four-year-old girl lisped forth, "Yes, sir."

"That was a very weak 'yes'," said Mr. Brown, shocked. "But it was very wrong, and don't forget it, please."

Then the children presented gifts to be sent to the welfare home on Randall's Island, a custom in vogue for three or four years, and which had served, said Mr. Sabine, to educate the children of the Sunday school to the fact that it is more blessed to give than to receive. "But," said good Mr. Sabine, as he noticed some dilapidated specimens, "don't give horses without legs and dolls without heads. The poor children want whole toys just as much as you do. Don't they, boys and girls?"

"Yes, sir," came the chorus.

Then came the real business of the evening, and it was hard to say whether the children found it more pleasing to give than to receive. Dolls, books, boxes of sweets, toys of all sorts, and more useful presents for the older children were distributed with wonderful recklessness. And all the time, Mr. Sabine told quaint little stories calculated to please juvenile minds, and the children roared with laughter. The Sunday school teachers flitted about like good spirits, dispensing pleasant smiles and happy words to their delighted charges. At last the big tree was bare, and as nothing further could be obtained from it, they left it to its fate.

Frequently church groups experimented with more Biblical substitutes for the Christmas tree, including evergreen-covered crosses, pyramids, wooden Jacob's ladders, and cardboard ships. But almost invariably, congregations went back to a tree the next year.

Sometimes Christmas observances exerted almost too much appeal. The presentation of Christmas trees covered with gifts created the Sunday school superintendents' problem of "Christmas bummers"—children who attended only during the holiday season in order to share in the fruits of the tree. Anne Gertrude Sneller, born in 1883 in New York State, recalled her childhood experiences with bummers in her evocative autobiography, *A Vanished World:* "Now it happened that a Sunday or two before Christmas, children would appear who had never been there before, but expressed their intention of being faithful comers thereafter. Somehow the present committee always failed to reckon with this influx although it was a fairly certain part of the Christmas season. There stood the Christmas trees. Here were the children—and no presents for them. Mother would come to Ethel and me and whisper, 'Little Gracie Drear and her little sister are here and there aren't any presents for them. You will have presents at home.' And into the outstretched hands of Gracie Drear, that well-named child, and Little Sister went our presents."

In New York City the Roman Catholics had a different problem. Mindful of the tradition that the Christ Child was born before daylight, they attended midnight mass on Christmas Eve. But by the 1870s the custom had to be abandoned because of drunken revelers who made the sacred services their last stop of the evening. The solution worked out was to postpone the first mass on Christmas Day until five o'clock in the morning when all the wassailers that were not in bed by that hour were usually guests at police stations. Thus an hour before dawn on Christmas morning in 1876, the city's fastest-growing denomination filled forty churches to overflowing.

# CHRISTMAS AT CHURCH

In the years ahead, countless midnight masses in other cities and towns also had to be rescheduled to five in the morning. Before that happened, Patrick Gallagher acquired poignant memories of a Christmas Eve service in Lancaster, Pennsylvania. According to Gallagher,

When I was eight, nine, ten, to walk a mile to church at 11 o'clock and to walk home at 1 o'clock in the morning was a very memorable occasion. Wondering whether I'd be able to stay awake during the mass was an excitement in itself. I kind of looked forward to the challenge.

I remember the way it felt to walk through the streets —sometimes on freshly packed snow—in the middle of the absolutely soundless night. We lived right on the edge of town so we didn't see very many other people until we got within four or five blocks of the church. That foot crunch and that clean air—cold air—would make the body feel a certain way. And it was all exaggerated by hunger.

Before the mass, we had to fast. If we ate supper we were not supposed to have anything to eat or drink during the evening. But throughout the evening my mother would be fixing the turkey for the next day. The aroma of all the fixins' would be throughout the house Christmas Eve. So my other specific recollection is one of intense hunger, walking to church through the cold night air—starving. Through the mass I tried to be reasonably devout. But I always knew my mother was going to break out the bird as soon as we got home; I have the most mouth-watering recollection of the way that the turkey and that plain bread filling would taste at two o'clock in the morning.

# CHRISTMAS AT CHURCH

Catholics were not the only churchgoers up before daylight. In Minnesota, after pancake breakfasts at about five o'clock, big families of Swedish Protestants bundled up against the cold, put hot bricks under blankets on sleigh floors, and, with harness bells jingling and torches flaring, drove through the pitch-black night to luminous candlelight services called *Julotta.* As they sang and prayed in their mother tongue, dawn broke. While singing *"Var Halsad"* ("Our Joy for this Morning") and *"Nar Jul Dajs Grimmer"* ("When Christmas Morn is Dawning"), sunlight filled the church and glistened on the snowbanks outside. Then straightaway they were off to home to milk their cows, sleighs skimming across the white snow like the long-gone swallows of summer.

By the nineteenth century, the Sunday school festival, with minor variations from place to place and from denomination to denomination, followed much the same pattern. As eager children entered the church door holding their parents' hands, they saw a big, present-loaded Christmas tree nearly as tall as the ceiling standing in one corner. Net stockings filled with nuts and candy, dolls, books, suspenders, mittens, and pocketknives hung from the tree and were piled about its base. Its branches were strung with strings of popcorn and cranberries, paper chains, and tin-foil tinsel, and a gold star was at the very top. Listen to Lewis Atherton's description of the scene in *Main Street on the Middle Border:*

## CHRISTMAS AT CHURCH

"Even the odor of the place seemed changed, a mixture of the smell of wet snow on clothing, of evergreens, of wax and tinsel, of oranges, all nicely mixed and flavored by drafts of hot air from stove or registers and the sharply biting cold which swept inside each time the door was opened."

Following an opening anthem and the saying of the Lord's Prayer, the superintendent greeted the scholars and guests. Then came singing, recitations, tableaux, and shadow pantomimes. Some children performed with aplomb, while others played their parts in an agony of trouser-hiking, belt-pulling, handkerchief-knotting embarrassment. A mere reading of the titles of some of the selections reminds one that the new Christmas was a product of Victorian romanticism. In the program at the Algona, Iowa, Congregational Church in 1886, little Georgie Horton recited "What Santa Claus Saw," and young Howard Robinson followed with "The Orphan's Christmas." Master Lee Reed then recited "My First Pants," and so it went until every youngster had performed. There were always as many parts as there were proud parents. Then came awards for Bible study and memorization. At a celebration in Winchester, Virginia, in 1869, the championship went to a boy who had learned 1863 verses during the year. And a little girl in the infant class won a doll as large as herself for memorizing 124 verses. When each child had received at least one gift from the illuminated tree, a hymn and the benediction closed the service—at which point everyone gave their wholehearted attention to tables overflowing with oranges and apples, pies and crullers, and other homemade treats.

A great deal of time was required for the preparation of elaborate Christmas pageants. Dr. Bruce Grove always remembered the many rehearsals at a little church five miles from his home at Muddy Creek Fork, Pennsylvania. From the time he and his brother were old enough to stand up and recite until they were in high school, there seemed to be no getting out of taking part. Going home from a rehearsal one night, alone in their father's sleigh, they both fell asleep. When they awoke at about three o'clock in the morning, they were safe at home. Their horse, Charlie, had pulled the sleigh into their barn.

In his unpublished autobiography, Ralph Flachman, born in Iowa at the turn of the century, recalled the days when church services held by immigrant congregations were still mostly in native tongues. "It was always my luck to have to speak my piece in German. With the folks always speaking English at home, it was difficult for me to memorize the piece. I stood up there and shook like a leaf when I gave the recitation."

Flachman also remembered, "A tree well lighted with candles, kerosene lamps and a wood stove contributed to the danger of fire. There were eight big kerosene lamps in the old Union Church, two pairs hung on ropes from the ceiling. When you pulled one pair down to light them, the other pair went up. We always had two people with a wet swab on a long stick to watch that the candles would not ignite the tree."

## CHRISTMAS AT CHURCH

Historian Carl Van Doren never forgot his first sight of Santa Claus at a church in a crossroads town on an Illinois prairie. He was four or five at the time. During the Sunday school festival, the sound of sleighbells was heard outside the church. There was a stirring among the congregation, particularly among the excited children, as the jangling bells got closer and closer, then were heard outside one wall. Suddenly the top part of a high window was pushed down, and a bearded, fur-coated Santa Claus made his way along a ladder that ran from the window to the top of a big chimney and fireplace prop at the front of the room. Frightened, little Carl hid his face in the lap of his grandmother, a grave, quiet woman, part New England and part Iroquois. Comforted by her, he looked up in time to see Santa Claus as he descended another ladder and emerged from the fireplace.

Once launched, the Protestant church Christmas was carried forward by an irresistible momentum. By the last decade of the nineteenth century, all the major Protestant denominations had adopted Christmas observances with the proverbial enthusiasm of the convert.

## Chapter 16

## GOING ALL OUT FOR CHRISTMAS

**C**hristmas, with
its emphasis on generosity
and goodwill, provides
its enthusiasts with broad
opportunities for
self-expression. Let me begin
this collection of tales about wholehearted efforts on behalf of the day with a few examples of gigantic edibles.

For Christmases at Mount Vernon, Martha Washington used to make a cake by this recipe, preserved by one
of her grandchildren: "Take 40 eggs and divide the
whites from the youlks and beat them to a froth. Start
working 4 pounds of butter to a cream and put the whites
of eggs to it a spoonfull at a time until it is well work'd.
Then put 4 pounds sugar finely powder'd to it in the
same manner. Then put in the youlks of the eggs and 5
pounds of flower and five pounds of fruit. 2 hours will

bake it. Add one-half ounce of mace, one nutmeg, half a pint of wine and some fresh brandy."

At the Christmas fair at St. John's Church in Bridgeport, Connecticut, in 1871, it took four strong men to carry the chicken pot pie that was served. It contained one hundred chickens. There is no record of how many men, women, and children it took to consume it.

Not quite so big, but large by most standards, was the mince pie served in a railroad baggage car on Christmas Day in 1901. The occasion was the third annual Christmas festival of the crew of the Pennsylvania Railroad's train number 273–283, which ran between Point Pleasant, New Jersey, and Jersey City. Three years before, the crew found that the holiday schedule called for their train to leave Point Pleasant early in the morning, return at noon, and lay over until evening. With the aid of their wives, they organized a Christmas dinner to fill the afternoon. They enjoyed it so much and talked about it so much that the next year the train's passengers made so many donations to the event that the men set a table and invited a number of other train crews to join them.

In 1901 innumerable commuters and almost every station along the line contributed something: several roasted turkeys, all manner of side dishes and delicacies, a Christmas tree and other greens, and enough cigars to keep the men supplied for a month or more. When all the gifts and about thirty invited guests were squeezed in, the baggage car was taxed to the limit of its capacity.

Before the train left Jersey City, a pie company's horse-drawn wagon delivered a steaming mince pie four feet in diameter and six inches deep, ordered by a wealthy regular passenger. The enormous tin plate had had to be specially made. As everyone at the railroadmen's feast agreed, it was a huge success.

For the Thanksgiving of 1909, the bakers of Jersey City and New York decided to send President William Howard Taft a similarly great mince pie. Mysteriously, without so much as a crumb of evidence remaining, it disappeared somewhere between New York and the capital. At Christmas, it was decided to send a replacement. The bakers, not taking any chances, packed it in a heavy wooden box, four feet square, nailed with tenpenny nails; and all the way from New York to Washington four delegates of the bakers' union sat on the cover, one on each corner. The nation's largest chief executive enjoyed the nation's largest pie.

That same year, a giant plum pudding was produced and consumed in Wall Street. In order that the Christmas spirit might have full sway, business on the Consolidated Exchange was suspended half an hour early the Friday before Christmas. Half a dozen football teams scrimmaged with gusto on the floor of the exchange. After they had finished tackling each other, the traders adjourned to the restaurant in the exchange where they tackled a six-hundred-pound plum pudding. They made away with it in short order.

This country's largest Christmas confection on record is a candy elephant made and exhibited by a Reading, Pennsylvania, candy maker in 1878. His hard candy creation was five feet high, seven and one-half feet long, and two and one-half feet wide.

On Christmas Eve in 1893, Sampson Getholtz, a Newcastle, Pennsylvania, farmer, decided to surprise his family by impersonating Santa Claus and sliding down an old-fashioned chimney. He made the passage all right until he reached the center of the chimney, where he stuck fast. He yelled for aid, but the other members of his family did not recognize his muffled voice and ran from the house terror-stricken. Neighbors were summoned, but it was only after a long time and much difficulty that Getholtz made himself known. The chimney was torn down level with the roof, a rope was lowered, and by the united efforts of three men, Getholtz was pulled out.

In New York City in 1911, another Santa Claus stuck fast in a chimney. All day long on December 24, as he finished his own preparations for Christmas, Alderman Frank J. Dotzler had looked forward to playing Santa Claus for all the children of his neighborhood.

Dotzler was well fitted for the part, for he weighed in the neighborhood of 375 pounds. There was the rub. The property man who set the stage for the Christmas festival in the yard of 244 East Third Street forgot what a big man the alderman was, or else planned a joke that was really unkind.

A chimney of tin and wood was built and, inside, a ladder was placed for Dotzler to use to come down to the

# GOING ALL OUT FOR CHRISTMAS

sidewalk to greet the children and distribute the contents of his pack. About nine o'clock the play began, and from a hidden point Dotzler entered the chimney. When he did not appear at the opening at the bottom, an investigation was begun, and it was found that Santa Claus was stuck fast in the middle of the chimney and could not get up to freedom or down to finish his part. The chimney had to be cut to pieces to release him.

Dotzler's assistants in the Santa Claus play were his fellow members of the East Side Fat Man's Club, and as none of them was qualified to make a successful descent through the chimney, that part of the program was abandoned.

Then two of the smallest members, Phil Fecher, at 240 pounds, and Martin Max, at 235 pounds, got hold of a peddler's pushcart. With Dotzler sitting inside on a chair, surrounded with his sacks of candy, oranges, and nuts, his fellow fat men drew the cart through the streets, stopping here and there to distribute the Christmas cheer to the children that flocked behind by the hundreds.

You never had to be rich to enjoy Christmas, but enjoy it the rich did.

On Christmas Eve in 1886, Philadelphian George W. Childs, the millionaire publisher of *The Public Ledger*, stayed at his office late. For several hours he was steadily engaged in stuffing and sealing envelopes. On the desk before him were piles of crisp, new banknotes: a small pile of five-hundred-dollar notes, a very respectable pile of one-hundred-dollar notes, an even larger one of fifties, and a large box of ten-dollar bills. On a stand next to the desk was a box crammed with envelopes bearing names and a note in one corner saying "With the best wishes of Mr. Childs."

The newspaperman was engaged in his usual Christmas work of sending presents to every one of his employees and other persons, many of them poor and needy families. It was tedious work, but Mr. Childs did not seem to mind it. Once he made a mistake and picked up two fifty-dollar bills instead of one, as they were stuck together. Looking at the name of one of his printers on the envelope, he said, "Well, he buried a child this year—I guess he'll need it." Few received less than fifty dollars. In an adjoining room two men were busy packaging books and other gifts. Including the envelopes to his employees, Mr. Childs gave away $25,000 that Christmas.

In New York on Christmas Eve in 1889, a surprise masked ball was given for Mrs. William Astor by seventy of her friends under the leadership of Mrs. Bradley Martin. The ladies wore white satin dominoes, an old-fashioned masquerade costume consisting of a robe with a hood and a half-mask, trimmed with holly. Each gentleman had made a Santa Claus of himself, donning a long brown mantle and a cap trimmed with white fur. By a piece of strategy, the ballroom at the Astor mansion on Fifth Avenue had been elaborately decorated without Mrs. Astor's knowledge. In the three drawing rooms burned grate fires, and cut flowers banked the mantels. The doorway into the ballroom was draped with evergreens, and in the gallery overlooking the room, musicians were tuning up. There were masses of holly and laurel everywhere, and snowballs of white carnations, and white violets almost completely covered the silver candelabra. In the alcove between the ballroom and the dining room was suspended a big snow-capped Santa Claus dressed in fur. Two rows of thirty-six small silk and satin stockings of varied colors were stretched across the ebony fireplace, and representatives of Santa Claus had filled them with bonbons and toys. A large bough of mistletoe hung from the balcony.

Immediately after their surprise arrival the friends began a cotillion. The first part was danced in costume. During a pause, a floral sleigh of smilax and holly, bound with broad ribbons of red, green, and gold, was pushed about the ballroom. It was filled with beautiful miniature Santa Clauses, harlequins, and all sorts of expensive favors. Supper was served at twelve-thirty and afterward the cotillion resumed.

In 1893 financial mogul John Pierpont Morgan was the Santa Claus who made Christmas Day a happy time for two hundred homeless boys temporarily cared for at an institution. Mr. Morgan had instructed the superintendent to provide a first-class dinner for the boys at his expense. On Christmas afternoon the boys had all the turkey, vegetables, pies, cakes, and ice cream that they could possibly eat. If he had been present, "J.P." would have seen how heartily the boys enjoyed his hospitality and with what tremendous enthusiasm they sang together at the close, "For He's a Jolly Good Fellow."

On other Christmases Morgan enjoyed having his librarian, Miss Belle da Costa Greene, read aloud Dickens's *A Christmas Carol* from the original manuscript, part of his collection. As the red-letter day approached again in 1911, Morgan had a new toy: a home movie projector. On Christmas Day, "motion views" were shown following dinner at his residence on Madison Avenue. Recently returned from abroad, Mrs. Morgan was hostess for a small family dinner, after which about fifty relatives and friends, including many children, were asked in to see a *Kinemacolor* motion picture of the coronation of George V and Queen Mary. In addition to the coronation, there were color movies of the launching of the steamship *Olympic*, a sunset on the Nile, a stag hunt in Exmoor, England, and views of Italy.

Several other novel entertainments were given that year by members of New York society. On Christmas afternoon in the drawing room of Mrs. Edwin R. Hewitt, an old-fashioned Christmas masque was performed, written by Mrs. Hewitt herself and entitled "Time and Eternity." Numerous adults as well as twenty children took part, each wearing a fancy costume. Ashley Cooper Hewitt, Mrs. Hewitt's eldest son, played Father Time, Miss Candace Hewitt assumed the role of Life, Miss Lucy Hewitt was Eternity's Child, and Abram S. Hewitt (who had defeated young Theodore Roosevelt for mayor in 1886) played the part of the Magpie.

Two days later, another children's masque was pre-

# GOING ALL OUT FOR CHRISTMAS

sented at a party given in the Washington Square home of Mrs. Benjamin S. Guiness. A series of tableaux was presented in which children took the parts of the subjects of many well-known paintings, including Gainsborough's *The Blue Boy,* Sir Joshua Reynolds's *Age of Innocence,* and Hans Holbein the Younger's *Henry VIII.*

On December 23, 1912, the combination third-birthday party and Christmas party for Vinson Walsh McLean, the son of Mr. and Mrs. Edward Beale McLean, was celebrated at the home of his parents in Washington, D.C. It exceeded in lavishness any children's entertainment ever given in Washington, a city that had been noted for luxurious children's Christmas parties for more than half a century. For a good three hours, the sixty young guests were in a fairyland that exceeded the wildest dreams of even the most sophisticated children present.

A great Christmas tree stood in the McLeans' largest drawing room. It presented a dazzling spectacle, lit from top to bottom with fancifully shaped electric lights. At its base were leopards; soldiers in uniforms that had been made by regular military tailors; dolls dressed by the finest dressmakers in Washington, New York, and Paris; horns, drums, pianos, doll carriages, bats and balls, and horses almost as large as real ponies, covered with the natural skins of the animals. There were also a bull moose and a reindeer, stuffed by skilled taxidermists. For the little girls, there were beautiful pieces of jewelry that they would treasure all their lives. Probably the present that Master McLean and his young friends liked best of all was a real live donkey and a beautiful cart.

Everyone invited brought the little host some precious gift, while he, with all the naturalness of a baby, clung to a rubber ball. Not the least wonderful sight of the celebration was a table with a mammoth birthday cake on it, gleaming under electric candles. Nearby was a smaller Christmas tree, laden with more beautiful toys and glistening in the reflected light of a big pond, where there were ducks and boats and all sorts of mechanical toys, and in which swam real goldfish.

The Russian ambassador, the Belgian and Swedish ministers, assorted viscounts and viscountesses, and a glittering representation of Washington society were there to see the children enjoy the wondrous scene. While the children dined at their fairylike table and Master Vinson Walsh McLean cut his birthday cake, the elder folk enjoyed a more substantial repast in an adjoining drawing room.

Another story: One Christmas morning in California during the 1880s, Mrs. George Hearst, wife of the millionaire senator who had made his money in mining, had their green lawn covered with snow in the form of several inches of crushed ice, just to make a house guest from Vermont feel at home.

One more: For the Christmas of 1892, Jeremiah Nunan, the richest man in Jacksonville, Oregon, gave his wife, Delia, a prefabricated twenty-two-room mansion. Ordered from the catalog of a firm in Knoxville, Tennessee, the parts—lacking only the foundation, roof, and chimney—were shipped in fourteen boxcars. The present came complete with draperies, carpets, gaslights, wallpaper, plumbing, and a foreman named Big Mick, who hired local labor for fifty cents per day.

From colonial times onward, the Moravians in eastern Pennsylvania had made more of Christmas than any other religious denomination in the country. Although they were among the first to embrace the Christmas tree custom, the Moravians' particular passion was the *putz*, an elaborate crèche in a miniature naturalistic landscape that they constructed beneath their Christmas trees. In the Moravian communities of Bethlehem and Lititz, the custom can be traced back to the eighteenth century. By the 1840s even the humblest Moravian home had a little table covered with a white cloth and a creditable artistic scene of wax shepherds tending their sheep on moss-covered hilltops created from small piles of rocks and dirt. The little scene was generally backed by evergreen branches, from which tin stars and choirs of wax angels were suspended, and it was illuminated by beeswax candles in tin holders.

By the very nature of the fact that they were labors of love, taking weeks of evening work, putzes invariably became ever larger and more elaborate productions. They were copied from nature by skilled craftsmen, with extraordinary attention paid to detail and realism. In one case, in Lancaster, mountains were achieved with an estimated half-ton of rocks. Carefully selected upside-down tree stumps were used to create the grottolike stable where the Christ Child was born. By the 1870s in many cases putzes had grown as large as the size of a parlor would permit, and sometimes were set among mountains five feet high, with real water lakes, cascading mountain streams, and waterfalls—ingeniously self-feeding or else fed from a cistern in an upstairs room. In Moravian communities, Christmas Eve was the great putz-seeing time. All homes held open house, and everybody went to see everybody else's handiwork. The family that, by consensus, had the outstanding putz could enjoy the fame for twelve months.

In the small city of Lancaster, putz building spread beyond the Moravians, and secular subject matter joined the biblical scenes. Men vied with each other for supremacy in mechanical invention. Ingenious crank and clockwork devices turned windmills, powered tiny sawmills, and moved trains, boats, and carriages through a Lilliputian world. In 1876 John Rohrer had a Christmas tree as high as the ceiling of his handsome residence, laden with paper and glass ornaments. Beneath it was a pond filled with live fish, a complete farm, bridges, mountains, and watercourses. But the extraordinary scene was on the other side of the drawing room. On a large table were arranged perhaps a hundred moving figures: a cat swallowing a mouse, a monkey playing a hand organ, an entire orchestra of cats playing violins, a man playing a banjo, dancers dancing, ice skaters skating on a mirror rink, horses racing along pulling carriages, a couple on a seesaw, a miniature mill—all moved by a little steam engine, which also made a hand organ play perpetual music. Mr. Rohrer had erected this Rube Goldberg invention himself, somehow getting all the hidden pulleys to perform their contrary and intricate motions.

Another example of extraordinary effort is the story of Mrs. Joseph Able, a Christmas artist working in the German Valley area of eastern Pennsylvania from the latter 1890s to about 1910. Mrs. Able is remembered as a tall, heavy woman who had no time for the tiny figures that her neighbors put under their trees. She preferred to make life-size figures for her Nativity scene. She had to make a small concession when it came to the size of her camels, but she made full-size sheep and donkeys, constructed on wood frames sturdy enough that children could sit on them.

Each year Mrs. Able started to set up her display in November, using the first floor of her farmhouse, with the exception of the kitchen. The furniture was removed to the kitchen and back porch. The parlor was devoted to a representation of the stable and manger scene. Other rooms provided a setting for the Magi, the shepherds, the angels, and various animals that wouldn't fit into the crowded stable. Though Mrs. Able was a completely untrained artist, her people and animals were remarkably real. She was able to make, for instance, a donkey so lifelike and natural in its stance that people almost expected it to twitch its ears and walk away.

Despite her veneration of Mary, Mrs. Able had little

time for Joseph. While he was among her figures, visitors usually found him with his face turned toward the wall, or else consigned to the kitchen, depending on her convictions of the moment. She felt her display should rightly be placed in her church, but since the church was small, permission for the display was annually denied, to Mrs. Able's considerable and forcefully expressed annoyance.

Her outsize crèche figures were famous and a recognized part of Christmas in her region. People traveled for miles to see her display and, if truth be told, to enjoy listening to her colorful commentary, spontaneous and unrestrained, that accompanied each showing. After her death, the big figures were thrown away, but they are still recalled each Christmas in the memories of those who can remember seeing them as children and marveling at the skill that went into their creation.

On a farm, Christmas morning or not, there are chores that have to be done. This fact led to a unique custom observed in Pulaski County in mountainous southwest Virginia, in the middle of the last century. As Christmas approached, a farmer would issue an invitation to all his neighbors that he and his wife would hold an open house Christmas Day. To no one's surprise, it began at three o'clock in the morning, at which time the neighbors arrived, children included, and spent three hours socializing over eggnog. Promptly at six o'clock, a huge farm breakfast was served.

Each family then returned home to attend to regular morning chores. After these were taken care of, they returned and the party continued with a shooting match for the men, a bountiful, game-rich Christmas dinner, and a religious service in the afternoon consisting of Bible reading, prayers, and hymns. Since everyone had been up half the night on Christmas Eve, they left in time to feed the stock and get early to bed on Christmas night.

Early in this century, across the continent in San Diego, California, the elaborate decorating of the stalls at the city market was becoming a Christmas tradition. On Christmas Eve in 1904, there were many delightful displays at the Bay City Market, but the one that caught the eye of virtually everyone was at a large butcher shop belonging to a hardy gentleman appropriately named Hardy. Two immense dressed hogs, one weighing 642 pounds, the other a tad over 628, guarded the entrance. One had been raised by a farmer, and the other had been fattened by Mr. Hardy himself. A giant swordfish, caught a week before and kept in cold storage for this display, and a 425-pound deep sea bass were other conversation pieces. On the counter of the pork stall stood a representation of Santa Claus and his sleigh. But instead of reindeer, he was driving a team of six dressed pigs that looked good enough to eat without cooking. In front of the poultry stall was a lighted Christmas tree hung with dressed poultry. At another counter, there were many artistic decorations rendered in colored lard, among them portraits of Teddy Roosevelt, Washington, and Lincoln. The festive market in general, and Mr. Hardy's premises in particular, were crowded until very late in the evening by overloaded basket-bearing shoppers and Christmas-present-laden sightseers, all in the best of humor.

When it came to such old-fashioned decorating for Christmas, some ideas were touching in their simplicity as well as in their sincerity. On December 19, 1908, in New York City, the distinguished members of the Queensboro Bridge Celebration Committee met and announced plans to decorate the enormously intricate steelwork bridge then nearing completion. On Christmas morning, huge stockings were to be filled with good things to eat and then hung low enough to be within reach of the boat hooks of tugboat men. Besides the fat stockings, scores of sou'westers were to be strung along the bridge for the rivermen. To add to the joy of the occasion, a few photographs of girls willing to marry seafaring husbands would decorate the bridge within reach of eligible hands.

Not every tree decorated at Christmastime in the old days was an evergreen. In Little Germany, on the east side of New York, on Christmas Eve in 1874, a reporter

# GOING ALL OUT FOR CHRISTMAS

saw a scene he could hardly believe. He was attracted to the sight of a strange, gigantic Christmas tree as tall as the houses. From afar, it appeared to be lighted by flashing torches. On closer examination, it proved to be a butcher's sign giving notice of his holiday wares in unique fashion. Pine branches were fastened to the naked limbs of a tree, and rabbits, poultry, links of sausage, and torches were hung all over it. With a ladder that reached the lower limbs, a boy could climb to the very top to bring customers any game they might fancy. It was a shop in the air, as well as a Christmas tree, and it made the whole neighborhood bright and cheery.

A somewhat similar tree was recorded in Marion, Ohio, for the Christmas of 1920. It stood behind the home of Warren G. Harding. So many people had showered the President-elect with holiday game that Mrs. Harding hardly knew what to do. Turkey, opossums, capons, wild ducks, and geese by the hundredweight had been delivered in profusion. In the cold, clear air, one of the backyard apple trees fairly bent under the weight of the dinners hanging from its limbs.

One of the most exciting Christmas trees ever seen was brought before the longing gaze of children at New York's Trinity Church on the afternoon before Christmas in 1886. An eager crowd completely filled the evergreen-decorated sanctuary. Following the service, an immense Christmas tree was rolled in, illuminated by upward of two hundred gas jets, all ablaze. The perfectly proportioned tree was actually a tree-shaped construction of gas pipes to which green boughs had been carefully wired, and every branch was laden with gifts for the children.

On New Year's Eve in 1879, Thomas Edison demonstrated his light bulb to the public for the first time in Menlo Park, New Jersey. Only three years later, in 1882, the first Christmas tree illuminated by electric light bulbs was in the New York City home of the president of the Edison electric company. In 1884 the first electrically illuminated public tree appeared at a festivity for children. The huge Christmas tree stood loftily in the First Reformed Episcopal Church in New York. On the night after Christmas, loaded with gifts of every description, it turned red, and green, and blue, and white, while four hundred youthful voices longed to cry "Oh!" and didn't dare because they were singing a hymn in church.

More than one thousand miles from those big-city Christmas trees, during a winter in the 1870s, two cowboys were holed up like hermits in a dugout shanty along the snow-covered banks of Bonte Creek in Wyoming, forty miles from Fort Fetterman, the nearest civilization. William Hooker and Nick Huber had little except their internal clocks to inspire them to celebrate Christmas. Neither had seen a calendar in a year. As they talked about Christmas, they weren't sure how close it might be. Only Hooker was sure it was December. After several days of talking about it, one morning he announced to his partner that he was going to the fort to find out what date it really was. He was sure from the way he felt that it was very close to Christmas.

Trotting through the snow like an Indian, Hooker

reached the tiny settlement outside Fort Fetterman at eight that night. In the general store, as he was buying a skinning knife as a present for Huber, he was shocked to learn that it was Christmas night. Later, Christmas or not, he was denied entrance to the fort. He spent the rest of the bitter-cold night huddled in a blanket among box elders along the creek. Staying the day after Christmas in town, he left on the morning of the twenty-seventh and only reached home late in the evening of the twenty-eighth, his return trip slowed by cold and by the weight of sixty pounds of supplies. A surprise awaited him: He found his partner with a Christmas tree. Nick Huber had been traveling too—more than fifty miles upcountry to Laramie Peak, where evergreens grew. His pine tree was decorated with German-style paper flowers impro vised from white, brown, and red soap wrappers. The normally taciturn "bullwhacker" had worked as a young man in his uncle's toy factory in Nuremberg in his native Germany. With his jackknife he had whittled a jumping jack and a whistle as presents for Hooker. Years later, William Hooker recalled that he had never had the nerve to tell his friend that, in reality, they celebrated Christmas three days late that year.

In 1895 George Washington Vanderbilt, the thirty-three-year-old grandson of railroad baron Commodore Vanderbilt, chose the Christmas holidays for the house-warming of his newly built mansion, Biltmore House, near Asheville, North Carolina. To celebrate the occasion, he and his young wife, Edith, had one of the largest Christmas trees that the world had yet seen. All the im-

# GOING ALL OUT FOR CHRISTMAS

mediate members of the Vanderbilt family were invited, and they arrived in private railway cars bringing with them an army of servants and trunks full of presents.

The gala party on Christmas Eve was described in *The Asheville News and Hotel Reporter*:

> On Tuesday evening the guests gathered in the banquet hall where there was a Christmas tree forty feet high, beautifully decorated. Under the tree was a round table piled high with gifts, which the guests exchanged with one another. The Imperial Trio furnished music for the occasion, and the rich costumes of the ladies, the soft lights and the tastefully draped garlands of evergreen and mistletoe, interspersed with shining leaves and red berries of the holly created a scene beautiful to look upon.

At eleven o'clock the next morning, the employees of the estate and their families were welcomed to the mansion by its genial young owner and his wife, a lifelong helpmate in all his projects. The distribution of presents to the servants was made by Mr. Vanderbilt, assisted by several of his guests.

A huge tree and a Christmas tree party for the staff became a tradition at Biltmore House. On Christmas afternoon in 1905, Mr. and Mrs. Vanderbilt provided a party for nearly a thousand children of Biltmore estate employees in the banquet hall of the château. The girls received dresses; the boys, suits of clothes. Over five hundred pounds of candy were distributed, as were many wagonloads of oranges, apples, and fruits.

# Going All Out for Christmas

The big tree that year was again lighted with hundreds of candles. Mrs. Vanderbilt preferred them to the five hundred newly fashionable electric lights that had been wired to the Christmas trees at the house in 1900.

Erecting such enormous Christmas trees presented interesting engineering problems. An account from Coronado, California, gives a good idea of the difficulties involved. Early on the morning of December 23, 1902, the gigantic tree for the children's party at the Hotel del Coronado arrived outside the rambling, 750-room clapboard hostelry by the sea. Fifteen men "yeo-heaved and yeo-hoed" the tree up the steps of the porch, where a block and tackle was attached and it was dragged through the big doors. The trunk measured fourteen inches in diameter at the butt, and the only way of sufficiently compressing its branches to get it through the doors was to wrap them tightly with ropes.

When the tree was finally in the hotel's huge ballroom, and a block and tackle had been put in place forty feet above the floor, all hands heaved with a will. Up went the tree a foot or two—and then the heavy manila rope broke. Another rope was attached, and a double tackle was tried. The anchor rope of one of the blocks snapped. Mr. Lucas, the hotel manager, undaunted by this series of accidents, had a chain attached to the dome of the ballroom eighty feet above the floor, and another attempt was made. Not until a late hour that night was the tree finally in an upright position. Its dimensions were the wonder of all: thirty-three feet high, with a spread of twenty-six feet at the widest part. The following morning it was loaded with candles, tinsel, colored balls, and several hundred toys.

In 1912 a committee of private citizens conceived the idea of giving New York City a giant electrically lighted outdoor Christmas tree, and the idea of community Christmas trees was born. To celebrate the occasion of their tree's lighting, a festival of international Christmas music was planned for Christmas Eve.

Shortly after noon on Saturday, December 20, an evergreen of magnitude corresponding to its advance publicity arrived at Madison Square Park, at Fifth Avenue and Twenty-third Street, hauled on a contractor's horse-drawn steel girder truck. The big pine was sixty-three feet high, its huge trunk was eighteen inches in diameter, and each of its lower branches had a sweep of twenty feet when the tree was finally set upright. The Adirondack club that had donated the tree had carefully selected the largest and most beautiful tree its members could find in that forested upstate region. A large crowd, including reporters and newspaper cameramen with their flashpowder, was on hand to watch. A crowd of workmen got busy with ropes, timbers, and guy wires. Several tall trees growing in the park were used as derricks to haul the great conifer upright. A six-foot hole had been dug in the center of the park, and into it, with extraordinary effort, the tree was set. Twenty-five men and four bosses were required to complete the job, which took until midnight. Then a big block of concrete was poured to hold the tree firm in all kinds of weather. Beginning early Monday morning, electricians from the city's Edison electric company, which donated the more than six thousand feet of wire and the 2,300 eight-candlepower lights, undertook the wiring of the huge tree.

At 1:10 A.M. on the morning of December 24, as the tree stood dark and still in the center of the park bordered by the imposing silhouettes of 1912-style skyscrapers, the weatherman began putting the finishing touches in place as he shook the feathery flakes of New York's first snowstorm of the winter out of the sky. Throughout the night and morning, until 3:40 in the afternoon it snowed at the rate of almost an inch an hour—11.8 inches in all. As night fell, with the sound of snow shovels heard in all directions, a large crowd of happy people was quietly gathering for the tree-lighting festival. At 4:50 P.M., 450 chimes from the adjacent Metropolitan Insurance Building tower sounded the first notes of Christmas music. Ten minutes later, as the last note of the chimes was followed by a moment of absolute silence, bells all over the city and across the East River in Brooklyn began jubilantly pealing Christmas anthems in a festival of bells that lasted half an hour.

The bright evening star that had been seen in the southern skies for a week appeared, peering down over the Flatiron Building into Madison Square. The star twinkled as stars only twinkle in clear, cold, winter weather, and the moon spread its pale light abroad, lighting the scene like a theater. Suddenly, at 5:30, just as the last church bell fell silent, the heavenly star was blotted out by the only cloud in the sky. Moments later, another star appeared. Dim at first, it became increasingly brilliant. It was the Star of Bethlehem, atop the Tree of Light. At the same time, from north and south, east and west, the sound of trumpets was heard. As both the incandescent star and the brass fanfare from *Lohengrin* reached their most electrifying point, the colored lights on the branches below winked into being, one cluster after another, until the whole tree was aglow, a pyramid of red, blue, green, and white lights.

Applause burst from the ten thousand spectators, and almost simultaneously there was a burst of song from many throats. To the south of the tree, a bandstand had been erected, wired not only for electric lighting but for electric heating as well, and in it were arrayed singers and musicians. From the moment that the tree was lighted until exactly midnight, there was a continual program of carols and instrumental music. The stillness of the night, aided by the carpet of snow, made it possible to hear individual voices distinctly at the extreme edge of the park and beyond. The music could be heard half a mile away in the shopping district and helped to attract the crowds that came and went during the evening.

From 5:30 to 7:00 P.M., choruses and singing societies, including the MacDowell chorus of the Schola Cantorum, a chorus of red-cheeked Welshmen, and a chorus from a Negro settlement house, sang Christmas carols. Everyone was asked to join the singing in his native tongue, and a great many did. From 7:00 to 8:30 P.M., well-known soloists sang carols, among them "The First Noel," the old French carol "Shepherds Leave Your

# GOING ALL OUT FOR CHRISTMAS

Flocks," the German "From Highest Heaven to Earth We Come," "While Shepherds Watched Their Flocks By Night," and "Good King Wenceslas." Then "Oh, Little Town of Bethlehem" was sung in a clear tenor voice by Ludwig Hess, who was greeted by the greatest applause of the evening, and he repeated parts of the song several times. He sang through a megaphone, his breath billowing out the big end of the megaphone in vapor.

Throughout the park, on every path, to a large degree unmindful of the cold, stood a reverent audience, applauding the concert and praising the idea of a public Christmas tree. It was one of the best-humored and most orderly crowds ever assembled. At about nine o'clock, word was passed to a policeman, who took it to one of the attendants at the bandstand, that an old woman in the crowd was suffering from the cold. The attendant hurried to the woman and invited her to the music stand, where the electric heaters had been installed for the benefit of the performers. The woman hovered over a heater, and when she had thawed out she said, "I want to stay until midnight and hear them sing 'My Country 'Tis of Thee.' I want to sing with them. I'm so happy here." It was arranged that the woman should stay, and an escort of four Boy Scouts took her to her home in Brooklyn afterward. Throughout the evening, a large contingent of scouts performed duties, from getting planks for women and children to stand on to keep their feet from getting cold, to running messages from the bandstand to singers and musicians keeping warm in a church across the street while waiting their turn to perform.

Christmas shoppers bearing packages, families with children, sober citizens and citizens not so sober, ministers, mechanics, groups of pretty girls, and roving crowds of urchins made up the ever-shifting kaleidoscopic throng of people who came and went, some staying half an hour and others the entire evening. Here and there, some members of the crowd warmed their hands over charcoal and coke burners used by workmen in winter.

The comments of the people, many of whom had journeyed all the way from Brooklyn, the Bronx, and nearby New Jersey towns, were often picturesque.

*"Ach, das kostet Geld!"* exclaimed a stout, thrifty German housewife to her red-nosed mate.

"Some piece of timber, all right," commented one of two boyish-looking sailors from Wyoming, miles from home. Most Americans, however, used the phrase "Ain't it pretty!" to express their rapture.

"The Almighty put snow on the tree to make it prosper," said one old woman who hobbled along on crutches.

From nine o'clock until midnight a brass band played Bach chorales, hymns, famous marches, national anthems, and folk music from many nations. One man in the crowd, his eyes glistening as the band played *"Ein Feste Burg ist Unser Gott"* ("A Mighty Fortress Is Our God"), when asked if he were German, replied with a thick German accent, "I am American!" More than five hundred spectators who witnessed the first lighting of the tree remained and were part of the crowd of more

# GOING ALL OUT FOR CHRISTMAS

than two thousand at midnight. Exactly at twelve o'clock the band crashed out the strains of "My Country 'Tis of Thee," and the crowd around the tree joined in the singing with patriotic fervor.

Taking one last wondering look at the biggest, most colorful Christmas tree the world had ever seen, people headed happily for home. The tree remained lighted throughout the night, until dawn on Christmas morning, and every night until New Year's, the lights going out for the last time as daylight broke on the first day of the new year.

One last story: A few days before Christmas in 1901, it was snowing briskly, and darkness had already fallen as throngs of homebound businessmen surged along Nassau Street near City Hall at the lower end of Manhattan. A snow squall had come on suddenly, covering the street with half an inch of slippery snow. Small boys were making a slide down the steeply pitched hill on Nassau Street. In a twinkling, it took on a surface of icy slickness. After a quick, running start, the participants slid nimbly, standing up, using nothing for their swift descent but their own leather-soled shoes. As brokers, lawyers, and counting-house clerks paused to watch the fun, the parallel lines of spectators grew longer and thicker until the white pathway between the sidelines looked like a tunnel. Young men and apple-cheeked office boys joined in the sport. Then along came a gray-haired old fellow grown stout with age. As he paused at the brow of the slope, sizing up the situation, a small lad sped past him, struck the ice gracefully, and disappeared down the hill between the black lines of onlookers. The old man's eyes brightened, and he started to button up his coat. Then he shook his head sadly, as if deciding he was too old to take the risk. More boys and one or two men, chuckling with mirth, took the slide. Then the old boy's jaw shut firmly; he tossed aside his newspaper, and with two or three light skips, he started down the glassy chute.

Biff! Bang! A youngster lammed him with a rolled up newspaper, while another banged him on the back as he shot by. With his arms out like a chicken running across the barnyard and his feet wide apart, the old gentleman kept to the middle of the course and landed safely near the curb at Maiden Lane. Then he straightened up and fairly gurgled with glee as he turned and saw that younger men than himself had failed to keep their footing.

"D'ye see me take that slide just like a boy?" he asked a nearby man in one of those sudden bursts of confidence that are often begotten by excitement. "By thunder! Do you know I ain't had a slide like that for nearly forty years? Honestly, I didn't know I could still do it. You've got to have the knack, you know. Feet wide apart, and your legs bent at the knees—body bent over a little and your hands out to balance you. Fifty years ago I was a 'champeen' at that sort of business. That was up in Pennsylvania—Wayne County—where the hills are good and steep, and where there's ice from the first of December to the last of April. It beats all how it stirs one's blood to take a slide again. Makes me feel glad again it's Christmas. Before I took that slide I didn't care if Christmas never came."

Under the electric lights, one reporter noticed that the old man had two bright red spots on his cheeks, and that his eyes gleamed with excitement. Then, exultingly he hurried along toward the Brooklyn Bridge.

And that, dear reader, is a brief description of a few of the joys of old-fashioned Christmases

GODEY

CHRISTMAS

1871

## ——— Acknowledgments ———

This book has been
a long labor of love. As
the work comes to an end,
I'd like to thank those to whom
I am beholden. In writing
history, one builds,
necessarily, upon the works and knowledge of many others. I have already mentioned my enormous debt to the American newspaper reporters of Christmases past. Also of immense value in the course of my reading were the works of James H. Barnett, Charles W. Jones, and Alfred L. Shoemaker, the Christmas historians on whose firm foundation I've built. Likewise, Don Yoder's introduction to Shoemaker's *Christmas in Pennsylvania* is the best summary of eighteenth- and nineteenth-century religious attitudes toward Christmas ever published.

# Acknowledgments

I am profoundly grateful to John R. Roberson, my wise and supportive friend of a quarter-century. Again, as with my first book, he provided advice and editorial assistance at several stages of my manuscript's development. By helping me condense a far longer work, he made this book possible.

I would like to acknowledge, too, the great skill and contribution of Cynthia Vartan, my editor at Dodd, Mead. To have had her as editor for this book constitutes the happiest circumstance for myself and my readers.

I am grateful to the staff of the New York Public Library and particularly to Richard Hill, the head librarian at the newspaper file. His interest in this project helped add the warmth of friendship to the years of solitary research.

In medicine, as well, I have amassed many debts of gratitude. Simply stated, without the New York Cornell Medical Center in general, and Dr. A. Lee Winston in particular, and Dr. John Kastor, Dr. Alden H. Harken, Dr. Leonard N. Horowitz, and Dr. Mark E. Josephson, together with the staff of the Hospital of the University of Pennsylvania, this book would never have been completed.

To other individuals and institutions I'm indebted for invaluable help and small but useful contributions. In many different ways their assistance has found its way into these pages. I owe thanks to Ned Baker, Andreas Brown of the Gotham Book Mart, where an old-fashioned Christmas can still be found each December, Roy Coggin, Claire Counihan, Mary Catherine Cutter and

# Acknowledgments

Jack Cutter, the late Leslie Dorsey, Leonard Flachman, Charles Flynn, Linda Franklin, the late Patrick Gallagher, Dr. Bruce Grove, Betsy Haviland and Neal Haviland, Jack Henry, Lou Ann Horstman, Elfreda Kraege, Paul McDonough, Walter Moreth, Jim Morrison, the staff of the New York Historical Society Library, the staff of the New York Society Library, Jack Reynolds, Earl Shorris, Virginia Squair, and Donald Vining. In addition I'd like to thank Mr. Joseph Van Why, Director, and Ellice A. Schofield, Curator, The Stowe-Day Foundation, Hartford, Connecticut, for their permission to use the previously unpublished account of Harriet Beecher Stowe's Christmas tree in 1850. And I'd like to thank the editors of *Gourmet* for their permission to use a portion of Chapter I, first published in that magazine. And I take this occasion to thank warmly Bill Reiss, my agent at Paul R. Reynolds, who never lost faith in me or this book, despite years of rejections.

Finally, I am obliged to my friend and colleague, Doug Fais, who drew a new alphabet used in the design of this book. It is based on the fondly remembered, old-fashioned A&P trademark, associated in my mind with the Christmases of my own youth.

# Bibliography

Aasheim, Magnus, ed. *Sheridan's Daybreak: A Story of Sheridan County and Its Pioneers.* Sheridan: Sheridan County, Montana Historical Association, 1970.

Agnew, James B. *The Eggnog Riot: The Christmas Mutiny at West Point.* San Rafael: Presidio Press.

Albright, Raymond W. *Focus on Infinity: A Life of Phillips Brooks.* New York: Macmillan, 1961.

Allen, Walter. *Transatlantic Crossing.* London: Heinemann, 1971.

Anderson, Hugh G. *Lutheranism in the Southeastern States, 1860–1886.* The Hague: Mouton, 1969.

Ashdown, Dulcie M., ed. *Christmas Past: A Selection from Victorian Magazines.* London: Elm Tree Books, 1976.

Ashton, John. *A Righte Merrie Christmasse.* New York: Benjamin Blom, Inc., 1968.

Atherton, Lewis. *Main Street on the Middle Border.* Bloomington: Indiana University Press, 1954.

Bailey, Adrian. *The Cooking of the British Isles.* New York: Time-Life Books, 1971.

Bailey, Olive. *Christmas with the Washingtons.* Richmond: The Dietz Press, 1948.

Barnett, James H. *The American Christmas.* New York: Macmillan, 1954.

Bauer, John E. *Christmas on the American Frontier.* Caldwell, Idaho: The Caxton Printers, Ltd., 1961.

Birmingham, Nan T. *Store.* New York: G. P. Putnam's Sons, 1978.

Bishop, Robert, and Patricia Coblentz. *The World of Antiques, Art, and Architecture in Victorian America.* New York: E. P. Dutton, 1979.

Bonney, Catharina V. *A Legacy of Historical Gleanings.* Albany, N.Y.: J. Munsell, 1875.

# BIBLIOGRAPHY

Boorstin, Daniel J. *The Americans: The Democratic Experience.* New York: Random House, 1973.

Bridenbaugh, Carl. *Mitre and Sceptre: Transatlantic Faiths, Ideas, Personalities, and Politics, 1689–1775.* New York: Oxford University Press, 1962.

Buckler, Ernst. *Ox Bells and Fireflys.* New York: Alfred A. Knopf, 1968.

Buhl, Wolfgang. *Der Nurnberger Christkindles Markt.* Wurzburg: Echter, 1976.

Burdick, J. R. *Pioneer Postcards.* New York: Nostalgia Press, 1956.

Carpenter. *Frank G. Carp's Washington.* New York: McGraw Hill, 1960.

*Christmas in California.* San Francisco: California Historical Society, 1956.

Coffin, Robert P. Tristram. *Christmas in Maine.* New York: Doubleday, 1941.

Coffin, Tristram P. *The Illustrated Book of Christmas Folklore.* New York: Seabury Press, 1973.

Count, Earl W. *4000 Years of Christmas.* New York: Henry Schuman, 1948.

Cutler, R.V. *The Gay Nineties.* New York: Doubleday, Page and Company, 1927.

Davis, Hubert J. *Christmas in the Mountains: Southwest Virginia Christmas Customs and Their Origins.* Murfreesboro, North Carolina: Johnson Publishing Company, 1972.

DeGroot, Adriaan D. *Saint Nicholas: A Psychoanalytic Study.* New York: Basic Books, 1965.

Dow, George F. *Every Day Life in the Massachusetts Bay Colony.* New York: Benjamin Blom, 1935.

# BIBLIOGRAPHY

Ebon, Martin. *Saint Nicholas: Life and Legend.* New York: Harper & Row, 1975.

Emrich, Duncan. *Folklore on the American Land.* Boston: Little, Brown, 1972.

Engle, Paul. *An Old Fashioned Christmas.* New York: The Dial Press, 1964.

Foley, Daniel J. *The Christmas Tree.* Philadelphia: Chilton, 1960.

Genovesse, Eugene D. *Roll Jordan, Roll: the world the slaves made.* New York: Pantheon Books, 1974.

Gray, Nada. *Holidays: Victorian Women Celebrate in Pennsylvania.* Lewisburg: Union County Historical Society, 1983.

*Grove's Dictionary of Music and Musicians.* New York: St. Martin's Press, 1955.

Hadfield, Miles and John. *The Twelve Days of Christmas.* Boston. Little, Brown, 1961.

Haswell, Charles H. *Reminiscences of un Octogenarian of the City of New York.* New York: Harper & Brothers, 1896.

Hechtlinger, Adelaide. *The Seasonal Hearth: The Woman at Home in Early America.* Woodstock, New York: The Overlook Press, 1977.

*International Book of Christmas Carols.* Englewood Cliffs, New Jersey: Prentice-Hall, Inc., 1963.

*John Udell's Journal 1858.* Los Angeles: N. A. Kovach, 1946.

Jones, Charles W. *Saint Nicholas of Myra, Bari, and Manhattan: Biography of a Legend.* Chicago: The University of Chicago Press, 1978.

Jones, E. Willis. *The Santa Claus Book.* New York: Walker and Company, 1976.

Kane, Harnett T. *The Southern Christmas Book.* New York: Bonanza Books, 1953.

# BIBLIOGRAPHY

Ladd, C. E. and Eastman, E. R. *Growing Up in Horse and Buggy Days.* New York: Nesterman Publishing Company, 1943.

Loeper, John J. *Mr. Marley's Main Street Confectionery: A History of Sweets & Treats.* New York: Atheneum, 1979.

Martin, George. *The Damrosch Dynasty.* Boston: Houghton Mifflin Company, 1983.

Marzio, Peter C. *The Democratic Art: Pictures for a 19th-Century America.* Boston: David R. Godine, 1979.

McCabe, James D., Jr. *Lights and Shadows of New York Life.* Philadelphia: National Publishing Company, 1872.

Miall, Anthony and Peter. *The Victorian Christmas Book.* London: J. M. Dent & Sons Ltd., 1978.

Miles, Clement A. *Christmas Ritual and Tradition, Christian and Pagan.* London: T. Fisher Unwin, 1912.

Moore, Clement C. *The Night Before Christmas.* With a life of the author written by Arthur N. Hosking. New York: Dodd, Mead, 1934.

Morgan, Helen M., ed. *A Season in New York: Letters of Harriet and Maria Trumbull.* Pittsburgh: University of Pittsburgh Press, 1969.

Muir, Frank. *Christmas Customs and Traditions.* New York: Taplinger Publishing Co. Inc., 1977.

Myers, Robert Manson. *Handel's Messiah: A Touchstone of Taste.* New York: Macmillan, 1948.

Nevins, Allan and Milton Halsey Thomas, eds. *The Diary of George Templeton Strong.* New York: Macmillan, 1952.

Notestein, Wallace. *The English People on the Eve of Colonization.* New York: Harper & Row, 1954.

Patterson, Samuel W. *The Poet of Christmas Eve.* New York: Morehouse-Gorham, 1956.

Pimlott, John A. *The Englishman's Christmas: A Social His-*

# BIBLIOGRAPHY

*tory*. Atlantic Highlands, New Jersey: Humanities Press, 1978.

Richards, Katharine L. *How Christmas Came to the Sunday-Schools*. New York: Dodd, Mead, 1934.

Riemerschmidt, Ulrich. *Weihnachten*. Hamburg: Schroder, 1962.

Robacker, Earl F. *Old Stuff in Up-Country Pennsylvania*. Cranbury, New Jersey: A. S. Barnes & Company, 1973.

Rose, Harold Wickliffe. *The Colonial Houses of Worship in America*. New York: Hastings House, 1963.

Sanson, William. *A Book of Christmas*. New York: McGraw-Hill, 1968.

Shackleton, Robert. *The Boston Book*. Philadelphia: The Penn Publishing Co., 1916.

Shoemaker, Alfred L. *Christmas in Pennsylvania: a Folk-Cultural Study*. Kutztown. Pennsylvania Folklore Society, 1959.

Smith, Lillian. *Memory of A Large Christmas*. New York: W. W. Norton, 1961.

Smith, Matthew H. *Sunshine and Shadow in New York*. Hartford: J. B. Burrows and Company, 1869.

Sneller, Anne Gertrude. *A Vanished World*. Syracuse: Syracuse University Press, 1964.

Staff, Frank. *The Picture Postcard and its Origins*. London: Lutterworth Press, 1966.

Sullivan, Ed. *Christmas with Ed Sullivan*. New York: McGraw-Hill Inc., 1959.

Wright, Louis B. *Life in Colonial America*. New York: G. P. Putnam's Sons, 1971.

Yoder, Don. *American Folklife*. Austin: University of Texas Press, 1976.

# BIBLIOGRAPHY

## NEWSPAPERS

*The Brooklyn Eagle,* 1883 and 1912
*The Erie Daily Times,* 1889
*The New York Herald,* 1835 through 1900, and 1912.
*The New York Evening Post,* 1801 through 1900, and 1912.
*The New York Times,* 1851 through 1930.
*The New York Daily Tribune,* 1841 through 1920.
*The New York Sun,* 1833 through 1900.
*The New York World,* 1860 through 1900, and 1912.
*The San Diego Union,* 1902 and 1904.
*The Washington Post,* 1904.
*The Washington Star,* 1912.


## PERIODICALS

*Americana,* May/June 1981.
*American Heritage,* December 1963.
*Antiques,* December 1976.
*The Clarion,* Winter 1981.
*Colorado,* November/December 1976.
*Early American Life,* December 1974 and December 1975.
*Gourmet,* December 1967.
*Harper's Weekly,* Decembers 1869, 1873, and 1883.
*High Fidelity,* April 1959.
*Modern Maturity,* December/January 1976/77.
*Yankee,* December 1977

# ——List of Illustrations——

# Index

# INDEX

# INDEX

# INDEX